NEW LABOUR'S OLD ROOTS

**Revisionist Thinkers in Labour's History
1931–97**

Introduced and Edited by
Patrick Diamond

IMPRINT ACADEMIC

Published in the UK by Imprint Academic
PO Box 200, Exeter EX5 5YX, UK

Published in the USA by Imprint Academic
Philosophy Documentation Center
PO Box 7147, Charlottesville, VA 22906-7147, USA

ISBN 0 907845 894

A CIP catalogue record for this book is available from the
British Library and US Library of Congress

Contents

Acknowledgements

The editor and publishers would like to thank the following for permission to reproduce extracts from copyright material:

Random House for *The Future of Socialism* by C.A.R. Crosland; The Fabian Society for the extracts from Fabian Tracts and pamphlets; David Higham Associates for *Socialism in the New Society* by Douglas Jay and *The Unprincipled Society* by David Marquand; Maggie Pearlstine for *Choose Freedom: The Future of Democratic Socialism* by Roy Hattersley; Routledge for *Equality* by R.H. Tawney and *The Politics of Democratic Socialism* by E.F.M Durbin; Taylor & Francis for *Practical Socialism for Britain* by Hugh Dalton; Macmillan for *Crosland and New Labour* by Dick Leonard and *Socialism Without the State* by Evan Luard.

Every effort has been made to acknowledge copyright material that appears in this book; the publisher apologises if, by being unable to trace copyright holders, there are any omissions to the above list.

Foreword

I very much welcome the publication of this book. It explores an important strand of Labour's intellectual history, no less relevant today despite the fact that the huge controversies surrounding the views of the authors now appear far distant.

The strength of the Labour Party has always been its values – simple truths that hold party members together and bind them to the people of Britain. The story of Labour over the last generation is the story of a party that has returned to its roots. We have re-discovered the ideals of community, equality and solidarity that are the foundation of our party, applying them in new ways to the massively changed world in which we live.

In setting out the case for change and renewal, the party has struck a chord with the British people. They never deserted Labour values, but sometimes doubted that the party could ever implement them. Our project would never have been possible without hard and rigorous thinking, and a willingness to challenge conventional assumptions and sentimental attachments. Goodwill and a warm heart would not have been enough. That is why through the generations, the contribution of the Labour intellectuals celebrated in this book has been of outstanding and irreplaceable value.

I am proud of the way that New Labour has taken the best of the party's values, and restated them afresh for a new generation and a new world. We owed it to the people of this country to establish ourselves as a modern party of government.

I hope that this book will be read by everyone who wants to know something about Labour and its history, and about the improvements that it has brought to Britain in the past.

But it also urges us to look forward. We must not allow ourselves to run out of steam. Neither must we wait for a return to opposition before we tackle the challenge of renewal. Learning from the past will ensure that we prepare rigorously for the future.

The editor and publishers have done us a great service by bringing this collection together.

Rt. Hon. Tony Blair MP
May 2004

Preface

This book is an exploration of some historical problems of the British Labour Party, and their relation to some of the current concerns of British politics and the British state. It examines the British revision-ist tradition and the emergence of 'New' Labour as a strategy to re-cast the historical Labour Party.

With 'New' Labour, it could at last become a successful party of government, undertaking a transformation of British politics, and averting Britain's long-term economic and social decline. The book nonetheless argues that such a revolution is far from complete.

As a body of work, it is concerned with Labour's ideological development as a social democratic party, and does not put the record of the Labour Government since 1997 to the revisionist test. That task awaits us.

These arguments are explored by reproducing revisionist argu-ments taken from their original sources, charting the course of the party's ideological transformation since 1931. The editor has written an introduction to each extract, as a guide to each thinker's contribu-tion to debates about revisionism.

This is a specific, and relatively narrow, method for the historian of political ideas. Some attention is also paid to such published sources as the books, pamphlets, and periodicals that are the main receptacles of British social democratic thought during this period.

The study draws additionally on diaries and biographical mate-rial, as well as interviews with several of the leading protagonists in the ideological debates of these years. Many friends and colleagues have helped me to write this book. I am grateful to them all. Special thanks go to Claire McCarthy, without whom it would simply not have been possible.

My intellectual debts are too many to mention — though special reference goes to Professor Peter Clarke and Professor Andrew Gamble. Their influence will be apparent throughout this book.

The original style of each essay has been retained, despite the presence of language that is now considered sexist. It is a male-dominated affair, reflecting the dominance of men in the post-war Labour Party — a situation that it is hoped 'New' Labour will reverse.

This book is not uncritical either of the revisionists or 'New' Labour. It was put together in the belief that socialist ideas are greater and more important than whoever happens to be leader of the Labour Party, or in the Labour Cabinet at any one time.

A party of blind obedience and mindless loyalty has no long-term future.

PD

May 2004

Introduction

New Labour's Old Roots: Revisionist Thinkers in Labour's History 1931–97

Introduction: The Future of Socialism

This book explores one of the central themes of modern British politics: the relationship between 'New' Labour and social democracy in twentieth-century Britain. It asks what are the philosophical roots of 'New' Labour?[1] Does it represent a radical break in post-war Labour politics, or merely affirm historical continuities? Does it constitute a credible programme for the modernisation of the British state; can Labour forge an irreversible progressive settlement in British politics?

The book aims to assess and stimulate that debate further. It argues 'New' Labour stands in a line of descent with modernising forces in the party, especially the revisionists of the 1950s and 1960s, and the ethical socialists of the pre-war years. Its common heritage is conscience and reform, while its shared ideal is national renewal — the creation of a 'New Britain'. A central thrust of the book is that Labour can only succeed when it embraces national goals for the country, averting the decline of the British economy, and fundamentally re-casting the British state and British politics.

Post-war revisionism in Britain, as in Germany, emphasised the ethical value of equality in contrast to the instrumental value of pub-

---

[1] 'New' Labour has remained a highly contested project since the revision of Clause IV (iv) in 1994–95. Notably, The Labour Party recently removed the pre-fix 'New' from the party membership card.

lic ownership. The role of collective planning and nationalisation have been dominant themes in revisionist writings since the 1930s. No issue has more divided the Labour Party since its birth than the ownership of productive assets, and the future of British capitalism.

But social democratic revisionism, as this book will show, addressed itself to wider concerns than the dispute over public ownership and Clause IV (iv). In its method, it drew on Eduard Bernstein's *Evolutionary Socialism* (1899). This sought to revise Marx's theory of capital and surplus value, as doubt was cast on predictions of inevitable economic collapse and working-class revolution in the late nineteenth century. Revisionists insisted that the classical orthodoxies of the past offered no guidance to a future in which capitalism had been transformed out of existence.

British revisionism has its origins in Edwardian social liberalism, in R.H. Tawney's ethical socialism, and in the strenuous efforts of Hugh Dalton and the Fabian Research Bureau in the 1930s to devise an account of political economy that embraced J.M. Keynes' revolutionary *General Theory* (1936).

In refuting Marx, revisionism assailed the Labour left. But the target of their revisionist zeal was wider than a narrow Marxism. At its core was the belief that for a century, British socialists had clung stubbornly to a flawed class analysis. Since the late nineteenth century, Labour had suffered successive defeats because too often it conceived its constituency as a homogenous industrial working-class whose interest the labour and trade union movement uniquely encompassed.

Four Phases of Revisionist Thought Since 1931

An essential insight of the revisionists and 'New' Labour is that Labour as a class party, representing labour interests against capital and the state, had to be fundamentally reconstructed. Four phases of revisionism since the 1930s are described in this book, beginning with Tawney's Equality (1931), and concluding with Gordon Brown's essay Equality — then and now (1997), published immediately after the 1997 election.

- Phase I: Laying revisionist foundations. Pre-1945, when the precise role of public ownership was being explored in the construction of a credible economic policy informing Labour's ideology and programme. A new synthesis of planning and Keynesian theory subsequently emerged after 1931.

- Phase II: Revisionism's high tide. Post-1945, the development of revisionism as the Attlee Government's programme was completed, and the perceived inadequacies of rival attitudes to public ownership and socialism became starker, leading to deepening confrontation in the 1950s.

- Phase III: Revisionism revised. The fading appeal of revisionist social democracy after 1970 as bitter ideological conflicts resurfaced in response to the failings of the Wilson administration, leading eventually to the split and formation of the Social Democratic Party (SDP) in 1981, and the electoral disaster of 1983.

- Phase IV: Revisionism re-born. The process of ideological change from the late 1980s that built the foundations of 'New' Labour, culminating in the revision of Clause IV in 1994–95, and the apparent completion of the original revisionist project.

The essays in this collection provide strong evidence for continuity between 'New' Labour and its revisionist past, and succinctly represent the intellectual contribution of each author.

Labour's Identity Crisis

Revisionist ideas in Britain were an attempt to grapple with the fundamental structural weaknesses of the Labour Party. Labour has suffered in previous generations because as the social historian Gareth Stedman-Jones[2] suggests, rather than presenting a credible plan for the future, each faction in the party was too often concerned with winning the internal battle to write the past more vividly than its opponents.

Labour's identity was riddled with contradictions, leading to embittered relations between the party rank and file, and the parliamentary leadership. In the 1950s, Labour was unable to recover the sense of purpose it had lacked once the unity engendered by the desperate poverty and mass unemployment of the 1930s, and the immediate tasks of post-war reconstruction, had faded. In truth, it continually exposed itself to conflict because it had no consistent idea of what socialism in practice should look like.

From its earliest days, Labour sought to reconcile the necessity of managing capitalism with a radical rhetoric promising to replace capitalism with an alternative economic system. In the 1960s, a tem-

---

[2]   Stedman-Jones (1983).

porary truce between revisionists and fundamentalists was achieved only by concealing profound disagreements concerning the very nature and purpose of democratic socialism and public ownership. Harold Wilson depicted planning as an ideologically coherent link between the scientific revolution and the British socialist tradition.

But the economic crisis that ensued after 1967 exposed the implausibility of this strategy, sealing a decade of protracted consolidation and retreat. Neither Labour nor Conservative Governments could defy the international orientation of British economic policy, and achieve the goal of expansion without price inflation, breaking the 'stop-go' cycle.[3]

The whole strategy of expansion and modernisation depended upon an increased public expenditure dividend from growth. It also required the co-operation of the trade unions, accepting pay restraint in exchange for the prospect of faster growth in living standards. Both policies depended in the short term on governments finding some way to expand the economy that would not lead to a balance of payments or sterling crisis. In the absence of any resolution to this dilemma, it was clear that the old priorities of the social democratic consensus − full employment and rising living standards − could no longer be maintained, fuelling internal party conflicts.[4]

The identity crisis was also reflected in the party's changing perceptions of its performance in office. In the late 1950s and 1960s, the predominant tone of discussion of the 1945 administration, on both left and right, was highly critical. For the right, it identified Labour too closely with obsolete shibboleths like nationalisation, and the cloth cap. For the left, it represented a failure to capture the commanding heights of the economy and a capitulation to market forces, the civil service and the cold war. Yet, in the light of the failings and frustrations of the Wilson-Callaghan years, the post-war Labour Government came to be seen as a golden age.[5]

British revisionism was a theoretical critique both of Labour's traditional left and right, defined in Kenneth O. Morgan's terms, as 'those who cling to the basic principles of the creed and favour speedy advance towards the party's goals, and those who are will-

---

[3]   See Beckerman (1972).

[4]   See Coates (1980).

[5]   See Shaw (1994).

ing to trim the doctrine and to proceed at a slower, more cautious pace'. Both were complicit in the party's historic under-performance, the revisionists argued, preventing it from developing into the natural governing party that could fundamentally re-cast the terrain of British politics.[6]

Herbert Morrison's maxim that 'socialism is what a Labour Government does' was as vehemently criticised as left fundamentalism. Morrison's appeal to consolidation had left the party directionless after losing office in 1951, opening the way for the revisionist charge that an appeal to the past was insufficient to sustain Labour in power. This had sealed the fate of the Attlee administration by the late 1940s, leading *The Times* to conclude harshly in 1951:

> The strongest argument for rejecting the Labour Government is that after six testing years in office they have largely exhausted their capacity for creative thinking . . . The Labour Party is left with no distinctive contribution to make to the solution of the nation's problems.

This sense of disillusionment with the 1945 Government also fuelled long-running disputes about the prominence of nationalisation in Labour's doctrine and programme, culminating in the battle over Clause IV (iv) in 1959–60. Nye Bevan, a leading Minister in the Attlee Government believed that nationalisation and planning were both economically efficient and morally just:

> Our main case is and must remain that in a modern complex society it is impossible to get rational order by leaving things to private economic adventure. Therefore I am a socialist. I believe in public ownership.[7]

By the early 1950s, as Bevan staked out his personal testament *In Place of Fear*, Clause IV of the Labour Party constitution had emerged as a sacred text. It was Labour's equivalent of the Old Testament, written by the social reformer Sidney Webb, and formally adopted by the party in 1918. It demanded 'the common ownership of the means of production, distribution and exchange', reflecting the socialist view that private ownership of industry and land was inherently exploitative. Over decades, Clause IV became a totem of earlier idealism, though no Labour Government had ever contemplated such a radical programme of nationalisation.

---

[6]   Morgan (1987).

[7]   Bevan (1951).

The revisionists of the 1950s always recognised the compelling arguments for the pragmatic nationalisation of inefficient industries. Planning and rationalisation had economic benefits. But they wholly rejected Nye Bevan's view that the essence of socialism was public ownership. Anthony Crosland wrote in *The Future of Socialism*,

> The worst source of confusion is the tendency to use the word [socialism] to describe, not a certain kind of society, or certain values which might be attributes of a society, but particular policies which are, or are thought to be, means of attaining this kind of society or realising these attributes.

The desire to sideline nationalisation was controversial among party activists, since it appeared to represent a fundamental betrayal of the class struggle, and abandoned the goal of a socialist society in which all property is collectively owned. Emphasising enduring ideals as the touchstone of socialist doctrine imperilled Labour's founding myth of a new, post-capitalist world in which the economic system is drastically re-ordered eliminating private profit and greed — a myth that like the party's origins itself, owed more to Methodism than to Marx.[8]

This deep-seated ambiguity in Labour's doctrine concerning the legitimacy of public ownership, collective planning and competitive markets persisted until Clause IV was revised in 1994–95.

It was a decisive moment in Labour's history. By refusing to undertake an explicit process of theoretical reconstruction, Labour for generations had detached its policies and methods from the enduring socialist values of liberty, equality and social justice. At a stroke, it enacted its own ideological liberation — able to formulate a socialist doctrine for Britain's future.

'New' Labour thus exemplifies the project of revisionist social democracy in Britain.[9] But 'New' Labour's roots — its common heritage — extend beyond disputes over Clause IV and nationalisation. The three tenets of revisionism are its fundamental appeal to ethical values, the disciplined rigour of its analysis, and its strategy for securing power within a changing society. 'New' Labour weaves each of these elements into its project for the revitalisation of the British economy, and the British state.

---

[8]   Pelling (1965).

[9]   See also Fielding (2003).

'New' Labour set out to revive the Labour Party in British politics following the sudden decline of post-war social democracy, and the emergence of Thatcherism. Having suffered a dramatic collapse of support in the 1980s, it had to find a new programme and a new appeal. It did so by retaining its historic commitment to social justice while appealing to the aspirant middle-class. 'New' Labour rejects the elevated status previously accorded to public ownership, and in its economic aims embraces global market forces and competitive enterprise.

The strategic purpose of 'New' Labour, shared by its revisionist predecessors, is to create a new progressive coalition in British politics. This progressive alliance is built on feasible reform, not class struggle. It sees conscience rather than class as the key to radical politics. It appeals to equity and compassion, not militancy or greed. Fundamentally, it believes that by adhering to its principles, Labour can establish itself as the natural party of government within the British state.

'New' Labour: A Fundamental Breach?

The pervasive interpretation of 'New' Labour, however, continues to assume a fundamental breach with the party's traditions. 'New' Labour is seen to represent a clean break with the past. In this interpretation, the category of 'Old' Labour refers indiscriminately to all wings of the party, to the policies of all previous Labour governments and oppositions, and to the trade unions and Labour local authorities.[10]

This dichotomy of 'Old' and 'New' Labour was applied enthusiastically in the mid-1990s. But unhelpfully, it appeared to detach the party from its ethical and intellectual roots, and served to perpetuate long-standing confusion about Labour's identity. It was accused of abandoning historic goals — Keynesian demand management, employment protection, defence of the trade unions, and fiscal redistribution. This enabled 'New' Labour's opponents to portray it as 'Thatcherism Mark II'.[11]

These criticisms were fuelled by claims in the early 1990s that social democracy — as a historical force seeking to counter the unregulated individualism of the market — was itself in crisis. The

---

[10] See Gamble (2003).

[11] See Heffernan (2000).

political theorist John Gray has argued that social democracy, 'embodies assumptions and modes of thought that belong to a historical context that has vanished beyond recovery'.[12] Pervasive resistance to penal rates of taxation, and the global mobility of capital, compromise the use of contemporary welfare states for egalitarian purposes.

In Gray's view, social democratic institutions presuppose a closed economic regime that is now under persistent threat from downward harmonisation and intensive competition over labour costs. This analysis is, however, totally inconsistent with the enduring vitality of Nordic social democracy.[13]

It also exaggerates the extent to which Thatcherism has shaped 'New' Labour. There have been deep and irreversible changes in the structure of the world economy and British society since 1979, far more complex than Gray depicts.[14] In the great firestorm of the 1980s, the Thatcher Governments merely hurried on the restructuring of British capitalism, destroying many industries that remained.

Certainly, Thatcherism also sought to reverse the trend towards a larger state, dismantling corporatist institutions, reducing public expenditure, and reshaping the post-war compromise between capital and labour, creating the conditions for a free economy.

But to suppose that Thatcherism determined 'New' Labour is manifestly far-fetched. The fundamental weakness of the argument is its suggestion that one particular phase of Labour's development contains the essence of what Labour is, and always should be. Such a procedure naturally elevates the 1945–51 Attlee Government as Labour's finest hour, since it laid the foundations of the post-war welfare state and mixed economy. But to imply that the Attlee administration sets the standard against which Labour will always be judged seems misplaced.

There are some accounts that are disinclined to treat the post-war Labour Government as sacred.[15] Moreover, if Labour actually adopted this approach it would quickly descend into irrelevance, as over the years it perpetuated steadily more outdated means. By the 1980s, a ferocious debate had taken hold concerning the relative decline of post-war Britain, and the loss of economic supremacy. The

---

[12] Gray (2000).

[13] Callaghan (2000).

[14] Gamble (1981).

[15] Dell (2002).

charge that 'New' Labour is inherently 'right-wing' ignores the necessity of carefully considering the contrasting contexts in which political actors operate. The labels of 'left' and 'right' have been constantly re-defined since the French revolution gave birth to them in 1789.

In fact, 'New' Labour's evolution has to be seen as a long, drawn out historical process. The purpose of this book is to trace these roots in long-standing debates within the Labour Party over its evolving doctrine and strategy.

'New' Labour Isn't New

It explores three themes in particular.

Most obviously, 'New' Labour isn't really new at all. It has old roots in ethical socialism and revisionist social democracy. By revising Clause IV in 1994–95, 'New' Labour had accomplished the task that revisionists had set out to achieve in the early 1950s. This removed the doctrinal ambiguity over public ownership from the party's ethos. In this sense, 'New' Labour merely restates the enduring themes of revisionist social democracy, preserving and updating its central ideas.

Second, neither historical interpretation of 'New' Labour, by critics or sympathisers, is remotely satisfactory.[16] 'New' Labour has not discarded the defining tenets of social democracy as its enemies allege. Nor, on the other hand, has it evolved an entirely distinct ideology forged in the mid-1990s. Both of these arguments confuse rather than illuminate. They fail to uphold the means–ends distinction that is central to revisionism, and they defer to a misleading conception of 'Old' versus 'New' Labour.

Finally, 'New' Labour is strengthened if it situates itself within the social democratic lineage. 'New' Labour's mission is to transform the party into an agent of reform in British society, promoting fairness and opening up institutions once dominated by privileged elites. It should fit seamlessly into the British progressive tradition, casting its identity in these terms. Efforts to distance 'New' Labour from its social democratic past are not merely inaccurate. They are strategically inept, heightening accusations of betrayal, and perpetuating the fundamental historical confusion over Labour's identity.

---

[16] See Heffernan (2000) and Gould (1998).

Negative memories of previous Labour administrations did provide powerful symbols of the party's incompetence and inability to govern. Such images had haunted the British electorate since the IMF crisis of the mid-1970s, and industrial action in the public sector that led to the 'winter of discontent' in 1978–79. But, with the benefit of hindsight, the category of 'Old' Labour involves a deceptive and confusing conflation of disparate historical events that led 'New' Labour to deny its obvious attachment to prevailing revisionist assumptions.

The former Labour leader Hugh Gaitskell is barely referred to in Peter Mandelson and Roger Liddle's *Blair Revolution*, widely regarded as a formative 'New' Labour text. This reluctance to associate the new revisionist leader with the old in the mid-1990s is striking. It indicates that in the early days of 'New' Labour, the party's hierarchy perceived that proximity to revisionist social democracy damaged its cause — despite the fact it had been so obviously shaped by its fundamental tenets.

The long-standing emotional intensity of doctrinal disputes in the 1950s aroused fears of a return to factionalism, providing justification for this breach with its ancestry. But this was not without a price for 'New' Labour, heightening the misleading impression that it was vacuous, devoid of ideological or intellectual roots.

In fact, New Labour's origins are to be found in revisionist ideas, exploring the changing nature of the British state, the British economy, British politics, and the British socialist tradition, as the chapters in this book reveal.

The Enduring Aim: Social Justice and a Classless Society

A view has arisen of the stereotypical revisionist as Oxbridge-educated with a lifestyle far removed from that of the typical Labour voter.[17] Though the revisionists are an eclectic tradition with disparate perspectives and interests that foreclose such generalisations, theirs was a shared endeavour. This is encapsulated by two assumptions that prevail within their political approach — and suggest strong affinities with 'New' Labour.

The first is a strategic claim, envisaging Labour as the moderate and progressive force in British politics. To fulfil its potential as the natural governing party, Labour must reach far beyond its traditional frontiers. The party had to reject the tribalism inherent in the

[17] See Jeffreys (1999).

founding myth of labourism, a tendency to divide the world up into 'Us' and 'Them' captured by the refrain of its anthem: 'while cowards flinch and traitors sneer, we'll keep the red flag flying here'. Otherwise, it would continue to confound a simple tenet of political theory, since it could not succeed as the representative of a single interest group.

In a 1939 essay J.M Keynes has asked: 'why cannot the leaders of the Labour Party face the fact that they are not secretaries of an outworn creed, mumbling moss-green demi-semi Fabian Marxism, but the heirs of eternal liberalism?'[18] Revisionism was underpinned by a psephological analysis that led the Labour leader Hugh Gaitskell to claim in 1958, 'working-class people are week by week becoming less working-class, less class-conscious, and more allergic to such old appeals as trade union solidarity or class loyalty'.[19]

The assertion that Labour had to govern for the nation was a logical response to the relative decline of the manual working class in Britain. This was in tune with the radical thinking sweeping through other socialist and social democratic parties during those years. The conflict between capital and labour had been transcended. For Labour to live up to its own values, it had to purge itself of class prejudice. A classless society was best achieved by breaking down class barriers, rather than the enforced supremacy of one class over the other.

The revisionists were determined to show that Labour was no longer a class party driven by outdated ideology. For Gaitskell the self-defeating effect of Labour's ideological purity was embodied in the original Clause IV. By 1959, Labour was increasingly and damagingly identified as the party of nationalisation. To enshrine such an undesirable, and largely unattainable, aspiration in the party's constitution merely scared away the majority of the British people who were not socialists, but who may well have found Labour's humanising, egalitarian values attractive.

The devastating political impact was reflected in the unprecedented electoral humiliations of the 1950s. The Conservative share of the vote remained constant at 48–50%, but the Labour share dropped from 48.8% in 1951, to 46.4% in 1955, and 43.8% in 1959. Labour seemed unwilling to embrace important social changes created by the emerging consumer society, a set of attitudes to owner-

[18]   J.M Keynes, *The New Statesman* (January 1939).

[19]   Williams (1983).

ship and consumption that the left instantly found contemptible. Yet, the pace of rising prosperity was remarkable — living standards in Britain rose faster in 1951–58 than 1918–39.[20]

This culminated in Gaitskell's failed efforts to revise Clause IV in 1959–60, leading to retaliation and further conflicts with the trade unions over Labour's stance on unilateral nuclear disarmament.

The defence question belonged to lively debates concerning Britain's role in the world, Britain's relationship with Europe and America, and British national sovereignty. There was general agreement about the importance of NATO. Only through the Atlantic alliance could Britain continue to play a global role, defending the West from the Soviet threat. The Atlantic alliance and the ideas set out in Denis Healey's essay 'Power Politics and the Labour Party' (1952) had remained intact as the bedrock of moderate Labour politics since the 1940s.

But there was less unity on the future of Europe among the revisionists of the 1950s and 1960s. Indeed, their differences over Europe were eventually to divide them irredeemably. While for Roy Jenkins the growing unity of Europe was central, Douglas Jay opposed Britain's entry into the European Economic Community. Anthony Crosland was developing a pose of 'studied boredom' on the subject. His preoccupation remained the construction of social democracy within the nation-state.

The second assumption broadly shared between the revisionists and 'New' Labour is ideological — based on a notion of equality and liberty as indissolubly linked, leading to a conception of the state as developmental and 'enabling'. Rights in a free society only have real meaning where individuals possess the economic and political strength to exercise them. Freedom is more than the absence of restraint or the assertion of the rudimentary rights of citizenship. Protection from coercion by state, private or corporate power of any sort is only the first step towards liberty.

Socialism was a means of practical freedom for individuals. The origins of this claim can be found in the early twentieth-century social liberalism of T.H. Green, L.T. Hobhouse, the Hammonds, and Graham Wallas. Peter Clarke brings out the relationship between

---

[20] Nield (1959).

social liberalism and revisionist social democracy, arguing: 'the New Liberalism was not proto-socialist, but revisionist'.[21]

Green had insisted: 'The mere removal of compulsion, the mere enabling a man to do as he likes, is in itself no contribution to true freedom'.[22] This advocated a positive view of freedom, of liberty as autonomy, the ability of people to freely control and govern their own lives. Not freedom from interference, especially the state, as espoused by the Conservatives, but the right to human dignity and fulfilment through the security and opportunity afforded by collective social provision. Hobhouse had justified restraints on unfettered economic individualism declaring that, 'liberty without equality is a name of noble sound and squalid result'.[23] In *Choose Freedom*, Roy Hattersley had declared: 'Socialism exists to provide — for the largest number of people — the ability to exercise effective liberty'.

Social democrats seek to guarantee a fair distribution of opportunities despite the dominance of competitive markets, prioritising equality and redistribution, and therefore the public services. Revisionists were sceptical that state ownership per se would necessarily produce a higher level of social welfare.

By the late 1940s, revisionists were boldly questioning whether 'public enterprise', as Morrison depicted it, effectively realised social democratic aspirations. Most favoured a 'case by case' approach, rationalising natural monopolies, or replacing investment resources diminished by redistributive taxation. For example, Douglas Jay favoured it for aircraft, and Hugh Dalton, Anthony Crosland and Hugh Gaitskell for machine tools.[24] But the ideals of social justice and a classless society were not necessarily promoted by the nationalisation of industry.

These strategic and ideological assumptions defined Labour as a progressive party using an enabling and democratic state to achieve its social democratic objectives. This accepted the limits to what socialism could achieve in the new society. To win, Labour had to stress modern visions of socialism rather than a desire to nationalise the commanding heights of the economy. Revisionist social democ-

---

[21]   Clarke (1978).

[22]   See Nettleship (1885–8).

[23]   Hobhouse (1909–10).

[24]   See Brivati (1996).

racy and 'New' Labour were propelled forward as they sought to modernise outdated doctrine, and discard redundant truths.

This fundamental reinvention of the social democratic model can be summarised in the following terms:

- Labour should affirm its steadfast commitment to social democratic values, but seek innovation in the means of delivery.

- Labour must re-conceive the state in social democratic politics, especially the relevance of nationalisation and public ownership.

- Labour should be a party of production as much as distribution and fair outcomes, enlarging growth within a mixed market economy.

- Labour must reclaim ground invaded by the right, refusing to surrender centrist territory on consumer rights in the 1950s, or crime and immigration in the 1990s.

- Labour seeks a liberal socialism where its core commitment to social justice through collective action is enriched by its commitment to personal freedom.

- By the late 1970s, it was clear that Labour had to incorporate dynamic and emerging currents in British thought and society, from communitarianism, to environmentalism and feminist politics.

Each proposition requires the deployment of an enabling state that stands up for the individual, vigorously promoting equality in life chances and a classless society across the economy, politics and culture.

'New' Labour has developed much of its doctrine by implicitly drawing on the past. It has assimilated the key political and ideological assumptions of revisionist thinkers in devising its own governing philosophy. This is the case not only for post-war social democracy, but the first stage of revisionism that preceded it, and the critique of the corporatist central state in the 1970s and 1980s.

The argument put was that earlier revisionists had been naïve about the state as an instrument for realising their ideological objectives. The challenge was apparently to seize the state apparatus and employ it for socialist ends. This led to overload and the collapse of the Keynesian consensus in the early 1970s, questioning Labour's ability to govern. The centralisation of the post-war British state corrupted its efficiency, and was ill suited to a world in which deferential attitudes were in terminal decline.[25]

Hugh Dalton and Evan Durbin's commitment to planning and collectivism has obvious contemporary limitations. But despite this, and the later failings of the Gaitskellite revisionists, it is remarkable how far the 'New' Labour project of the 1990s has drawn on their ideas and themes. This shared vision is best encapsulated by Hugh Gaitskell's commentary on the group of intellectuals, including Dalton and Durbin, who had strongly influenced him in the 1930s:

> They were not just interested in protesting against the ills of the present, they wanted to get rid of them in a practical kind of way . . . they were before everything, realistic. They were not interested in Utopianism. They believed in making the economy more efficient; they believed in the possibility of full employment; they believed in social reforms that would gradually undermine the class structure, so that in due course a happier and more socially just society emerged. These were the ideals they held in front of them, and it was in order to advance these that they had gone into politics.[26]

On their outlook, Gaitskell wrote:

> They were realistic in politics and critical of armchair politicians who, not understanding what the British electorate were really like, were forever making bad political judgements. Above all, while accepting the ultimate emotional basis of moral valuation, they had great faith in the power of reason both to find answers to social problems and to persuade men to see the right. They were for the pursuit of truth to the bitter end, through the patient and unswerving application of logical thought. They wanted no barriers of prejudice to obstruct the free working of the mind or blunt the sharp edge of intellectual integrity.[27]

Hugh Gaitskell set out the social democratic priorities in a famous speech at the post-mortem party conference after the 1959 general election. These have found an explicit echo in 'New' Labour, though the language has inevitably been revised. The list of objectives shared by the revisionists and 'New' Labour had five common elements: a protest against the poverty and squalor arising from capitalism; a wider concern for social welfare; a belief in equality and classlessness; a rejection of competition in every sphere of life and the embrace of co-operation; and a protest against capitalist inefficiency.

---

[25] See Mackintosh (1982).

[26] Williams (1983).

[27] Gaitskell (1954).

In Crosland and Gaitskell's view the struggle against poverty, and economic inefficiency, had largely lost their relevance by the 1950s as the capitalist system was being transformed. They expressed supreme confidence that the economic problem of wealth creation had been solved, and astonishing faith in the power of indicative planning and demand management. Mass unemployment, for example, was an unthinkable social evil.

That is why social welfare and equality were held out as enduring socialist values in the 1950s. The idea of a co-operative social purpose raised too many problems for revisionists who could not work out clear commitments arising from such a principle, foreshadowing later difficulties for 'New' Labour in giving substance to its communitarian ideals.

Social democrats in the 1970s and 1980s acknowledged that the underlying growth potential of Britain was far weaker than Gaitskell and Crosland had assumed, and the continuation of British prosperity was threatened by deficiencies on the supply side of the British economy. Some commentators, notably J.P. Mackintosh, have criticised the complacent assumptions of British social democracy in the 1950s and 1960s.[28]

After Labour's decisive defeat at the 1979 election, another line of attack was opened up from within the revisionist tradition itself, gravely weakened by the death of Crosland. It was argued that the basis of this political approach — economic growth, high spending and redistribution — had steadily collapsed during the course of the 1970s, reflecting a deeper crisis of the British state.[29]

Since Crosland's time, there have also been some obvious and important changes in the world. Globalisation and the rise of the service economy. Women's inclusion in the labour market. The decline of class in general, and the manual working-class in particular. A taxpayer's revolt.

How far these changes have taken us and the implications for social democracy have been hotly contested since the 1950s. But, as David Lipsey suggests, 'it is the absolute need to revise that matters most of all. Reformulating the party's policies and strategy in the

---

[28] Marquand (1982).

[29] Marquand (1979).

light of changing circumstances, as "New" Labour has sought to do, is pure revisionism.'[30]

Revisionism as Cast of Mind

The thesis of this collection, enunciating a direct and explicit parallel between revisionist social democracy and 'New' Labour, seeks to restore a more precise historical definition to revisionism.

Over the years, the original intentions of the revisionist thinkers, and the subtlety with which they explored major intellectual questions about the future of the economy and society, have been obliterated out of existence.

This has fed an industry of misleading, and largely unfavourable comparisons between revisionist thinkers and their 'New' Labour heirs. For example, the explicit abandonment of Keynesian macroeconomic policy is not an adequate explanation for discontinuity between 'Old' and 'New' Labour.[31] We have to accept the essential revisionist premise that policies exist to be revised in the light of changing circumstances.

Revisionism can be better understood as a cast of mind. The revisionist account of one generation is the orthodoxy of the next, requiring a new revisionism to test it against changing circumstances, keeping ossification at bay. The enduring feature of politics is values, the fundamental benchmark against which policies and programmes are measured and developed. The importance of the distinction between ends and means is one of the revisionists most insistent themes.

In practice, Labour has been flexible in its economic aims, irrespective of the formal doctrine enshrined in its constitution. Clause IV was a compass, not a commitment. Labour's policies have undergone continuous transformation since the late nineteenth century. The economic programme of the 1930s linked socialism to planning, and Keynesian policies. 1950s revisionism shifted from nationalisation and national credit controls to welfare state redistribution. Labour's victory in 1964 espoused the 'white heat' of industrial modernisation, emphasising supply-side efficiency, skills, planning, and science as the engine of the 'New' Britain.[32]

---

[30] In Lipsey & Leonard (1981).

[31] See R. Heffernan (2000a).

[32] Wilson (1964).

Indeed, a decisive parallel between revisionist social democracy and 'New' Labour is that both understand the fate of Britain in terms of the contentious thesis of relative national decline. After 1945, the British economy suffered from the effects of conflict, achieving a rate of growth lower than Japan and similar economies in Western Europe. The long-term legacy of past greatness appeared to be inexorable decline: the dissolution of Empire, the emergence of Celtic separatism, and the inability of British industry to compete in world markets.

Three ideas were central to this claim of a dramatic collapse in Britain's world influence, and the relative decline of the economy, threatening the continuance of British prosperity. First, world competition, from the East in particular, was a threat to jobs and living standards without a dramatic reorientation of British economic policy. Second, irresistible forces were also driving structural changes, from 'automation' in the 1950s to 'globalisation' in the 1990s. Third, after long neglect, education and skills should be placed at the centre of a strategy for national revival.[33]

In responding to these dramatic perceptions of decline that cast a long shadow over British life, Labour's leaders always sought to convey 'newness'. This lay behind Keir Hardie's rupture with liberalism, Ramsay MacDonald's progressive coalition in the 1920s, Crosland's *The Future of Socialism* (1956), the social reforms of the 1960s and the Open University, and 'New' Labour's embrace of the technological revolution in the mid-1990s. Novelty enables the party to revive itself as times change.

What distinguishes the revisionist tradition is its coherent analysis of the economic and social structure of post-war Britain, and its insistence on distinguishing means and ends.

Both 'New' Labour and revisionism develop their strategies by precisely distinguishing between policies and underlying values. Moral values are the ends. These are constant. But means that might be considered relevant in one generation are wholly irrelevant to the next, and are, therefore, dispensable. In this sense, 'New' Labour is in line with social democratic thought since Bernstein.

Crosland spearheaded this drive in the 1950s by defining socialism in terms of greater equality, rather than state control. In fact, the revisionists were directing their case less at Marxism than at tradi-

---

[33] See Gamble (1981).

tional Fabianism. Its idea of a gradual collectivist road to socialism via nationalisation was unattractive and outdated.

Meanwhile, the puritanical attitude of the Webbs to liberty, leisure and culture offended the impeccable libertarian credentials of the revisionists, who believed that markets and the price mechanism were essential for liberty. Social democrats should embrace the choices afforded by the emerging consumer society, Anthony Crosland argued in 1955:

> Generally I have never been able to see why high consumption and brotherly love should be incompatible — why should not the brothers be affluent, and the love conducted under conditions of reasonable comfort?[34]

Crosland reminded the 'elite' that ordinary people do want rising consumption:

> My working-class constituents . . . want washing machines and refrigerators to relieve domestic drudgery; they want cars, and the freedom they give on weekends and holidays; and they want package tour holidays to Majorca . . . why should they too not enjoy the sun?[35]

Socialism must acknowledge the benefits of acquisitive materialism, and come to the defence of prosperous mass democracy.

There is a more significant and compelling dimension to these debates, however, that forms a bridgehead between revisionist social democracy, 'New' Labour, and the theme of British national decline. Revisionists, new and old, understood that Labour's failure to emerge as the natural governing party within the state stemmed from its leaders' inability to make the strategic choices necessary to secure the long overdue modernisation of the economy and society in Britain. This was compounded by its deeply confused identity and its ambivalent relationship to the market economy that was symptomatic of debates over nationalisation and Clause IV.

We can detect in revisionist ideas the ultimate objective of liberating the Labour Party from outdated shibboleths, so that it could formulate a coherent strategy for the modernisation of industrial capitalism, and fulfil its wider ambitions for the country. In 'New' Labour, this goal had at last been realised. But it still represents an unfinished revolution in the task of re-casting the historical Labour Party, and fundamentally re-shaping Britain.

---

[34] Crosland (1955).

[35] Crosland (1974).

'New' Labour and Equality

Nonetheless, the charge that there is an unbridgeable divide between the revisionists and 'New' Labour persists. In his incisive biography, *Hugh Gaitskell*, Brian Brivati ends with a controversial historical judgement. 'New' Labour, he argues, has sacrificed Gaitskell's memory. Equality is no longer the formal aim of Labour in power. The revolution in political economy instigated by the right after 1979 has forced it to discard the essential ethical objectives of social democracy.

But to conclude that the revisionists and 'New' Labour are separated fundamentally over aims is mistaken. We have to distinguish between 'New' Labour's vocabulary, its stated doctrine, and its programme. Nor can equality simply be conflated with redistribution and higher rates of income tax. When they debated taxation, Jay and Crosland concentrated more on inherited wealth than earned income.[36]

These misunderstandings have complex origins and reflect internal confusions that have persisted throughout Labour's history about the precise meaning of 'equality'. In the 1970s the term was demonised by neo-liberals, implying everything from levelling down in public services, to welfare state dependency, and penal taxation rates.[37]

There has also been disagreement among historians about what precisely the revisionists meant by the invocation of equality as a value. This indicates its vulnerability to neo-liberal attack, though it has been the strongest ethical inspiration of virtually every socialist doctrine since the late nineteenth century.

If we treat Crosland's *The Future of Socialism* as an outstanding exposition of the revisionist case for democratic equality, it is clear that Crosland saw equality as a carefully negotiated compromise between 'opportunity' and 'result'. Meritocracy was central to the revisionist conception of the classless society. But it depended on a prior distribution of income guaranteed by the state. Crosland was anxious that a wholly meritocratic society would merely substitute one form of social stratification for another, creating 'an aristocracy of talent'. Significant income redistribution was therefore justified, but social mobility and meritocracy were also desired ends.

---

[36]   See Reisman (1997a).

[37]   See Plant (1981).

Brivati's argument that 'New' Labour constitutes a dramatic break with the past also idealises the party's previous disposition and achievements. Labour Governments of the 1960s and 1970s, for example, were frequently criticised on the grounds that they did not possess a sufficiently effective or comprehensive egalitarian strategy. Successive reports demonstrated that the link persisted between social class, housing tenure, and other measures of prosperity, sickness and death, despite the 1964–70 and 1974–9 Labour Governments. Peter Townsend fired his charge in 1975:

> poverty is more extensive than is generally or officially believed and has to be understood not only as an inevitable feature of severe social inequality but also as a particular consequence of actions by the rich to preserve and enhance their wealth and so deny it to others.[38]

The revisionists also saw 'class' and stratification in broader terms than statistical measures of income and wealth. Their overriding concern was the abolition of the class society, and the undesirable status inequalities it produces. This disdain for class partly reflected revisionist ideas about efficiency, but also the ethical nature of society. Class was inefficient, reinforcing stagnation in the economy. It wasted talent, and prevented the most able from rising up the occupational ladder. And it stifled the innovation, creativity, and freedom that were essential to an economy and society struggling to shake off post-war sclerosis.

The final charge is that 'New' Labour has negated personal liberty in contrast to the post-war social democrats, who were determined to discard Labour's tendency to show, in Crosland's words, 'more orthodoxy than a bench of bishops'. Revisionists placed a high premium on liberty, enjoyed pleasure and even a little hedonism, and saw Labour as freedom's guardian in post-war Britain.

Once again, allegations of a fundamental breach with 'New' Labour appear wide of the mark. 'New' Labour has been careful to distinguish its rights and responsibilities approach to civic duty from the re-assertion of tolerance in the private domain — though it has embarked on a project to re-moralise civic life in an age when traditional solidarities are waning. Fundamentally, it has built on Jenkins' achievements in the 1960s, rather than dismantling them.

---

[38] Townsend (1975).

Both would subscribe to Jenkins' view that, 'There is the need for the state to do less to restrict personal freedom'.[39]

There is a further point of fundamental commonality. Both have adopted a strategy of what the historian and leading intellectual in the Campaign for Democratic Socialism (CDS) Rita Hinden terms, 'advance on many fronts'.[40] Social democrats should not depict their reforms instrumentally, as raising living standards, and expanding the frontiers of the public sector. Social democracy should be understood somewhat differently, as altering the essential characteristics of British society, embracing education, culture and industrial democracy. This seeks to re-cast the fundamental structures of economic and political power within the state.

The pursuit of egalitarian ideals demands rather more than the redistribution of income and wealth. New concerns have arisen since 1945 embracing environmentalism, social cohesion, democratisation, and personal liberty. As Crosland puts it: 'Total abstinence and a good filing system are not now the real sign posts to the Socialist Utopia: or at least, if they are, some of us will fall by the way side'.[41] As society becomes richer, attention gradually shifts from the economy to the social and psychological causes of unhappiness and distress.

'New' Labour has learnt much from the errors and tactical miscalculations of its modernising predecessors. But it has also drawn inspiration from their achievements. Tawney's Christian socialism; Durbin's riposte to Communism in the 1930s that 'to betray democracy is to betray socialism'; the post-war settlement; Crosland's legacy as Education Secretary and *The Future of Socialism*; Jenkins' reforms as Home Secretary and Chancellor, and his pro-European values; Healey's courage as Defence Secretary, and his determination to save the Labour Party from the fundamentalist left in 1981.

These are achievements that continue to influence 'New' Labour, just as many of its key preoccupations have a long pedigree in the party. The making of 'New' Labour, above all its new statement of values and its wider electoral appeal, fulfils the revisionist ambitions set out by Giles Radice in *Labour's Path to Power: The New Revisionism*.

The New Clause IV was expressed in terms of ideals, rather than specific policies. With it Tony Blair argued, 'The Labour Party has

---

[39] Jenkins (1972).

[40] See Appendix (CDS Manifesto, 1962).

[41] Crosland (1956).

reclaimed its basic values'.[42] In the early 1990s he had gone further, claiming: 'The battle over theoretical forms of economic organisation is dead'.[43] These are classic revisionist statements because they distinguish ends and means, values and policies. Indeed, they define socialism in ethical terms, establishing the party in the mainstream of European social democracy. But fundamentally, they enable the Labour Party to formulate a distinctive project to revolutionise British society through steady, but persistent, social reform.

Fulfilling Revisionist Aims

'New' Labour has therefore accomplished the first stage of the revisionist project to which Dalton, Gaitskell and Crosland became devoted in the 1950s and 1960s. It has removed the party's doctrinal ambiguity over the market economy, and discarded the obsolete link between nationalisation, public ownership and social justice. Indeed, it has formally abandoned the party's founding myth of a future socialist commonwealth built on public ownership of the means of production, widely regarded as redundant and doctrinaire.

It has therefore ended a persistent contradiction in Labour's history. This sought to combine the necessity of managing capitalism with a radical rhetoric envisaging the replacement of capitalism with an alternative economic system. Instead, Labour's future no longer relied on evasion or obfuscation. It could espouse with clarity its values and aims in power, no longer shrouded in confusion over its real intentions towards British capitalism.

'New' Labour triumphed in 1994–95 where Gaitskell failed in 1959–60 because the terms of debate on public ownership, within and outside the party, had been transformed. The privatisation of nationalised utilities in the 1980s led to a more receptive climate on the left, as Labour gradually abandoned its re-nationalisation commitments after the 1987 election.[44]

In truth, the new Clause IV meant no substantive or far-reaching transformation of its programme, since the leadership had formally accommodated itself to the preservation of competitive markets in

---

[42]   Blair (1994).

[43]   Blair (1991).

[44]   Shaw (1994).

the late 1980s.[45] It was first and foremost an act of clarification, reassuring the electorate as to its true intentions. It also signalled the triumph of the revisionists in the battle for the party, delayed for thirty-five years. A strategic dilemma seldom anticipated has nonetheless arisen since the early 1990s: what to put in its place.

The first stage of the revisionist project is to discard the features of its party's doctrine that are obsolete. The next step is to re-configure its ideological identity, articulating a positive definition of what it is for. Revisionist social democracy is a two-stage exercise.

The new doctrine should serve as a compass for future Labour Governments, guiding them in a world of lost ideological certainties. Critically, it must enable the party to govern on its own terms, not those of its opponents, permanently reshaping the contours of domestic British politics.

This raises the theme of what 'New' Labour now stands for. What are its guiding principles and governing ideals given that public ownership has been relegated in importance, and the old Clause IV revised out of existence?

'New' Labour has instigated a genuine process of theoretical reconstruction in which centre-left parties around the world have been engaged since the late 1980s. It has abandoned traditional shibboleths, while reappraising the out-worn assumptions of post-war social democracy.

In its place, 'New' Labour has inserted an abstract communitarian ideal, according to which 'we achieve more together than we achieve alone' (Clause IV (iv)). But whether this goal has the emotional power and clarity to supersede Labour's historic commitment to nationalise the commanding heights of the British economy remains uncertain.

The unfulfilled task of revisionism is to lay claim to the centre-ground of politics transforming social democracy into a permanent governing force. 'New' Labour is the vehicle to realise this historical objective, breaking the unhappy sequence of defeats suffered by the British centre-left in the twentieth century. Its purpose — to correct the inefficiencies and injustices of the market order — to modernise Britain and its institutions — creating a society that is more equal, free and just, less disfigured by human misery and suffering.

The inclusive appeal of the new Clause IV embodying 'New' Labour's doctrine and identity has also led inevitably to problems

---

[45] See *Meet the Challenge, Make the Change* (The Labour Party, 1989).

and contradictions. According to some analysts, it lacks a clear, precise definition.[46] This has inhibited the struggle for ideological dominance that is necessary for Labour to become a natural party of power, and to undertake the drastic re-orientation of British economic and social policy that is necessary to finally break free of the dismal failures of the post-war years.

'New' Labour has seemed to lack a clear, positive definition for several reasons.

Most obviously, it was defined at its inception as neither the new right of the conservatives, nor traditional social democracy. This emphasis on 'triangulation' enabled the party to gain credibility and definition, bringing into sharper focus the novelty of its appeal to the electorate.[47] As a popular movement for social reform, 'New' Labour has been practically orientated towards social ills, rather than abstract philosophical debates. In turn, it has re-cast the traditional categories and parameters of social and political thought. For example, it envisages the interests of market and state working in harmony, and seeks to resolve the dialectical relationship between individual and community.

This gave 'New' Labour distinctive qualities, as it transcended the forces of left and right. The transformative capacities of an ideology should be judged by how far its progressive tide shifts the centre of gravity towards the left.[48] But to sustain its hold over the domestic landscape, 'New' Labour has to continue setting out with clarity what it is for, not merely what it is against — redefining the strategic choices facing Britain.

The forces of 'moral' and 'mechanical' reform are evidently in tension within the 'New' Labour project, further obscuring its real identity.

This reflects a historical ambiguity within Labour's culture and traditions concerning its view of the state, famously elaborated by Peter Clarke in *Liberals and Social Democrats*. 'Moral' reformers take an optimistic view of progress. Moral change, a change of heart and a new consciousness, will be the agent and sanction of a transformation within society.

In contrast, the pessimistic 'mechanical' reformer has no such confidence. Change must be made from above if spontaneous forces fail.

---

[46] See Jones (1996).

[47] See Gould (1998).

[48] Freeden (1978).

This was a significant deficiency of the social democratic middle way, as David Marquand demonstrates in his lucid essay *The Unprincipled Society*. There were limits to how far Keynesian fine-tuning and higher public expenditure could secure a more just and efficient society.

Socialism had to discard its corporatist ethos, Evan Luard argued in a brilliant, but little known essay in the late 1970s.[49] At root, Labour's inability to emerge as a more potent governing instrument within the British state partly reflects these persistent, and unresolved ambiguities about moral and mechanical reform.

Labour's institutions in the past have been swept away as it failed to secure an enduring legacy. Only path-breaking achievements, notably the National Health Service, have survived since 1945. In future, social democracy must ensure that its reforms have sufficient support and legitimacy to live on, becoming accepted by its successors, and coalescing into an irreversible progressive settlement.

This is the challenge for 'New' Labour. This book urges a return to the themes and ideas explored by revisionists, as it seeks to re-cast British society and institutionalise itself as a party of government.

Britain has been transformed since 1979. There can be no return to the 'golden era' of post-war social democracy. Economic reforms carried out during the 1980s have reshaped the post-war compromise between capital and labour. Constitutional reforms have profoundly altered the nature of the British state.[50] Debates about decline that preoccupied the political class during this prolonged contraction of British power have ebbed away. What sort of country should Britain now seek to become? As it rises to this challenge, 'New' Labour should confidently reclaim its heritage.

'New' Labour's Old Roots

'New' Labour is the unfinished revolution in British politics. It has transcended Labour's ambiguous commitment to public ownership and nationalisation of the means of production, distribution and exchange. But if Labour is to govern in the future on its own terms — becoming a more effective instrument for the realisation of radical aims, while re-casting British society and British politics — it must furnish the party with a stronger, more confident social democratic

---

[49] Luard (1979).

[50] See Gamble (2003).

doctrine, anchored in values and commitments, providing a wider frame and narrative that makes sense of political activity and involvement.

'New' Labour has accorded iconic status to liberal thinkers and practitioners, notably L.A. Hobhouse, William Beveridge and J.M. Keynes.[51] This liberal progressive tradition counteracts the statist and centralising nature of British social democracy.

As this anthology demonstrates, such a view rests on a narrow appreciation of the richness and diversity of social democratic thought in Britain.

In the twentieth century, revisionist thinkers from within the Labour tradition assimilated and synthesised liberal and progressive ideas.

It is a defining premise of this book that the fate of the Labour Party and the transformation of the structures and institutions of the British state, are intertwined. Labour needs a coherent perspective on Britain's role within the world economic and political system, demonstrating how the domestic problems of modernisation and restructuring should be tackled. A book such as this can hardly provide all the answers — but as a historical tract, it can restore Labour's confidence in its own future.

---

[51] See Marquand (1991).

Laying Revisionist Foundations

R.H. Tawney — Liberty and Equality (1931)

R.H. Tawney's outstanding achievement was to furnish Labour with a basic political philosophy. His ideas permeated deep into the political consciousness of the party, and he was in key respects the father of Labour's ethical socialist tradition. At a Memorial Service in 1962 Hugh Gaitskell declared of Tawney: 'I always think of him as the Democratic Socialist par excellence'.

He was born in 1880 in India, educated at Rugby and Oxford, and had worked in London's East End at Toynbee Hall before becoming a pioneer of the Worker's Educational Association and a distinguished academic. Like the Fabian G.D.H. Cole, the theorist of self-governing industrial guilds, and Harold Laski, political thinker and inspirational teacher of generations of students at the London School of Economics, Tawney was a leading intellectual figure in the twentieth-century Labour Party.

Tawney's vision was defined by its commitment to equality. He advanced a dual definition of equality as an essential socialist objective. He did not think of it in the naïve sense of equality of talent, merit, or personality. First, he argued that everyone possesses equal moral value. We are all worthy of equal consideration by virtue of being human. Second, he used it to legitimate differences in material conditions, providing society collectively could justify them, as a precursor to John Rawls' 'theory of justice'.[1]

---

[1]   Rawls (1999).

Tawney's target was unwarranted material inequality. Differences in wealth and power were justified only where they fulfilled a wider social purpose, such as mobilising scarce talent. The level of reward should reflect the extent of service to the community. But in the world of the 1930s, most inequalities did not support the common good at all. They were founded on privilege. Persistent social and economic inequalities prevented large sections of the population from achieving their full potential, both as human beings and citizens.

He vigorously attacked the traditional economic arguments in favour of inequality. Tawney proposed instead to enlarge the British state so that it could provide the means of emancipation. These goods such as education and social welfare were required by individuals to make the most of their potential. Equality of provision did not therefore mean identity of provision, clearly preceding 'New' Labour's notion of the enabling state.

But public ownership was also regarded as an essential step in securing control over private economic power, and as a spur to modernise Britain's economy, and its institutions.

Equality was necessary for freedom. Tawney's work proved compelling as a statement of the essence of democratic socialism.

Tawney's commitment to working-class emancipation was expressed through service, as President of the Workers Educational Association between 1928 and 1944, and through a succession of education committees and working groups. His influence is writ large over the history of education policy in Britain. He helped shape the 1944 Butler Act, establishing universal secondary education. Tawney was closely involved in the practical effort to return Labour to office in the 1920s and 1930s, and lent his support to the Campaign for Democratic Socialism (CDS) in the early 1960s.

By marrying liberal idealism with Christian values and economic history in Equality *(1931), Tawney provided British socialism with a coherent doctrine rooted in a fundamental belief in individual moral worth, equality of opportunity, and social responsibility. State intervention, changing existing circumstances to make society more ethically organised, was the essence of Tawney's socialism. In emphasising the social and moral case for equality alongside nationalisation and public ownership, Tawney's synthesis had a lasting impact on later revisionist accounts of socialism.*

R.H. Tawney's publications include The Acquisitive Society *(1921),* Religion and the Rise of Capitalism *(1926),* The Attack and Other Papers *(1953), and* The Radical Tradition: Twelve Essays on Politics, Education and Literature *(1964).*

Selected Text[2]

Equality

What a community requires, as the word itself suggests, is a common culture, because, without it, it is not a community at all. And evidently it requires it in a special degree at a moment like the present,[3] when circumstances confront it with the necessity of giving a new orientation to its economic life, because it is in such circumstances that the need for co-operation, and for the mutual confidence and tolerance upon which co-operation depends, is particularly pressing. But a common culture cannot be created merely by desiring it. It must rest upon practical foundations of social organisation. It is incompatible with the existence of sharp contrasts between the economic standards and educational opportunities of different classes, for such contrasts have as their result, not a common culture, but servility or resentment, on the one hand, and patronage or arrogance, on the other. It involves, in short, a large measure of economic equality — not necessarily in the sense of an identical level of pecuniary incomes, but of equality of environment, of access to education and the means of civilisation, of security and independence, and of the social consideration which equality in these matters usually carries with it . . .

It is obvious, indeed, that as things are today, no redistribution of wealth would bring general affluence, and that statisticians are within their rights in making merry with the idea that the equalisation of incomes would make everyone rich. But, though riches are a good, they are not nevertheless, the only good; and because greater production, which is concerned with the commodities to be consumed, is clearly important, it does not follow that greater equality, which is concerned with the relations between the human beings who consume them, is not important also. It is obvious, again, that the word 'equality' possessed more than one meaning, and that the controversies surrounding it arise partly, at least, because the same term is employed with different connotations. Thus it may either purport to state a fact. Or convey the expression of an ethical judgment. On the one hand, it may affirm that men are, on the whole, very similar in their natural endowments of character and intelli-

---

[2]   Tawney, R.H., *Equality*, London: Bell & Sons, 1930. [Footnotes in this section are editorial.]

[3]   Tawney wrote *Equality* in the context of the 1931 economic crisis.

gence. On the other hand, it may assert that, while they differ profoundly as individuals in capacity and character, they are equally
entitled as human beings to consideration and respect, and that the
well-being of a society is likely to be increased if it so plans its organisation that, whether their powers are great or small, all its members
may be equally enabled to make the best of such powers as they
possess . . .

The equality . . . which these thinkers emphasise as desirable is not
equality of capacity of attainment, but of circumstances, institutions,
and manner of life. The inequality which they deplore is not inequality of personal gifts, but of the social and economic environment.
They are concerned, not with the biological phenomenon, but with a
spiritual relation and the conduct to be based on it. Their view, in
short, is that, because men are men, social institutions — property
rights, and the organisation of industry, and the system of public
health and education — should be planned, as far as is possible, to
emphasise and strengthen, not the class differences which divide,
but the common humanity which unites, them . . .

It is true that human beings have, except as regards certain
elementary, though still sadly neglected, matters of health and
development, different requirements, and that these different
requirements can be met satisfactorily only by varying forms of provision. But equality of provision is not identity of provision. It is to be
achieved, not by treating different needs in the same way, but by
devoting equal care to ensuring that they are met in the different
ways most appropriate to them, as is done by a doctor who pre-
scribes different regimens for different constitutions, or a teacher
who develops different types of intelligence by different curricula.
The more anxiously, indeed, a society endeavours to secure equality
of consideration for all its members, the greater will be the differentiation of treatment which, when once their common human needs
have been met, it accords to the special needs of different groups and
individuals among them.

It is true, finally, that some men are inferior to others in respect of
their intellectual endowments, and it is possible — though the truth
of the possibility has not yet been satisfactorily established — that
the same is true of certain classes.[4] It does not, however, follow from
this fact that such individuals or classes should receive less consider-

---

[4]   Tawney's remark reflects the popularity of genetic theories in the 1920s and
       1930s for explaining ethnic and social characteristics.

ation than others, or should be treated as inferior in respect of such matters as legal status, or health, or economic arrangements, which are within the control of the community . . .

Everyone recognises the absurdity of such an argument when it is applied to matters within his personal knowledge and professional competence. Everyone realises that, in order to justify inequalities of circumstance or opportunity by reference to differences of personal quality, it is necessary . . . to show that the differences in question are relevant to the inequalities. Everyone now sees, for example, that it is not a valid argument against women's suffrage to urge, as used to be urged not so long ago, that women are physically weaker than men, since physical strength is not relevant to the question of the ability to exercise the franchise, or a valid argument in favour of slavery that some men are less intelligent than others, since it is not certain that slavery is the most suitable penalty for lack of intelligence.

Not everyone, however, is so quick to detect that fallacy when it is expressed in general terms. It is still possible, for example, for one eminent statesman to ridicule the demand for a diminution of economic inequalities on the ground that every mother knows that her children are not equal, without reflecting whether it is the habit of mothers to lavish care on the strong and neglect the delicate; and for another to dismiss the suggestion that greater economic equality is desirable, for the reason apparently, that men are naturally unequal. It is probable, however, that the first does not think that the fact that some children are born with good digestions, and others with bad, is a reason for supplying good food to the former and bad food to the latter, rather than for giving to both food which is equal in quality but different in kind, and that the second does not suppose that the natural inequality of men makes legal equality a contemptible principle . . .

Many services are supplied by collective effort today which in the recent past were supplied by individual effort or not supplied at all, and many more, it may be suspected, will be so supplied in the future. At any moment there are some needs which almost everyone is agreed should be satisfied on equalitarian principles, and others which are agreed should be met by individuals who purchase what their incomes enable them to pay for, and others, again, about the most suitable provision for which opinions differ. Society has not been prevented from seeking to establish equality in respect of the first by the fear that in so doing it may be perpetrating a scientific impossibility. Nor ought it to be prevented from moving towards equality in respect of the second and third, if experience suggests that greater equality in these matters also would contribute to greater efficiency and to more general happiness . . .

Perhaps, therefore, the remote Victorian thinkers, like Arnold and Mill,[5] who dealt lightly with mumbo-jumbo, and who commended equality to their fellow-countrymen as one source of peace and happiness, were not speaking so unadvisedly as at first sight might appear. It is the fact that, in spite of their varying characters and capacities, men possess in the common humanity a quality which is worth cultivating, and that a community is most likely to make the most of that quality if it takes it into account in planning its economic organisation and social institutions — if it stresses lightly differences of wealth and birth and social position, and establishes on firm foundations institutions which meet common needs, and are a source of common enlightenment and common enjoyment. The individual differences of which so much is made, they would have said, will always survive, and they are to be welcomed, not regretted. But their existence is no reason for not seeking to establish the largest possible measure of equality of environment, and circumstance, and opportunity. On the contrary, it is a reason for redoubling our efforts to establish it, in order to ensure that these diversities of gifts may come to fruition . . .

So to criticise inequality and to desire equality is not, as is sometimes suggested, to cherish the romantic illusion that men are equal in character and intelligence. It is to hold that, whilst their natural endowments differ profoundly, it is the mark of a civilised society to aim at eliminating such inequalities as have their source, not in individual differences, but in its own organisation, and that individual differences, which are a source of social energy, are more likely to ripen and find expression if social inequalities are, as far as practicable, diminished. And the obstacle to the progress of equality is something simpler and more potent than finds expression in the familiar truism that men vary in their mental and moral, as well as in their physical characteristics, important and valuable though that truism is as a reminder that different individuals require different types of provision. It is the habit of mind which thinks it, not regrettable, but natural and desirable, that different sections of a community should be distinguished from each other by sharp differences of economic status, of environment, of education and culture and habit of life. It is

---

[5]   Matthew Arnold was an influential nineteenth-century educationalist; John Stuart Mill was a leading advocate of utilitarian philosophy.

the temper which regards with approval the social institutions and economic arrangements by which such differences are emphasised and enhanced, and feels distrust and apprehension at all attempts to diminish them . . .

Most social systems need a lightning-conductor. The formula which supplies it to our own is equality of opportunity. The conception is one to which homage is paid today by all, including those who resist most strenuously attempts to apply it. But the rhetorical tribute which it receives appears sometimes to be paid on the understanding that it shall be content with ceremonial honours. It retains its throne, on condition that it refrains from meddling with the profitable business of the factory and marketplace. Its credit is good, as long as it does not venture to cash its cheques. Like other respectable principles, it is encouraged to reign, provided that it does not attempt to rule . . .

It is possible that intelligent tadpoles reconcile themselves to the inconveniences of their position, by reflecting that, though most of them will live and die as tadpoles and nothing more, the more fortunate of the species will one day shed their tails, distend their mouths and stomachs, hop nimbly on to dry land, and croak addresses to their former friends on the virtues by means of which tadpoles of character and capacity can rise to be frogs. This conception of society may be described, perhaps, as the Tadpole Philosophy, since the consolation which it offers for social evils consists in the statement that exceptional individuals can succeed in evading them. Who has not heard it suggested that the presence of opportunities, by means of which individuals can ascend and get on, relieves economic contrasts of their social position and their personal sting? Who has not encountered the argument that there is an education 'ladder' up which talent can climb, and that its existence makes the scamped quality of our primary education — the overcrowded classes, and mean surroundings, and absence of amenities — a matter of secondary importance? And what a view of human life such an attitude implies! As though, if they could, it were natural and proper that the position of the mass of mankind should permanently be such that they can attain civilisation only by escaping from it! As though the noblest use of exceptional powers were to scramble to shore, undeterred by the thought of drowning companions!

It is true, of course, that a community must draw on a stream of fresh talent, in order to avoid stagnation, and that, unless individuals of ability can turn their powers to account, they are embittered by a sense of defeat and frustration. The existence of opportunities to move from point to point on an economic scale, and to mount from humble origins to success and affluence, is a condition, therefore, both of social well-being and of individual happiness, and impediments which deny them to some, while lavishing them on others, are injurious to both. But opportunities to 'rise' are not a substitute for a large measure of practical equality, nor do they make immaterial the existence of sharp disparities of income and social condition. On the contrary, it is only the presence of a high degree of practical equality which can diffuse and generalise opportunities to rise. The existence of such opportunities in fact, and not merely in form, depends, not only upon an open road, but upon an equal start. It is precisely, of course, when capacity is aided by a high level of general well-being in the *milieu* surrounding it, that its ascent is most likely to be regular and rapid, rather than fitful and intermittent . . .

If a high degree of practical equality is necessary to social well-being, because without it ability cannot find its way to its true vocation, it is necessary also for another and more fundamental reason. It is necessary because a community requires unity as well as diversity, and because, important as it is to discriminate between different powers, it is even more important to provide for common needs. Clever people, who possess exceptional gifts themselves, are naturally impressed by exceptional gifts in others, and desire, when they consider the matter at all, that society should be organised to offer a career to exceptional talent, though they rarely understand the full scope and implications of the revolution they are preaching. But, in the conditions characteristic of the large-scale economic organisation, in which ninety per cent of the population are wage-earners, and not more than ten per cent employers, farmers, independent workers or engaged in professions, it is obviously, whatever the level of individual intelligence and degree of social fluidity, a statistical impossibility for more than a small fraction of the former to enter the ranks of the latter; and a community cannot be built upon exceptional talent alone, though it would be a poor thing without it. Social well-being does not only depend upon intelligent leadership; it also depends upon cohesion and solidarity. It implies the existence, not merely of opportunities to ascend, but of a high level of general culture, and a strong sense of common interests, and the diffusion throughout society of a conviction that civilisation is not the business of an elite alone, but a common enterprise which is the concern of all. And individual happiness does not only require that men should be able to rise to new positions of comfort and distinction; it also requires that they should be able to lead a life of dignity and culture, whether they rise or not, and that, whatever their position on the economic scale may be, it shall be such as is fit to be occupied by men.

Liberty and Equality

Liberty and equality have usually in England been considered antithetic; and, since fraternity has rarely been considered at all, the famous trilogy has been easily dismissed as a hybrid abortion. Equality implies the deliberate acceptance of social restraints upon individual expansion. It involves the prevention of sensational extremes of wealth and power by public action for the public good. If liberty means, therefore, that every individual shall be free, according to his opportunities, to indulge without limit his appetite for either, it is clearly incompatible, not only with economic and social, but with civil and political, equality, which also prevent the strong exploiting to the full the advantages for their strength, and, indeed, with any habit of life save that of the Cyclops. But freedom for the pike is death for the minnows. It is possible that equality is to be contrasted, not with liberty, but only with a particular interpretation of it.

The test of principle is that it can be generalized, so that the advantages of applying it are not particular, but universal. Since it is impossible for every individual, as for every nation, simultaneously to be stronger than his neighbours, it is a truism that liberty, as distinct from the liberties of special persons and classes, can exist only in so far as it is limited by rules, which secure that freedom for some is not slavery for others. The spiritual energy of human beings, in all the wealth of their infinite diversities, is the end to which external arrangements, whether political or economic, are merely means. Hence institutions which guarantee to men the opportunity of becoming the best of which they are capable are the supreme political good, and liberty is rightly preferred to equality, when the two are in conflict. The question is whether, in the conditions of modern society they conflict or not. It is whether the defined and limited freedom, which alone can be generally enjoyed, is most likely to be attained by a community which encourages violent inequalities, or by one which represents them.

Inequality of power is not necessarily inimical to liberty. On the contrary, it is the condition of it. Liberty implies the ability to act, not merely to resist. Neither society as a whole, nor any group within it, can carry out its will except through organs; and, in order that such organs may function with effect, they must be sufficiently differentiated to perform their varying tasks, of which direction is one and execution another. But, while inequality of power is the condition of liberty, since it is the condition of any effective action, it is also a menace to it, for power which is sufficient to use is sufficient to abuse. Hence, in the political sphere, where the danger is familiar, all civilised communities have established safeguards, by which the advantages of differentiation of function, with the varying degrees of power which it involves, may be preserved, and the risk that power may be tyrannical, or perverted to private ends, averted or diminished. They have endeavoured, for example, as in England, to protect civil liberty by requiring that, with certain exceptions, the officers of the State shall be subject to the ordinary tribunals, and political liberty by insisting that those who take decisions on matters affecting the public shall be responsible to an assembly chosen by it. The precautions may be criticized as inadequate, but the need for precautions is not today disputed. It is recognized that political power must rest ultimately on consent, and that its exercise must be limited by rules of law.

The dangers arising from inequalities of economic power have been less commonly recognized. They exist, however, whether recognized or not. For the excess or abuse of power, and its divorce from responsibility, which results in oppression, are not confined to the relations which arise between men as members of a state. They are not a malady which is peculiar to political systems, as was typhus to slums, and from which other departments of life can be regarded as immune. They are a disease, not of political organization, but of organization. They occur, in the absence of preventative measures, in political associations, because they occur in all forms of association in which large numbers of individuals are massed for collective action. The isolated worker may purchase security against exploitation at the cost of poverty, as the hermit may avoid the corruptions of civilization by forgoing its advantages. But, as soon as he is associated with his fellows in a common undertaking, his duties must be specified and his rights defined; and, in so far as they are not, the undertaking is impeded. The problem of securing a livelihood ceases to be merely economic, and becomes social and political.

The struggle with nature continues, but on a different plane. Its effi-ciency is heightened by co-operation. Its character is complicated by the emergence of the question of the terms on which co-operation shall take place.

In an individual civilisation, when its first phase is over, most eco-nomic activity is corporate activity. It is carried on, not by individu-als, but by groups, which are endowed by the State with a legal status, and the larger of which, in size complexity, specialization of functions and unity of control, resemble less the private enterprise of the past than a public department. As far as certain great industries are concerned, employment must be found in the service of these corporations, or not at all. Hence the mass of mankind pass their working lives under the direction of a hierarchy, whose heads define, as they think most profitable, the lines on which the common enterprise is to proceed, and determine, subject to the intervention of the State and voluntary organizations, the economic, and to a con-siderable, though diminishing, extent, the social environment of their employees. Possessing the reality of power, without the deco-rative trappings — unless, as in England is often the case, it thinks it worth while to buy them — this business oligarchy is the effective aristocracy of industrial nations, and the aristocracy of tradition and prestige, when such still exists, carries out its wishes and courts its favours. In such conditions, authority over human beings is exer-cised, not only through political, but through economic, organs. The problem of liberty, therefore, is necessarily concerned, not only with political but also with economic, relations.

It is true, of course, that the problems are different. But to suppose that the abuses of economic power are trivial, or that they are auto-matically prevented by political democracy, is to be deceived by words. Freedom is always, no doubt, a matter of degree; no man enjoys all the requirements of full personal development, and all men possess some of them. It is not only compatible with conditions in which all men are fellow servants, but would find in such condi-tions its most perfect expression. What it excludes is a society where only some are servants, while others are masters.

For, whatever else the idea involves, it implies at least, that no man shall be amenable to an authority which is arbitrary in its proceed-ings, exorbitant in its demands, or incapable of being called to account when it abuses its office for personal advantage. In so far as his livelihood is at the mercy of an irresponsible superior, whether political or economic, who can compel his reluctant obedience by *force majeure*, whose actions he is unable to modify or resist, save at the cost of grave personal injury to himself and his dependents, and whose favour he must court, even when he despises it, he may possess a profusion of more tangible blessings, from beer to motor bicycles, but he cannot be said to be in possession of freedom. In so far as an economic system grades mankind into groups, of which some can wield, if unconsciously, the force of economic duress for their own profit or convenience, while others must submit to it, its effect is that freedom itself is similarly graded. Society is divided, in its economic and social relations, into classes which are ends, and classes which are instruments. Like property, with which in the past it has been closely connected, liberty becomes the privilege of a class, not the possession of a nation.

Political principles resemble military tactics; they are usually designed for a war which is over. Freedom is commonly interpreted in England in political terms, because it was in the political arena that the most resounding of its recent victories were won. It is regarded as belonging to human beings and citizens, rather than to citizens as human beings; so that it is possible for a nation, the majority of whose members have as little influence on the decisions that determine their economic destinies as on the motions of the planets, to applaud the idea with self-congratulatory gestures of decorous enthusiasm, as though history were of the past, but not of the present. If the attitude of the ages from which it inherits a belief in liberty had been equally ladylike, there would have been, it is probable, little liberty to applaud.

For freedom is always relative to power, and the kind of freedom which at any moment it is most urgent to affirm depends on the nature of the power which is prevalent and established. Since political arrangements may be such as to check excess of power, while economic arrangements permit or encourage them, a society, or a large part of it, may be both politically free and economically the opposite. It may be protected against arbitrary action by the agents of government, and be without the security against economic oppression which corresponds to civil liberty. It may possess the political institutions of an advanced democracy, and lack the will and ability to control the conduct of those powerful in its economic affairs, which is the economic analogy of political freedom.

The extension of liberty from the political to the economic sphere is evidently among the most urgent tasks of industrial societies. It is evident also, however, that, in so far as this extension takes place, the traditional antithesis between liberty and equality will no longer be valid. As long as liberty is interpreted as consisting exclusively in security against oppression by the agents of the State, or as a share in its government, it is plausible, perhaps, to dissociate it from equality; for though experience suggests that, even in this meagre and restricted sense, it is not easily maintained in the presence of extreme disparities of wealth and influence, it is possible for it to be enjoyed, in form at least, by pauper and millionaire. Such disparities, however, though they do not enable one group to become the political master of another, necessarily cause it to exercise a preponderant influence on the economic life of the rest of society.

Hence, when liberty is construed, realistically, or implying, not merely a minimum of civil and political rights, but securities that the economically weak will not be at the mercy of the economically strong, and that the control of those aspects of economic life by which all are affected will be amenable, in the last resort, to the will of all, a large measure of equality, so far from being inimical to liberty, is essential to it. In conditions which impose co-operative, rather than merely individual, effort, liberty is, in fact, equality in action, in the sense, not that all men perform identical functions or wield the same degree of power, but that all men are equally protected against the abuse of power, and equally entitled to insist that power shall be used, not for personal ends, but for the general advantage. Civil and political liberty obviously imply, not that all men shall be members of parliament, cabinet ministers, or civil servants, but the absence of such civil and political inequalities as enable one class to impose its will on another by legal coercion. It should be not less obvious that economic liberty implies, not that all men shall initiate, plan, direct, manage, or administer, but the absence of such economic inequalities as can be used as a means of economic constraint.

The danger to liberty which is caused by inequality varies with differences of economic organization and public policy. When the mass of the population are independent producers, or when, if they are dependent on great undertakings, the latter are subject to strict public control, it may be absent or remote. It is seen at its height when important departments of economic activity are the province of large organizations, which, if they do not themselves, as sometimes occurs, control the State, are sufficiently powerful to resist control by it. Among the numerous interesting phenomena which impress the foreign observer of American economic life, not the least interesting is the occasional emergence of industrial enterprises which appear to him, and, indeed, to some Americans, to have developed the characteristics, not merely of an economic undertaking, but of a kind of polity. Their rule may be a mild and benevolent paternalism, lavishing rest-rooms, schools, gymnasia, and guarantees for constitutional behaviour on care-free employees; or it may be a harsh and suspicious tyranny. But, whether as amiable as Solon, or as ferocious as Lycurgus, their features are cast in a heroic mould. Their gestures are those of the sovereigns of little commonwealths rather than of mere mundane employers.

American official documents have, on occasion, called attention to the tendency of the bare stem of business to burgeon, in a favourable environment, with almost tropical exuberance, so that it clothes itself with functions that elsewhere are regarded as belonging to political authorities. The corporations controlled by six financial groups, states the Report of the United States Commission on Industrial Relations some twenty years ago, employ 2,651,684 wage-earners or 440,000 per group. Some of these companies own, not merely the plant and equipment of industry, but the homes of the workers, and streets through which they pass to work, and the halls in which, if they are allowed to meet, their meetings are held. They employ private spies and detectives, private police and, sometimes, it appears, private troops, and engage, when they deem it expedient, in private war. While organized themselves, they forbid organization among their employees, and enforce their will by evicting malcontents from their homes, and even, on occasion, by the use of armed force. In such conditions business may continue in its modesty, since its object is money, to describe itself as business; but, in fact, it is a tyranny. 'The main objection to the large corporation', remarks Mr Justice Brandeis, who, as a judge of the Supreme Court, should know the facts, 'is that it makes possible — and in many cases makes inevitable — the exercise of industrial absolutism.' Property in capital, thus inflated and emancipated, acquires attributes analogous to those of property in land in a feudal society. It carries with it the disposal, in fact, if not in law, of an authority which is quasi-governmental. Its owners possess what would have been called in the ages of darkness a private jurisdiction, and their relations to their dependents, though contractual in form, resemble rather those of ruler and subject than of equal parties to a commercial venture. The liberty which they defend against the encroachments of trade unionism and the State is most properly to be regarded, not as freedom, but as a franchise.

The conventional assertion that inequality is inseparable from liberty is obviously, in such circumstances, unreal and unconvincing; for the existence of the former is a menace to the latter, and the latter is most likely to be secured by curtailing the former. It is true that in England, where three generations of trade unionism and state intervention have done something to tame it, the exercise of economic power is, at ordinary times, less tyrannical than it once was. It still remains, nevertheless, a formidable menace to the freedom of common men. The pressure of such power is felt by the consumer, when he purchases necessaries which, directly or indirectly, are controlled by a monopoly. It is felt in the workshop, here, within the limits set by industrial legislation, and collective agreements, the comfort and amenity of the wage-earners' surroundings, the discipline and tone of factory life, the security of employment and methods of promotion, the recruitment and dismissal of workers, the degree to which the successive relays of cheap juvenile labour are employed, the opportunity to secure consideration for grievances, depend ultimately upon the policy pursued by a board of directors, who may have little love, indeed, for their shareholders, but who represent, in the last resort, their financial interests, and who, in so far as they are shareholders themselves, are necessarily judges in their own cause.

The effects of such autocracy are even graver in the sphere of economic strategy, which settles the ground upon which these tactical issues are fought out, and, in practice, not infrequently determines their decision before they arise. In such matters as the changes in organization most likely to restore prosperity to an embarrassed industry, and, therefore, to secure a tolerable livelihood to the workers engaged in it; methods of averting or meeting a depression; rationalization, the closing of plants and the concentration of production; the sale of a business on which a whole community depends or its amalgamation with a rival — not to mention the critical field of financial policy, with its possibilities, not merely of watered capital and of the squandering in dividends of resources which should be held as reserves, but of a sensational redistribution of wealth and widespread unemployment as a result of decisions taken by bankers — the diplomacy of business, like that of governments before 1914, is still commonly conducted over the heads of those most affected by it. The interests of the public, as workers and consumers, may receive consideration when these matters are determined; but the normal organization of economic life does not offer reliable guarantee that they will be considered. Nor can it plausibly be asserted that, if they are not, those aggrieved can be certain of any redress.

Power over the public is public power. It does not cease to be public merely because private persons are permitted to buy and sell, own and bequeath it, as they deem most profitable. To retort that its masters are themselves little more than half-conscious instruments, whose decisions register and transmit the impact of forces that they can neither anticipate nor control, though not wholly unveracious, is, nevertheless, superficial. The question is not whether there are economic movements which elude human control, for obviously there are. It is whether the public possesses adequate guarantees that those which are controllable are controlled in the general interest, not in that of a minority. Like the gods of Homer, who were not thereby precluded from interfering at their pleasure in the affairs of men, the potentates of the economic world exercise discretion, not, indeed, as to the situation which they will meet, but as to the manner in which they will meet it. They hold the initiative, have such freedom as to manoeuvre as circumstances allow, can force an issue or postpone it, and, if open conflict seems inevitable or expedient, can choose, as best suits themselves, the ground where it shall take place.

> Even if socialism were practicable without the destruction of freedom [writes Lord Lothian][6] would there be any advantage in converting the whole population into wage or salary earners, directed by the relatively few, also salaried, officials, who by ability, or promotion, or 'pull', could work their way to the top of the political machine or the permanent bureaucracy? . . . Is not that community the best, and, in the widest sense of the word, the most healthy, which has the largest proportion of citizens who have the enterprise, and energy, and initiative, to create new things and new methods for themselves, and not merely to wait to carry out the orders of somebody 'higher up'?

In view of the practice, in some parts, at least, of the business world, the less said about 'pull', perhaps, the better. But how true in substance! And how different the liner looks from the saloon-deck and the stokehold! And how striking that the conditions which Lord Lothian deplores as a hypothetical danger should be precisely those which ordinary men experience daily as an ever-present fact.

---

[6]   Lord Lothian was Private Secretary to Lloyd George, and co-author with J.M. Keynes of 'Can we conquer unemployment?' (1929).

For, in England at any rate, as a glance at the Registrar-General's reports would have sufficed to show him, not only the majority of the population, but the great majority, are today 'wage or salary earners', who, for quite a long time, have been 'directed by the relatively few', and who, if they did not 'wait to carry out the orders of somebody higher up', would be sent about their business with surprising promptitude. Unless Lord Lothian proposes to abolish, not only a particular political doctrine, but banks, railways, coal-mines and cotton-mills, the question is not whether orders guarantee that they are given in the general interest; but whether those to whom they are given shall have a reasonable security that, when their welfare is at stake, their views will receive an unbiased consideration.

Freedom may be, as he insists, more important than comfort. But is a miner, who is not subject to a bureaucracy, or at least, to a bureaucracy of the kind which alarms Lord Lothian, conspicuously more free than a teacher, who is? If a man eats bread made of flour produced to the extent of forty per cent by two milling combines and meat supplied by an international meat trust, and lives in a house built of materials of which twenty-five per cent were controlled by a ring, and buys his tobacco from one amalgamation, and his matches from another, while his wife's sewing-thread is provided by a third, which has added eight millionaires to the national roll of honour in the last twenty year, is he free as a consumer? Is he free as a worker, if he is liable to have his piece-rates cut at the discretion of his employer, and, on expressing his annoyance, to be dismissed as an agitator, and to be thrown on the scrap-heap without warning because his employer has decided to shut down a plant, or bankers to restrict credit, and to be told, when he points out that industry on which his livelihood depends is being injured by mismanagement, that his job is to work, and that the management in question will do his thinking for him? And if, in such circumstances, he is but partially free as a consumer and a worker, is not his freedom as a citizen itself also partial, rather than as Lord Lothian would desire, unqualified and complete?

Lord Lothian is misled as to liberty, because he has omitted to consider the bearing upon it of another phenomenon, the phenomenon of inequality. The truth is that, when the economic scales are so unevenly weighted, to interpret liberty as a political principle, which belongs to one world, the world of politics and government, while equality belongs — if, indeed, it belongs anywhere — to another world, the world of economic affairs, is to do violence to realities. Governments, it is true, exercise powers of a great and special kind, and freedom requires that they should be held strictly to account. But the administration of things is not easily distinguished, under modern conditions of mass organization, from the control of persons, and both are in the hands, to some not inconsiderable degree, of the minority who move the levers of the economic mechanism. The truth of the matter is put by Professor Pollard in his admirable study, *The Evolution of Parliament.*

> There is only one solution [he writes] of the problem of liberty, and it lies in equality . . . Men vary in physical strength; but so far as their social relations go that inequality has been abolished . . . yet there must have been a period in social evolution when this refusal to permit the strong man to do what he liked with his own physical strength seemed, at least to the strong, an outrageous interference with personal liberty . . . There is, in fact, no more reason why a man should be allowed to use his wealth or his brain than his physical strength as he likes . . . The liberty of the weak depends upon the restraint of the strong, that of the poor upon the restraint of the rich, and that of the simpler-minded upon the restraint of the sharper . . . Every man should have this liberty and no more, to do unto others as he would that they should do unto him; upon that common foundation rest liberty, equality, and morality.

Hugh Dalton — Towards Social Equality (1935)

Hugh Dalton made two compelling contributions to the development of revisionist ideas in the post-war Labour Party. In Practical Socialism *(1935), he produced an outstanding work of political economy that laid the foundations for the social democratic 'middle way' of post-war Britain. And he served as the first Labour Chancellor in the 1945 Government, where he urged radicalism in solving the country's economic crisis against the caution of Labour's consolidators.*

Hugh Dalton was born in August 1887 in Neath, educated at Eton and King's College, Cambridge. Son of a tutor to royal princes, the Tories later branded him a class traitor because of the contrast between his upper-class upbringing, and his socialist conviction.

He was first in a long line of eminent Labour economists who shared revisionist ideas. With his position on the National Executive of the Labour

Party, and his research post at the London School of Economics (LSE), Dalton encouraged a younger generation of academic economists to put their services directly at the disposal of the Labour Party. In the 1930s, Hugh Gaitskell, Evan Durbin, Douglas Jay, James Meade and other members of the New Fabian Research Bureau found their ideas eagerly pillaged leading to an agreed programme For Socialism and Peace (1934), revised three years later as Labour's Immediate Programme.

After fighting a succession of by-elections, he was elected as the MP for Peckham in October 1924. In 1929, he switched to represent Bishop Auckland. Dalton was elected to the Shadow Cabinet in 1925, and served as Under-Secretary of State at the Foreign Office in the second Labour Government of 1929–31. He temporarily lost his seat in 1931, but re-gained it at the General Election of 1935, and remained in the House of Commons until 1959.

In the mid-1930s, Dalton pressed for firm action to be taken against Hitler, and increased military expenditure. When Labour entered the Churchill coalition in May 1940, he was appointed as the Minister for Economic Warfare, and then President of the Board of Trade in 1942 where he laid the foundations of post-war regional policy.

In the newly elected Labour Government of 1945, Dalton became the first post-war Chancellor, where he rapidly implemented a series of far-reaching measures. The tax burden was increased to pay for reconstruction and the welfare state. The Bank of England was nationalised and the public sector expanded across a whole range of industries. He resigned in November 1947 after prematurely releasing details of emergency measures contained in his Budget. But he returned to the Cabinet in 1950, and remained a leading architect of the Attlee settlement.

Dalton's publications include With British Guns in Italy (1919), Principles of Public Finance (1923), Practical Socialism for Britain (1935), and a collection of memoirs.

His essays in Practical Socialism demonstrate Dalton's lucidity as a revisionist thinker. At Cambridge, he studied alongside J.M. Keynes and A.C. Pigou, translating economic theories into practical proposals for how through the taxation of unearned income, Britain could finance its war effort and undertake a modest redistribution of wealth. His specific idea for a capital levy was never implemented, however.

Unlike Keynes, Dalton stressed the importance of institutional changes, not content to rely on what were seen as short-term measures to tackle unemployment. This implied the need for a modernisation strategy that could equip the British economy to recover from the hardship of war. There was an implicit contrast between this socialist approach to planning deter-

mined within an egalitarian and collectivist frame of reference, and liberal Keynesianism that concentrated on regulating the level of demand to maintain full employment — as his essay, 'The Nature and Objects of Economic Planning', makes clear.

Dalton's socialism also attacked the deprivation and inefficiency of capitalism in the 1930s for wasting talent, restricting initiative, and retarding growth. It advocated liberation from want so that all had the freedom to develop. He was one of the first economists on the left to openly challenge whether nationalisation could further material equality. Public ownership could tackle under-performing areas of industry and increase efficiency. But Dalton was also alive to the dangers of a state apparatus controlled by cliques and oligarchs, and sought remedies to democratise industrial power.

With the ends of a classless society and social equality agreed in Dalton's socialism, the next step was to identify the means. Greater equalisation of outcomes could be achieved through steeply graduated death duties, a gifts-tax, a progressive income tax, and a reliable system of unemployment benefit and poverty relief. Improving the general level of schooling could provide further opportunities for empowerment, and was central to the abolition of class privilege.

Selected Text[7]

Towards Social Equality

Socialists seek, by the abolition of poverty and the establishment of social equality, to build a prosperous and classless society.

Complete economic equality — in the sense of absolute equality of individual income, or individual 'outgo' in the form of effort — is neither practically possible, nor ideally good.[8] Nor is it necessary to the attainment of social equality and the classless state. But what *is* necessary is a very great reduction in our present economic inequalities.

This implies that, while the average level of well being must be greatly raised, the rich shall become poorer and poor richer. The span of individual incomes in this country runs from well over £50,000 a year to much less than £1 per week, a ratio of much more than a thousand to one. This is grotesquely wide.

---

[7] Dalton, H., *Practical Socialism for Britain*, London: Routledge, 1935. [Footnotes in this section are original.]

[8] Because, to mention only two reasons, it makes no allowance for individual differences, either of need or performance.

But when we propose the reduction of economic inequality, we meet at once a whole procession of silly arguments. It is suggested that, once we admit absolute equality to be impossible, there is no more to say; or it is pretended that present inequalities of wealth correspond to inequalities of service, or merit, or intelligence, or 'social standing', and should not, therefore, be disturbed; or that these present inequalities are inevitable, because men are not 'equal in nature'; or it is claimed that, under capitalism, all men of exceptional ability can rise from humble beginnings to proud endings; or it is observed that a few gifted children of the poor have, in fact, climbed our steep and narrow educational ladder to the high roof of commercial and professional eminence.

The wealthy 'self-made man' is a familiar advertisement of the virtues of individualism. And:

> It is possible [as Mr Tawney says] that intelligent tadpoles reconcile themselves to the inconveniences of their position, by reflecting that, though most of them will live and die as tadpoles and nothing more, the more fortunate of the species will one day shed their tails, distend their mouths and stomachs, hop nimbly on to dry land, and croak addresses to their former friends on the virtues by means of which tadpoles of character and capacity can rise to be frogs. This conception of society may be described, perhaps, as the Tadpole Philosophy, since the consolation which it offers for social evils consists in the statement that exceptional individuals can succeed in evading them.[9]

Why is social equality desired by Socialists? Because Socialism means comradeship, and comradeship means social equality. Because great inequality is both unjust and ugly. Because it gives cake to a few, while many lack bread. Because it breeds servility, wastes talent, and restricts the sources of initiative and leadership.

Finally, because it makes a mockery of freedom. We have no freedom to spend money we have not got.[10] The millionaire and the coal miner are equally free, in theory, to drink champagne or travel round the world; their wives equally free to hire a lady's maid or to cook their husband's dinner with their own hands; their sons equally free to go to the University or to go down the pit. But, in prac-

---

[9]   Tawney (1931), p. 142.

[10] Intellectuals are apt to put too much stress on freedom of opinion and its expression. Even more fundamental is freedom to eat sufficient food, to occupy sufficient houseroom, to possess sufficient clothes, to enjoy sufficient comforts and amenities, to be able to live like a human being.

tice, wealth opens the gates of freedom and opportunity, and poverty closes them.

Social equality must rest on equality of opportunity and this in turn upon equality of environment, especially in childhood. Great social inequality looks its ugliest, when we see it strike the young.

What practical framework, of laws and institutions, does social equality require? The elements of such a framework,

> Belong [as Mr Tawney points out] to one or other of two principle types. There are those, in the first place, such as the extension of social services and progressive taxation, which mitigate disparities of opportunity and circumstance, by securing that wealth which would otherwise have been spent by a minority is applied to purposes of common advantage. There are those, in the second place, such as trade unionism and industrial legislation, which set limits to the ability of one group to impose its will, by economic duress, upon another, and thus soften inequalities of economic power. The co-operative movement and the extension of undertakings carried on as public services, with their practice of returning profits to the consumer, and their recognition of responsibility, not to investors, but to the community, combine, in some measure, the benefits of both.[11]

Of the so-called 'social services', some are destined to assume increasing importance with the advance of Socialism, others, one hopes, to dwindle into insignificance.

In the first class are public education and public health services, including the provision of houses.[12] Likewise, State pension schemes. All these are permanent functions of the State.

In the second class are unemployment benefit and poor relief. In proportion as Socialism succeeds in curing unemployment and poverty, these forms of provision will become unnecessary, as with many physical diseases now extinct among civilised nations. But, while these economic diseases continue, not to succour their victims is a social crime.

The rapid expansion of education and health services is essential, not only as a step towards social equality but as a social investment in human capacities, which we can ill afford to neglect. Educational advance is one of the main roads towards the abolition of class privilege. The Labour Party has declared that,

---

[11] Tawney (1931), pp. 165–6.

[12] Some speak glibly of 'revolution'. But what a revolution it would be if every family were decently housed.

> it stands for complete educational equality and for the final abolition
> of the system under which the quality of the education offered to
> children has depended on the income or social position of their par-
> ents.[13]

Such equality is not an unrealisable dream. But it looks remote,
when to-day the proportion of children in England and Wales entering secondary schools is less that one-seventh, and in some areas less
that one-tenth, of those leaving elementary schools, and when three-
quarters of the children reaching the age of fourteen plunge immediately into an overcrowded labour market.

The raising of the school leaving age to fifteen forthwith, and to
sixteen with the least possible delay, is urgent both on educational
grounds, including grounds of physical health, and as a blow at
unemployment.[14]

Complete equality requires not merely more, but better and more
varied education. For it is important to insist that, for a variety of
inclination and ability, equal opportunity means variety of opportunity. In concrete terms, there must be, for all children under eleven,
better buildings, smaller classes, ample facilities for practical work
and for play, with nursery schools, especially in the towns, as the
preliminary stage.

For children between eleven and sixteen, standards of staffing,
building, equipment and amenities, including playing fields and
provision for physical training, must be levelled up to the present
standards of the better secondary schools. And fees in secondary
schools should be abolished.

For young people over sixteen there must be such an increase of
scholarships to Universities and other centres of higher education
and professional training as shall secure that no advantage, in
respect of entry to such institutions, remains with wealth, but that
appropriate abilities alone decide the question. I have stated these
concrete requirements of educational equality in un-emphatic
words. But if they could be fully realised, we should have made a
real revolution in the lives and outlook of the young, and in the
future form of our society.

It is an important item in the Labour Party's policy that maintenance allowances should be paid to parents, in respect of children
kept at school beyond the age of fourteen. Personally I regard this as

---

[13] *Labour and Education*, p. 20

[14] See R.H. Tawney, *The School Leaving Age and Juvenile Unemployment*.

the thin end of the wedge of a national scheme of family allowances, which, by adjusting family income more closely to family needs, would be a bulwark of social equality. There is no sanctity, nor finality, in maintenance allowances only starting at fourteen. But such a national scheme, starting at birth, is not financially practicable yet, though I hope that we shall move steadily towards it. The same is true of the more ambitious national pension schemes, whose cost runs into hundreds of millions of pounds annually.

Health, it is often said, is a purchasable commodity, of which, within wide limits, a community can buy as much or as little as it cares. In this commodity we are practising criminal economies. Preventable death, disease and general ill-health bulk large in our national heritage.

A constructive health policy is many-sided. It includes an ample and efficient State medical service, which will care for men, women and children alike, without discriminations of the present system of National Health Insurance. It is closely linked with housing, with the provision of more open spaces and playing fields, with the abolition of unemployment and low wages, with shorter hours and healthier working conditions. Most closely of all it is linked with the schools, with more frequent and thorough medical inspection, to be followed in all cases by the prescribed treatment, — specially valuable if continued for all children until the age of sixteen, — with the provision of school meals and of a regular milk ration.

Chiefly to help the farmers, the National Government has done something to encourage milk drinking by school children. But the Board of Education has laid it down that free milk may only be given to children by a doctor as showing visible symptoms of 'malnutrition'. A cruel and ignorant pedantry! As Dr Somerville Hastings has observed, 'the effects of under-nourishment are by no means easy to detect by physical examination'.[15]

> Unfortunately [writes another high authority] we cannot make a sensational story out of malnutrition as it occurs to-day — it produces a slow silent rot of virility, vitality and fibre from which recovery soon becomes impossible. It takes a lot of ill-feeding to kill a child. It takes very little to sap his vitality seriously.

Industrial legislation must have a prominent place in any Labour programme. In its various aspects such legislation is a powerful aid to health, to leisure, to security and to the legitimate rights of organ-

---

[15] *The Lancet*, March 23, 1933.

ised labour; indirectly a powerful aid to social equality, through the levelling up of standards of life. A new Factories Act, a new Shops Act, a new Workmen's Compensation Act, an Offices Regulation Act, are long overdue. The next Labour Government should pass them into law. Likewise a new Mines Regulation Act, though the socialisation of the mines would, one hopes, make the requirements of such an Act mere ordinary routine. Likewise a legislative reduction of working hours. Likewise a restoration to Trade Unions of the rights taken from them by the most reactionary Act of 1927. I have not the special knowledge needed to discuss usefully here the details of these various branches of industrial legislation. But I wish to emphasis their practical importance,[16] and I know that in this field the Labour Party is exceptionally rich in experts.

The pace at which the social services can expand and industrial legislation goes forward, partly depends on the pace at which prosperity increases and Socialism goes forward. A greater flow of plenty, better distributed and safeguarded against interruption, is a necessary condition of rapid advance.

It is wrong to pitch hopes too high, or to date their complete fulfilment too early. There are limits to the practical possibilities of the redistribution of wealth based on high taxation within the framework. Our gains, as recent history shows, are not secure. Economy campaigns may come again, as in 1931 and 1922, intensifying inequality in the hope of reinvigorating capitalism.

> Since the standard of education, elementary and secondary, that is being given to the child of poor parents is already in very many cases superior to that which the middle class parent is providing for his own child, it is time to call a halt.

So spoke George May, from the depths of his heart! Such extravagance necessitates too high an income tax.

The Labour Party has always preferred graduated taxation of incomes, and of property passing at death to their sources of revenue. These must continue to be the mainstays of a Socialist Budget. But we should, I think, turn our minds also to the possibility of new taxes on luxury consumption.

---

[16] People who invent imaginary difficulties sometimes say that the next Labour Government must choose between the extension of social services and industrial legislation on the one hand, and the introduction of measures of socialisation on the other. On the contrary, it must choose both, and must vigorously pursue both lines of policy.

The next Labour Government will need all the revenue it can gather, both from old taxes and new. There will be heavy competing claims upon it, coming from many quarters. Some of these will have to be postponed in the early years, or only met in part. Only the growth of planned prosperity, and a heavy fall in unemployment, can ease the Budget problem. But gradually contributions from the surpluses of socialised enterprises should become an important aid to public revenue.

The problem of debt charges will take on a new aspect with the extension of socialisation. Some years ago the Labour Party proposed a capital levy, on a graduated scale, on all individuals owning capital worth more than £5,000, to be applied to debt redemption. Unfortunately, this sound policy was not adopted. In the last few years the burden of the dead-weight debt, previously increased by falling prices, has been somewhat diminished by conversions, and the debt problem has now receded to the second line of our preoccupations. But the burden on the Budget remains severe, and the opportunities of further relief by conversions are now small. It is my personal opinion that we have made good progress with socialisation, and the policy of the capital levy should be brought to the front again, to reduce both the dead-weight debt and that attached to socialised enterprises.

Last, but not least, of the measures for achieving social equality — for a Socialist, indeed, the most fundamental — is the extension of the 'socialised sector'. For this purpose, as for many others, I count the Co-operative Movement, both on its productive and distributive side, as a great public enterprise, and as a powerful engine of equality. It generates no large unearned incomes, no inflated salaries, no private profits, only a social surplus which all its members share. Between Co-operative and other forms of public enterprise, mutual goodwill should always find practical accommodation.

We must distinguish clearly between the initial act of socialisation and the subsequent process of socialised enterprise. The initial act, not being accompanied by any confiscation of private property rights, but only by a change in their form, makes no direct contribution to equality. But the subsequent process steadily promotes it. And even the change in form is significant. For the rentier is not well placed to play the bad citizen by trying to 'sabotage' government. In the last resort, he is the captive of his paymaster.

But social equality does not imply the abolition of private property. Quite the contrary.

The Nature and Objects of Economic Planning

Planning or drifting, looking ahead or living from hand to mouth, are two different styles of conduct. I should define Economic Planning, in its widest sense, as the deliberate direction, by persons in control of large resources,[17] of economic activities towards chosen ends. Planning is not, of course, a good thing in itself. It will be good or bad, according to who directs, towards what chosen ends, by what means, and with what skill. But a good plan, well executed, is always better than no plan at all.

Economic Planning is to be contrasted with *Laissez-faire*, Free Competition, Free Enterprise, the Free Play of Economic Forces, Service through Profit-seeking, Automatic Adjustments through the Price mechanism. These are the soothing phrases, or some of them, which do duty in this controversy.

Anti-planners worship the God of Free Market, in which all prices, including wages, move freely under the influence of ever-changing demand and supply, and by their movements bring a double stream of blessings to mankind: employment, on appropriately changing terms, not only to all labour, but to all capital and land as well, and satisfaction of consumers' preferences, for all who have money to spend, whether much or little. This stream, they tell us, will flow ever more abundantly, as capital accumulates and knowledge grows and profiteers adventure, always on one condition. Man must not tamper with the divine machine, nor defy the inexorable laws which rule the economic universe. All the world's woes today — poverty, unemployment, crisis — arise from such defiance. Man has tried to plan, and brought down ruin on his impious head.

Much time might be spent in examining these doctrines of Individualism. But I have neither space nor patience, in a book devoted to positive proposals, for so negative a task.

I desire to make only three points, in passing, on the individualist theory of the anti-planners. The 'freedom' which they worship has strict limits which they seldom emphasise. The free play of economic forces, which is to bring salvation, is to operate within the legal framework of capitalism. And this, as has been said already, frames social inequality. Though he resents State interference in general, it

[17] The qualification 'in control of large resources' is necessary, if we are to exclude from the definition the little economic 'planlets' of small firms, or individual producers or consumers. These are each too small for variations in the doings of any one of them to have any appreciable effect on prices or on total production or consumption.

is no part of the individual creed that the State should cease to interfere in one most important particular, namely to enforce the law, which in its turn enforces grave inequalities of wealth, status and opportunity. The policeman and the judge are not to be abolished. Private property in the means of production, most unequally distributed and perpetuated by inheritance; the sanctity of contract; the maintenance of law and order; the stiff class structure of society; these things would stand. In freedom and opportunity all citizens would be equal in law, yet grossly unequal in fact.

In second place, the 'free enterprise' of the individualists' theory is not, as some seem to argue, a present possession, to be defended at all costs against the planners. It belonged to a short and peculiar phase in our history, which has already passed away. Freedom to compete implied also freedom not to compete, but to combine. Private monopoly, in all its variations of degree and form — running from huge trusts and combines to mere unwritten 'gentlemen's agreements' — is both the child and the destroyer of freedom. Not only is this true within national frontiers. The understandings of financiers and industrialists cross frontiers and limit 'free enterprise' internationally.

Free enterprise, therefore, is not a phrase which accurately describes modern capitalism. In a large measure, free enterprise has vanished. But private enterprise, by no means the same thing, remains the dominant type of economic organisation.

Thirdly, a word as to price movements. The individualist of the more intellectual type makes a great parade of these. He shows, with great elaboration of argument, that they perform an indispensable function in an unplanned economy. They secure the most economical distribution of limited supplies of goods, and also of 'agents of production'. 'Most economical', in this context, means most closely in accord with effective demand, whether of consumers, or of business men, no account being taken either of inequalities of income, or of the social utility of rival demands. It is a pretty picture. Planning, individualists think, would smudge the picture, and be 'uneconomic'. Some go so far as to maintain that a Planned Socialist Economy could not be 'rational' since it could not reproduce, in the completeness, these indispensable price movements of 'free capitalism'.

Such arguments against Socialism — and they apply equally against the privately planned Monopolistic Capitalism, which is developing around us — over-reach themselves. They prove too much.

The practical application of this worship of price movements is illustrated by the following historical incident.[18] A famine was anticipated in an Indian Province. The Government was advised to build up a reserve supply of grain, but refused, on the ground that, if it were known that grain was stored, speculators would be inactive and prices would fail to rise in anticipation of a coming shortage and that, if prices failed to rise, the most economical use of grain would not be promoted. The Government, therefore, laid up no reserves, the famine came, and the people died like flies. This was *laissez-faire* in action.

What is it, of practical importance to a Socialist, which emerges from individualist disquisitions on price movements? Only this, that, in so far as we retain prices at all in our economic system, and a price mechanism — and on grounds of practical convenience we shall certainly retain it, though possibly its range will be narrowed — we must study the working of this mechanism, lest its unanticipated movements defeat our purposes.[19]

I turn from these reflections on Individualism to the consideration of Planning.

Planning is not the same thing as Socialism. Socialism is primarily a question of ownership, planning a question of control or direction. Planning is not necessarily in the public interest, nor are those who direct it necessarily the agents of the State. There is private planning towards private ends and social planning towards social ends. And these are quite distinct in theory, though in practice we find hybrid forms.[20]

Privately planned capitalism holds many ugly possibilities, some of which in various parts of the world have already begun to be experienced. Private monopolies may ruthlessly exploit the labour of vast populations and the natural wealth of great areas. Private

---

[18] Related by Professor Jacob Viner of Chicago in a lecture at the London School of Economics in 1933.

[19] It is one of the great merits of Mrs Wootton's book, *Plan or No Plan*, that she makes this study, and relates it to the Planned, as well as the Unplanned, Economy.

[20] Logically there are five alternative systems — extreme types between which, in reality, lie many intermediate, or mixed, arrangements. These five are Unplanned Capitalism, Privately Planned Capitalism, Socially Unplanned Capitalism, Planned Socialism and Unplanned Socialism. The last of these is, I think, of theoretical interest only, combining public ownership of the means of production with free movement of all prices. In practice this is a most unlikely combination. But perfectly possible, if any society chose to adopt it. See Professor Cassel's *Theory of Social Economy*.

monopolies may grow into giants, link arms with other giants, and tread the earth as masters, making their profits as much from buying governments, including judges and officials, as from selling goods. Their chosen ends are power and plunder. Their means are manifold. Sometimes they aim at building up demand by bribery, false statements or law breaking. Thus some armament firms and some drug traffickers, to take only two examples, have been known to collect business.

Sometimes, demand being given, they limit output in order to raise prices and bring profits to a maximum. These are the elementary economics of monopoly. And clearly, when output is deliberately restricted, below what would be forthcoming under competition, employment is likewise restricted. In this and other ways private planning under capitalism often creates unemployment. Thus 'rationalisation' schemes, justified at first sight on grounds of efficiency and lower costs, but pursued wholly without regard to social ends or any socially designed plan, make whole townships and industrial areas derelict, deserts from which the waters of enterprise have drained away, leaving behind them populations without work or hope and social capital — buildings, public services, public amenities — falling into ruin. The ghost towns on Tyneside, in South Wales, and other devastated districts, bear witness to these processes of private planning. A society, subject to such influences, it has been truly said, is 'more planned against than planning'.

Since, therefore, private planning is, at the best, non-social and in many cases plainly anti-social, and since, in any case, it is not an instrument strong enough to change chaos and poverty into order and prosperity, the minds of many who would not call themselves Socialists turn towards social planning, or towards plans, part private and part social.[21]

There are difficulties in the application of social planning within the framework of capitalism. But these are not, as some theorists

---

[21] There is a growing literature in England on this subject. Sir Arthur Salter's *Framework of an Ordered Society*, Sir Basil Blackett's *Planned Money* (a little too narrow to describe the book, which discusses also planning in industry), Mr Harold Macmillan's *Reconstruction, a Plea for a National Policy*, are examples of it. Rathenau in Germany was a forerunner. See his book *In Days to Come*.

allege,[22] 'inherently' insuperable. Such beginnings, moreover, may accelerate the transition to Socialism.

The practical Socialist will hold that, both in the expanding socialist sector and in the dwindling private sector, there should be social planning. I am concerned only with social planning, that is to say with the deliberate direction by agents of the community[23] of economic activities towards ends, chosen on grounds of social, not of private, advantage.

What are these chosen ends? 'Plan for what?' — our critics ask. There need not be only one object in our planning. There may be several, jointly pursued. And these may vary with circumstances. The two outstanding examples of planning on a large scale in recent times are furnished by the World War and by the Soviet experiment. The object of the former was to win the war. That and nothing else. And it is on record that the reluctance of British businessmen to abandon profit-seeking and the pursuit of 'business as usual' in the supply of shipping, food and munitions nearly lost the war.

The main objects of planning in the Soviet Union I have tried to summarise elsewhere as follows:

> To avoid the economic crises and trade fluctuations of capitalism; to keep the whole working population in continuous employment and to raise their standard of living, without permitting the growth of large inequalities, to a level higher than that of the workers in capitalist countries, to achieve a large measure of economic self-sufficiency and, as a means to this end, to stimulate to the utmost the industrialisation of the country.[24]

For Western Socialists, in peacetime, the general object of planning is the maximum social advantage. Our particular objects are to wage peaceful war on poverty, insecurity, social inequality, and war itself.

The surrounding conditions of British planning, and many of its methods, will differ widely from the Russian, but we shall have many objects, though not all, in common.

I have argued in an earlier chapter that in every modern community there is a nucleus of Socialism, a socialised sector, wide or narrow, in its economic life. Likewise in every community there is a

---

[22] Here some individualists and some communists are found chanting in unison.

[23] Men sometimes act, in effect, as agents of the community without express appointment. Those, for example, who founded and the carry on the work of the National Trust for the Preservation of Places of Historic Interest and Natural Beauty.

[24] *Twelve Studies in Soviet Russia*, p. 31 (Gollancz, 1933).

nucleus of social planning, chiefly within the socialist sector, but extending also into the private sector. Social progress in public education has been planned, and in public health. No 'invisible hand' of the God of the individualists brought these public services. No mere 'price movements' created them. Likewise the State Budget is, within its limits, a rudimentary form of planned economy.

Plans are seldom exactly realised, and should be always in process of revision. Planning is only a method of trial and error, an alternative to the trial and error of Unplanned Capitalism. Planners will make mistakes, miscalculate the future, sometimes waste wealth and opportunities, often change directions. But they, at least, have their eyes fixed, not on abstracts, but on realities.

Evan Durbin — Socialism and Democracy (1940)

Evan Durbin was a leading revisionist intellectual, and a key figure in Labour Party politics whose tragic and untimely death in 1947 cut short a brilliant career. He played a pre-eminent role in re-thinking the meaning of socialist economic planning for the party in the 1930s, laying the foundations for the great, reforming administration of 1945.

He was born in March 1906 in Bideford, Devon. After attending Taunton School, and winning a scholarship to New College, Oxford, he specialised in economics, becoming a lecturer at the London School of Economics (LSE) in 1930.

Durbin then worked at the New Fabian Research Bureau under the tutelage of Hugh Dalton, where he formed a close friendship with Hugh Gaitskell and Douglas Jay. He entered the Economic Section of the War Cabinet Secretariat in 1940, and became personal assistant to Attlee in 1942. In 1945, he was elected as the MP for Edmonton, and served briefly as Parliamentary Secretary at the Ministry of Works.

Through his numerous papers and articles, Durbin sought to counter the view of orthodox economic theory that low consumption was the cause of economic crisis. He argued that the depression of the 1930s had arisen because the plan-less anarchy of traditional capitalism allowed savings to be turned into a hoard, restricting investment as much as consumption and employment. Unlike Keynes, Durbin believed that only a state-directed economy, where the action of governments, banking, industries and trade unions was centrally co-ordinated, could overcome the trade cycle of boom and slump so characteristic of private capitalism.

More significantly as an ancedent to Labour's revisionism, Durbin elaborated a politics of moderation that rejected the crisis posturing of the Socialist League, and the Popular Front strategy of an alliance with Communism, whose support of the Moscow trials in the 1930s appalled him. He looked to parliamentary democracy as a necessary cushion against any social change that might destroy the equilibrium of the British polity. He defined democratic government as a means of resolving severe class differences. Parliamentary democracy was for Durbin integral to socialism, binding classes and parties into an organic nation underlining an emotional unity forged by patriotism.

Evan Durbin's published works include Purchasing Power and Trade Depressions *with Hugh Gaitskell (1933),* The Problem of Credit Policy *(1935), and* The Politics of Democratic Socialism *(1940). The extract published here is a classic revisionist analysis of a changing capitalist society that offered the left an escape from perpetual neo-Marxism.*

Durbin argued 'the managerial revolution' was creating a growing army of technicians, white-collar workers, and suburban householders. This changing social landscape also meant a growing proportion of manual workers had small property holdings, savings and mortgages. It was essential to redefine its traditional constituency, winning over the new middle class, if Labour was to sustain itself as a political force. Later revisionists were indelibly influenced by Durbin's analysis.

But Durbin's greatest achievement was to spearhead a wave of fresh economic thinking through which Labour could revive itself from the intellectual paralysis and splits of the Macdonald years. The need to reconcile freedom and planning as a stimulus to industrial modernisation was the paramount challenge. He was able to introduce into the Labour Party recently formulated Keynesian ideas on macro-economic intervention.

This renaissance in socialist thought led to a new synthesis. The state, the mixed economy and indicative planning would work together, enabling Britain to escape from austerity and hardship and reverse its long-term economic decline. The agenda for democratic socialists was to harness the virtues of a reformed capitalism to meet the need for security and equality. Political ideas did not matter for their poetry in Durbin's socialism. They counted only if they worked.

Selected Text[25]

Socialism and Democracy

If the method of dictatorship is an unlikely way to secure social justice, what alternative method is open to us?

I wish to argue that the only conceivable route to a better social order lies in the pathway of democracy, and that the political method of democratic government is an essential principle, not an accidental accomplishment of any just society.

If by the 'socialist commonwealth' we mean a society in which a larger measure of social justice has been established through the instrumentality of a planned economy, then I believe that the democratic method is an inherent part of socialism, and cannot be separated from it — any more than batting can be separated from cricket or love from life. They are all necessary parts of a complex whole.

I am now concerned to argue the validity of this contention; but before I do so, it is necessary to make it synonymous with the phrase 'the good society'. A community is a 'true' democracy only if all cause for sighing and weeping have passed away. Before such persons will call any society a democracy, it must be completely free from social inequalities and economic insecurity. J.A. Hobson used the term in this sense when he says 'effective political democracy in unattainable without economic equality'. In this use the term 'democracy' becomes identified with the conception of social justice itself, and is therefore remote from the political practice of any present society.

By using the word in this way it is possible to say, quite rightly, that we have not got 'democracy' in Britain, or America, or France, or Sweden. In none of these countries has inequality, or insecurity, or class antagonism, passed wholly away. Democracy, in its Utopian sense, does not yet exist within these nations. They only possess 'capitalist democracy', or *political* democracy. They do not possess 'economic democracy' or 'true democracy' or 'real democracy'.

Now it is perfectly open to anyone to use terms as they please. If some people choose to mean by 'democracy' what other people mean by 'Utopia' there is nothing to stop them doing so. The moon will still be the moon even if we call it the sun. Utopia by any other name will smell as sweet, and look as remote. But it is not in Utopia, nor in the perfect society, that I am, for the moment, interested. I

[25]   Durbin, Evan, *The Politics of Democratic Socialism*, London: Routledge, 1940.

wish to discuss a narrower thing, a single political habit, a method of taking political decisions, a practicable and actual condition of certain societies. In short, what I want to consider is the significance or value of what the Utopian 'democrats' would call 'mere political democracy'. In what does that consist? Of what value is it? By what arguments can it be justified or criticised?

It is obvious that the institution of 'mere political democracy' must exist in some real sense, even in a capitalist society, since it is possible to distinguish 'capitalist democracies' from 'capitalist dictatorships'. Even in his most fanatical moments the Communist has not denied the *possibility* of making the distinction, although he used to deny the *importance* of making it. There must be therefore some sense in which democracy is compatible with capitalism and consequently with economic inequality. It is with this limited form of political democracy, its meaning and value, that I am here concerned.

In what does 'democracy' in this sense consist?

I believe the correct answer to this question to be that political democracy consists in the possession by any society of *three* characteristic habits or institutions:

1.   The *first* and most typical of these characteristics is the ability of the people to choose a government.

Disagreement between individuals is of the very essence of human personality. As long as we are different persons, there will be some of us who like one thing and some who do not, some who desire one order of society and some another, some who believe justice to be realised in one set of circumstances and some who disagree with that judgment.

Now the course of action taken at any moment, and the form of society thus brought slowly into existence, are determined largely by the decisions of Government. The Government has its hands upon the controls of the 'apparatus of coercion', and is therefore the *immediate* authority determining social policy. The nature of the decisions taken by the Government will depend upon the character of the persons forming it. Consequently there can be no control of the form of society by us, the common people, unless it is possible to change the personnel of the Government and the legislature. That is the first and most obvious characteristic of political democracy — the existence of a government responsible to the people, and the dependence of it and of the membership of the legislative assembly upon the free vote of the people.

In our own history we have found that the essential thing to attain and preserve is the power of the people to dismiss a government from office. This negative power is in reality an important positive power, because ordinary men and women are moved more deeply by the disapproval of measures they dislike in practice, than by their less definite conception of what they desire in the future. Political change in democracies is more frequently induced by a slow accumulation of resentment against an existing government or institution, than by the growth of a positive idea of new social forms. Experience is more real than imagination, to un-imaginative people.

Every practising politician appreciates this fact. The enthusiasts composing the party machine through which he has to work may be animated by the clear vision of a new society; but they are, at the best, a small minority of the surrounding electoral masses, and the masses are rarely inspired by Christian's clear vision, from a great distance, of the Celestial City. This is not to say that constructive social imagination is not powerful in the affairs of men, but only that democracies proceed to realize the prophets' vision by careful processes of empirical test. By the slow testing of ideas and of institutional experiments, by rejecting all those of which they disapprove and insisting upon the gradual extension of the things they find by experience that they like, an intelligent electorate unconsciously constructs a society that in large measure contents it. Little as we reformists of the Left may like it, the absence of a reforming or revolutionary zeal in our communities is a tribute to the fundamental, and often unrecognisable, ways in which society has been adapted to suit the unconscious, but essential, requirements of the people composing it.

Of this I shall have more to say presently. For the moment I wish only to insist upon the importance of the negative power to destroy a government as part of the broader right to choose a government. It is the continuous retention of this power that I shall call the 'maintenance of democracy'.

2.   But the continued existence of this right implies and requires the existence of a *second*, and less obvious, political institution. If liberty is to exist, if the dependence of government upon the will of the people is to be real, there must always be a real choice before the people. This implies the steady maintenance of a critical and essential institution — *that of freedom to oppose the Government of the day*. Unless the electorate has more than one possible government before it; unless there is more than one party able to place its views before the country; unless, that is to say, the opposition is free to prepare itself

to take over power, and the Government to surrender it peacefully after an electoral decision against it; there is no choice before the people. Their choice is Hobson's choice — they may walk or go upon their legs, they may die or cease to live, they may eat bread or bread. The range of choice is no greater.

This obvious reflection reveals at once the sharp absurdity of the electoral practices of modern dictatorships. Modern dictatorships pay to the institutions of democracy the sincerest form of flattery — that of imitation. They cope the device of the 'General Election'. But it is an empty and silly imitation — like that of an ape reading a newspaper or a baboon playing on a violin. It deceives no one, except those who wish to be deceived. Of course, no amount of electoral machinery, nor platform eloquence, nor secret balloting, nor 'equal voting', has the slightest real significance if there is finally nothing to vote about, no choice before the voters. The contemporary German and Russian elections, in which one Party receives 98% or 99% of votes polled, may be a tribute to the efficiency of the terror by which these unfortunate peoples are governed; but they have no more political significance than the jabbering of a school of marmosets or the senseless and uniform hissing of a gaggle of geese.

This we can see at once by asking the critical question: *What is the choice before the German or Russian electorate?* There is only one party in the election. There is only one government that can be formed. There may be a choice of individuals, but there is no choice of party, no choice of government, no choice of policy. The alternative before the German people is the choice between Fuhrer Hitler or Fuhrer Hitler; before the Russian people Comrade Stalin or Comrade Stalin. They may choose in the one country, the National-Socialist Party or the National-Socialist Party; in the other, the Communist Party or the Communist Party. As Herr Goebbels said,

> All we National-Socialists are convinced that we are right, and we cannot bear with anyone who maintains that he is right. For either, if he is right, he must be a National-Socialist, or, if he is not a National-Socialist, then he is not right.

Comrade Stalin thinks very much the same. It is only odd that both these self-righteous regimes consider it worthwhile to spend so much time and money in marching the adult population mechanically and idiotically through the polling booths to affirm a meaningless slogan.

Here then is the acid test of democracy. Democracy may be defined by the toleration of opposition. In so far as it is tolerated — in so far as alternative governments are allowed to come into existence and into office — democracy, in my sense, exists. In so far as opposition is persecuted, rendered illegal, or stamped out of existence, democracy is not present, and either has never existed or is in process of being destroyed.

Obviously this is not a simple test. These are varying degrees of freedom permitted to those in opposition to the Government of the day in the various political systems of the world. In the older democracies, like our own, there is complete legal freedom for parties in opposition to the Government. Their rights in respect of political agitation are the *same* as those of the Government. From this extreme there is an almost infinite gradation of liberty, through the milder dictatorships of Poland and even Italy, to the savage and ruthless insistence upon uniformity that characterizes Germany and Russia. There is no precise line at which it is possible to say that all the communities on this side of it are democracies, and all on the other side of it are dictatorships. But, although the test is quantitative and complicated, it is nevertheless an acid test. The suppression of opposition, as distinct from sedition, is the proof of dictatorial ambition. It is by our judgment of that condition in society that we shall judge democracy itself.

3.   But there is a *third*, and still less obvious, characteristic necessary to the existence of democracy. Both the previous characteristics — those of responsible government and of legal opposition — are the definitive properties of democracy, but they are not the causes of democracy. When these conditions are present in a society, democracy in my sense is present also; when they are absent democracy in my sense is dead. But they do not cause democracy to become present; they simply define democracy. What then *causes* democracy to appear? What is the substantial social condition guaranteeing its existence and continuance?

Now I shall go on to argue, before this Part is finished, that the ultimate cause of stable democratic habits among a people is the possession by them of a certain type of emotional character. I shall argue that democracy is the epiphenomenon of a certain emotional balance in the individuals composing a nation, and I shall try to describe the kind of personality that, in my view, alone makes democracy possible. But there is a simpler and more immediate description of the *result* of the predominance of such persons in any society; and that is, in my submission, the most essential condition for the existence and maintenance of democracy. It is the existence of *an implicit undertaking between the Parties contending for power in the State not to persecute each other*. It is upon that agreement that I believe democracy can alone be securely founded. Mutual toleration is the keystone of the arch and the cornerstone of the building.

It is obvious, upon a moment's reflection, why this should be so. Let us imagine for a moment that this condition is not fulfilled. Let us suppose that the Conservative Party now in power in Great Britain has reason to believe that the Labour opposition has never accepted, or does not now accept, the obligations of this informal compact of toleration. The Government has reason to think that, if and when the Labour Party comes to power, it will use that power not merely to carry out its programme, but to break up and destroy the Conservative Party as a political organization, and to stamp out, by persecution, conservatism as an idea. That is to say, it is the known intention of the Labour Party — as it is now the known intention of the Communist and Fascist Parties — to use the apparatus of coercion, control over which is vested in them as the Government, to 'liquidate' the Parties that will then be in opposition to them. What will then follow? I suggest that in these circumstances the continuance of democracy is inconceivable. It is not even necessary that one of the large Parties in the community should intend to resort to physical cruelty. It may be certain that they will be forced to do so by the attempt to liquidate their opponents; but even if this is not the case, the mere desire on their part to prevent the other Party, by force, from ever holding office again is sufficient to make the maintenance of democracy impossible. Why is this so? Because the Party so threatened will never surrender power peacefully. There is every reason why it should not do so. To hand over the reins of government to the victorious Opposition is to court political death, to put a noose around one's own neck, to hand over the gun to a murderer. There would be no sense in such a procedure. Why should I present a knife to a man who is going to stab me in the back with it? Who would willingly hand over a machine-gun to a lunatic or a gangster?

These moral dilemmas need not delay us now, as we shall return to them before the end of this Part. I am merely trying to elucidate the conditions necessary for the existence of democracy as I have defined it. Democracy requires the peaceful alternation of Parties in government. This is impossible if the Government believes that the Opposition intends to liquidate them if and when they, the Opposition, attain power. The Government is not likely in these circumstances to surrender power peacefully. Even if they did, democracy would nevertheless cease to exist, since the victorious Opposition would then proceed, by the persecution of those who disagreed with them, to the destruction of democracy itself. Political liberty or democracy, in my sense, depends then, first and last, now and in the future, upon mutual toleration between opposing Parties.

It will be noticed that, in my description of democracy, there is no reference to social equality or distributive justice, or to any characteristic of the ideal society. It is therefore perfectly open to anyone to suggest that it is not a valuable institution. It is possible to say: 'If that is all you mean by democracy, I am not interested in it. It does not appear to me to be a particularly important or valuable political habit. I see no necessity to trouble myself greatly over its preservation.' We are therefore brought, at once, to a consideration of the advantages and disadvantages of this method of government. What are the arguments for democracy? What are the arguments against it? What are the forces that support or undermine it?

Great Britain

I value the social tradition in which we live. The services of this country to the cause of human happiness cannot be lightly dismissed. We have, for centuries now, led the world in the arts of government and in the discovery of the springs of social peace. We first applied the principles of reason to the tasks of economic organization and industrial production. By so doing we made possible, for all men, levels of prosperity and wealth that would have appeared Utopian, even fantastic, to generations that lived before the onset of the English Industrial Revolution. We have, from the beginning, made invaluable contributions to the advancement of science and learning. To-day through the generosity and long-sighted wisdom of one group of our scientists — the practising psycho-analysts — standing in marked and honourable contrast to the behaviour of most other professions, we have gathered into our society the most distinguished group of psychologists in the world, working in the forefront of contemporary science. We shall continue, in many fields of human endeavour, to lead and not to follow the generality of mankind.

We have, in this country, much of which to be ashamed. The distribution of income is nowhere less equal. The grip of class system that frustrates the search for comradeship between us, and wastes a monstrously high proportion of our natural talent, is extraordinarily strong, and is not the less strong, nor the less destructive, because it is so little resented. In this generation moreover, we have been guilty of the most terrible crimes of popular vandalism. We have torn down some of our finest buildings, and we have permitted the speculative builder and the profiteering landlord to drive hideous scars across our country-side; strangling in promiscuous rape the lovely body of our ancient agricultural civilisation. We have revealed ourselves to the world as ruthlessly uncultured, and our generation will go down to posterity as one of the most aesthetically destructive in our history — a rival in the popular demonology of the future of the unforgettable excesses of the Reformation and the Civil War. Although we have reason to be proud of our social tradition we have, therefore, no occasion to be contented with its chequered pattern.

The future of the British tradition is not secure. It is threatened from within and from without. There are dictatorial parties at home and there is the ever-present threat of attack from abroad. We could no longer walk quietly in our traditional paths of liberty if either of our violent parties grew to power, or if we were on the losing side in the present European war. Even victory in it will endanger the stability of our society. Hence peace was and is one, though not the sole or the first, of our vital interests.

When the peace of Europe is restored, and in so far as we have preserved the institutions of a free government, we have still a great service to perform for ourselves and for the world.

Every generation is in part united, and in part inspired, by some conception of a better and a more just society. The conception varies from age to age, and reflects in large measure the peculiar needs and the dominant philosophy of the time in which it enlivens men to hope. There is a rough law of compensation in its form. The deeper the distress of the world in which they live, the more Utopian is like to be the hope by which men sustain themselves in their daily labour. Despite the fear of aerial bombardment, ours is predominantly an age of quietness and comfort. The standard of living continuously rises about us, and our social life is not torn by deep religious or political conflicts, moving men to violent solutions. We can therefore afford modest dreams and practicable aspirations. We do not need the soothing vision of a perfect society to reconcile us to a bitter distress.

The conception of a better society, by which the broad trends of our policy can best be instructed, is therefore of a specific kind. We need not be content with anything less, nor need we ask for more, than a society in which property as a source of social inequality is made to wither slowly away, in which the establishment of a rational central control has restored expansion and created economic stability, in which political democracy is preserved and perfected as a method of government, and in which children may grow, free from secret fear, into a sociable and happy maturity. This is what I mean by a more just society. An important, indeed an essential, part of it is the constituent principle of Socialism. Within it the common happiness of mankind can be, for a long season, safely established.

Nor need we fear that this society is far away, or difficult to achieve. There is nothing in it that could not be established in a single generation, if we had the eyes to see, and the hearts to will, this reasonable programme to social betterment. We have only to open our eyes and stretch out our hands to pluck this precious fruit from the tree of knowledge.

I feel the conviction, ever more strongly as I grow older, that it is in this land, rather than in any other, that these hopes are likely to find their first fulfilment. We shall not be conscious of the birth in our midst of a new society, because we do not exercise our minds in self-analysis, or construct systematic social philosophies. But as I move about this island, in its quiet lands and in its crowded streets, meeting people of all classes and persuasions, I feel the life of a strong and quite people about me; more deeply united than they realise, more creative than they ever suspect. Here, if anywhere, the will for the common good is strong. From it and from the common friendliness we bear to one another we can continue to make, if we will, a society of which all men will be glad.

Revisionism's High Tide

Denis Healey — Power Politics and the Labour Party (1952)

Denis Healey's status as a revisionist thinker requires careful qualification. He was once described by his Oxford contemporary and rival Roy Jenkins as carrying 'light ideological baggage on a heavy gun carriage'. His self-declared position was that of 'eclectic pragmatist'. He was until the mid-1980s one of three or four Labour Party heavyweights, and the dominating advocate of Atlanticism. But he produced no great work of revisionist theory, and though a Gaitskellite, he maintained a problematic relationship with other leading revisionist thinkers, as Giles Radice records in his incisive account of the lives of Crosland, Jenkins and Healey Friends and Rivals *(2002).*

Healey was born in August 1917, and educated at Bradford Grammar School, and Balliol College, Oxford to which he secured an exhibition in Classics. He was politicised by Oxford and the threat of Hitler, and became the Communist-endorsed Chairman of the Labour Club until the outbreak of war. He served in the army throughout the war, and was promoted to the rank of major.

In 1945, Healey was appointed International Secretary of the Labour Party, where he derived considerable personal authority from his close relationship with the Foreign Secretary, Ernest Bevin. He also helped to bring about the new direction in foreign policy that led to the Marshall Plan, the Western European Union, and the establishment of NATO. He was regarded as one of the leading anti-Communist figures in the post-war Labour Party.

In April 1952, he was elected in a by-election as MP for East Leeds. He served in the Shadow Cabinet of the late 1950s, and was appointed Secretary of State for Defence by Harold Wilson in 1964 where he served until 1970. When Labour unexpectedly won the February 1974 election, Healey was appointed Chancellor of the Exchequer. Hyper-inflation, world oil price hikes, and fiscal and labour market policies preventing structural adjustment posed a deep threat to the British economy. By early 1978 Healey had brought the economy back under control. In delaying the election a year, Callaghan was subsequently defeated in 1979.

In the internecine warfare that followed, Healey was narrowly defeated as leader against Michael Foot by 139 to 129 votes in the PLP, but narrowly defeated Benn for deputy leader in the Electoral College by 50.42% to 49.57%, thereby saving the Labour Party from probable disintegration. After Labour's 1983 defeat, he resigned as Deputy Leader but continued to serve as Shadow Foreign Secretary, lending real authority to the first phase of Neil Kinnock's modernisation project.

Healey's expertise in defence and foreign policy detached him from more orthodox revisionist debates concerning the relationship between socialist values and the economy. His ambivalence in relation to Britain's participation in Europe had alienated him from Jenkins and the moderate social democrats by the early 1970s.

However, he was a member of the Campaign for Democratic Socialism (CDS), formed in response to the need for a more organised centre-right in the party at both parliamentary and constituency level. The principles and policies upheld by the CDS were unmistakably revisionist - and though Healey was not active in the CDS - he was engaged in successive struggles against the fundamentalist left within Labour's ranks. Yet his willingness to accept the 'constraints and disciplines' of party gave him a more pragmatic air than the rigidly principled Gaitskell.

In the essay 'Power politics and the Labour Party', originally published in the New Fabian Essays, Healey affirms the Atlantic Alliance as the bedrock of Labour's foreign policy. Like the Conservatives, Labour had to come to terms with a post-imperial political landscape dominated by the complex and unresolved choice between Europe and America.

The Attlee Government had played a key role in persuading the United States to assume global responsibilities both in security through NATO, and in the reconstruction of the world economy through the Marshall Plan, GATT, the IMF and the World Bank. There has been a strong revival of

Atlanticism under 'New' Labour, emphasising once again the importance of the Atlantic Alliance for Labour's politics.

Selected Text[1]

That external factors would one day dominate British politics was never conceived by the founders of British Socialism. Apart from one reference to the foreign policy of the Manchester School, the original volume of *Fabian Essays* never mentions the world outside Britain except to point to a domestic moral. Indeed, this sort of parochialism was the Fabians' greatest strength. They found socialism wandering aimlessly in Cloud Cuckoo land and set it working on the gas and water problems of the nearest town or village. The modern Welfare State is their monument.

But the very success of Fabianism as an instrument of domestic reform condemns it as a guide to world politics. The world as a whole has never resembled the delicately integrated democracy which Britain developed in the three centuries following the Civil Wars — nor have more than a tiny minority of the states within it. *Leviathan* is still a better handbook for foreign policy than *Fabian Essays*.

An understanding of the power element in politics is the first necessity for a sound foreign policy. The trade union movement, as the other main contributor to British socialism, can still, as so often in the past, go some way towards filling this gap in Fabian theory. But the trade union movement is even more afflicted by parochialism, and it tends to intervene in the formation of foreign policy to correct errors rather than to give positive direction.

The major positive influences on Labour Party thinking about world affairs have come from neither the Fabians nor the trade unions, but from the liberal-Nonconformist wing with its bias towards pacifism, and the neo-Marxist wing, stemming from continental Social Democracy and Communism.

Because the Party as a whole lacks any systematic theory of world affairs, it has too often fallen victim to the besetting sin of all progressive opposition movements — utopianism. In particular, it tends to discount the power element in politics, seeing it as a specific evil of the existing system rather than a generic characteristic of politics as

[1]   Healey, D., 'Power Politics and the Labour Party', in R.H.S. Crossman (ed.), *New Fabian Essays*, London: Turnstile Press, 1952.

such. The liberal utopian believes that if left to themselves men will automatically act for the common interest. The Marxist utopian exaggerates the influence of economic factors on human behaviour and believes that all social evils stem from a bad system of property relations. In both cases depreciation of the power factor entails an inadequate understanding of the techniques of power.

Conservative movements which represent the ruling class have the opposite temptation. For them the exercise of power easily becomes an end in itself and the sole aim of all political activity. In Mannheim's words: 'The Conservative type of knowledge originally is the sort of knowledge giving practical control. It consists of habitual orientations towards those factors which are immanent in the present situation.' Thus it makes obsolescent administrative techniques serve as a substitute for policy in a changing world.

The foreign policies of the British parties bear out these generalisations. The Conservatives have a congenital grasp of the rules of thumb for protecting British interests as defined in the Victorian heyday. But they are slow to recognise changes in those interests and even slower to understand changes in the world within which their rules of thumb must be applied.

The Labour Party, on the other hand, has always been more alive to change in world affairs than to continuity. It is highly sensitive to the economic factors in international life. But it tends to see power politics as a disease peculiar to capitalism and to under-estimate or misjudge the power factors in a given situation. At worst it is so little conscious of Britain's national interests that its attention can be attracted to world affairs only by high-flown formulas which quickly lose their relevance. Particularly when the Labour Party is in office, foreign policy becomes the last refuge of utopianism.

For the utopian, Heaven is always round the corner, every evil has a single cause and thus a single cure — there is always 'One Way Only'. Socialist attitudes to war provide many examples. Esperanto has always been popular among socialists on the grounds that nations would cease to fight one another if they all spoke the same language. Though war is at least 3,000 years older than capitalism, many socialists believe that capitalism is the only cause of war, and that therefore the Soviet Union could not commit aggression because it has a 'socialist' economy. Others maintain that the only serious danger of war springs from disparities between the living standards of the peoples; yet it is difficult to find a single war in modern times which was caused primarily by such disparities.

Between the wars this type of utopianism had a damaging influenced on Labour's attitude to world affairs. Despite the contribution of the two Labour Governments towards the maintenance of collective security through the League of Nations — above all in the Geneva Protocol — the first great crisis of collective security in Manchuria swept the Party into an ostrich-like policy of total war-resistance. In 1934 the trade unions forced the Party back to collective security and in 1935 Bevin led a crushing attack against the pacifism of Lansbury and the pseudo-revolutionary naïveté of the Socialist League. Yet much Labour propaganda continued pacifist in spirit right up to the outbreak of war, and the Party's attitude towards rearmament remains equivocal.

Most British socialists had been preaching for years that war was the inevitable consequence of capitalism and that no capitalist government could be trusted to use power for peaceful ends. This belief made nonsense of the Labour Party's policy for maintaining collective security through the League of Nations, which was indeed from that point of view an 'international burglars' union', as Sir Stafford Cripps maintained. But the bulk of the Party, while believing in the intrinsic wickedness of capitalism, expected capitalist states in the League to behave more altruistically than states have ever behaved in history. The League of Nations failed, as Arthur Henderson said, not because its machinery was imperfect, but because its members would not use the machinery against their own conception of their national interests. But when have states ever shown such altruism?

Parochialism also played its part. The shortcomings of British conservatism always stood between the Labour Party and the foreign scene. In the 'twenties many English socialists thought Britain more responsible than Germany for the First World War. In the 'thirties they thought the City of London responsible for Hitler. This sort of parochialism survived the Second World War: in the 'fifties a Labour Party Conference cheered the statement that Churchill was responsible for Stalinism in Russia. And it is not confined to socialists in Britain: Republicans in the USA maintain that the Democratic Administration is responsible for Communism in China.

These criticisms of the Labour Party's attitude to world affairs do not apply to the foreign policy of the two brief pre-war Labour Governments and still less to the post-war foreign policy of Ernest Bevin, a man whose qualities of character, judgment and imagination go to make a great Foreign Secretary. But they are still valid for the bulk of the Party membership. Indeed, Bevin's foreign policy never

obtained wholehearted approval from the more enthusiastic socialists in the Party, and many of those who did approve it believed that
it was not to any significant degree a socialist policy. Thus the Party
as a whole gave only reluctant support to the Government's handling of Great Power relations, though it took genuine pride in the
Government's Commonwealth and Colonial policy — above all, the
transfer of power in India.

There is no doubt that the Labour Government, because it was
socialist, showed far more understanding and sympathy for the revolutionary trends in Asia and Africa than the Conservative opposition. That Britain is now the one white country with genuine friends
in Asia is due to the speed with which power was transferred in
India and the economic assistance which the new states received:
both were opposed by the Conservatives. The Government showed
similar understanding for the Chinese revolution, though the fruits
of this policy will be slow to mature. British influence was instrumental towards changing Dutch policy towards Indonesia. It is easy
to say Britain should have done more to change French policy in
Indo-China in the same way, but at the critical time de Gaulle was
the French Prime Minister and British relations with France were
already strained over Syria.

The contrast between achievement in this sphere and the disap-
pointment in the wider field of world affairs is not, however, due to a
sudden failure of socialist principle in dealing with power politics,
for in its handling of the post-war situation the Labour Government
showed both an understanding and a moral strength which owed
much to socialist conviction.

The essence of British socialism lies not it its contingent analysis or
techniques, but in its determination to apply moral principles to
social life. It belongs to that stream of Christian thought which, while
insisting that the individual human personality is an end in itself —
indeed the only temporal end in itself — believes that all men are
brothers, and must realise their brotherhood in this world by creating a society in which they enjoy an equal right and duty to freedom
and responsibility. It is in this sense that our socialism is inseparable
from democracy.

As a political programme, socialism developed during the nineteenth century in a number of industrialised European democracies
as a protest against economic conditions which prevented working
men from enjoying the freedom Liberalism claimed to have won for
them in the political field. The analysis it made of those economic

conditions and the techniques it invented to change them are still relevant to societies which resemble the industrial capitalist democracies of the nineteenth century, but elsewhere they have less guidance to offer. Confronted by modern American capitalism and primitive peasant societies, socialists must make a new analysis and develop new techniques by which to fulfil their moral principles. This is even more necessary in dealing with the affairs of the world as a whole.

By choosing the phrase 'Social Democracy' to distinguish their policy from that of other parties, socialists assume that society has already realised political democracy. But in world affairs the political foundations on which the theory of Social Democracy is built have yet to be laid. Indeed the basic problem which socialists face in the world as a whole is almost the opposite of that which they have hitherto faced in national societies. Instead of adjusting the economic system to realise a community already established in the political field, they must adjust political relations to realise a community already existing in the technological field. They must build a world society before they can build a socialist world.

The problem is primarily political, not economic or social. It concerns the acquisition, organisation and distribution of power. Power is not, of course, the only reality in world affairs. But it is a pervasive reality which has its own laws and fixed the limits within which moral criteria can operate. The central problem of politics arises from the fact that every time a political entity grows in size, strength or solidarity, it tends to obscure the fundamental brotherhood of its members with the members of other entities and thus to license immoral behaviour towards them. *Un bon pere de famille est capable de tout*. 'If we had done for ourselves what we have done for Italy', said Cavour, 'what scoundrels we would have been'.

In foreign as in domestic affairs, socialists should aim at changing the existing system so as to realise the fundamental brotherhood of all men and to check the selfish will to power. It is a fact that power tends to corrupt, but it is also a fact that men and even governments may resist corruption without sacrificing power. The urge to brotherhood is no less real a political fact than the will to power. In social as in personal life, moral progress is possible, although it is not automatic. Here the socialist already operates within a framework of law, they can make the necessary changes by consent through legislation. But in world affairs law is rarely able to override power and power is frequently exercised in its crudest form as physical force.

Many socialists believe that the political entities from which a world society must be built are social classes or political movements extending across the frontiers of nation states. This belief has always been a basic principle of Communist theory. It was Sir Stafford Cripps' reason for opposing sanctions against Italy in 1935. It often appeared in Labour criticism of Bevin's foreign policy.

In fact, however, the world has so long been divided into geographical units, each developing at a different rate and in a different direction, that there is little basis of interest or sentiment to unite classes occupying roughly similar positions in the social pattern of their various states.

The industrial proletariat, to which this theory is usually applied, is comparatively unimportant except in Western Europe and the United States of America. Even where the proletariat is a major element in its nation state, it does not automatically agree either in theory or practice with the proletariat of other states — still less with the peasant population of its own state.

Though the majority of workers in Britain and Scandinavia support socialism, their comrades in France and Italy are Communists, while in North America they believe in free enterprise capitalism. In Argentina they form the backbone of General Peron's dictatorship. Further disagreements appear on practical problems. Italian and Polish miners can testify that trade unionists are as anxious as employers to protect their livelihood from foreign competition. The Lancashire textile workers join the Lancashire mill-owner in opposing the common interests of textile workers and employers in Japan. Thus the popular injunction to side in all cases with the workers is no guide to foreign policy.

A policy based on socialist solidarity is still more difficult to apply. Democratic socialism is even less widespread and powerful than trade unionism and even more coloured by national interests. Every democratic socialist party aims primarily at achieving power in its own nation state and is thus obliged to consider the interests of its own state first. Indeed, to the extent that the internal structure of a given state satisfies the need of the workers within it, to that extent a socialist party will tend to put the national interest before international solidarity. It is no accident that in their approach to European unity since 1945 the socialist parties of Britain and Scandinavia have been most conservative — for they have most to conserve. Economic factors reinforce the trend towards nationalism in a governing socialist party: in a world predominantly capitalist, national economic planning may often be inconsistent with forms of international co-operation a laissez-faire government would be quite willing to accept.

The fact is that the nation state is by far the most important political entity in world affairs. Nationalism is the one force strong enough to defeat all comers, whether the imperialism of the past or the totalitarianism of the present.

Many British socialists share the liberal belief that every nation state is a moral entity with natural rights and duties which are ultimately compatible with the rights and duties of other nation states. But nation states are political entities, not moral entities; with interests and desires, not rights and duties. Liberal theory gives all states the right to security. But the security of Russia's western frontier is incompatible with the security of Germany's eastern frontier, and both Russia's security and Germany's security are incompatible with the existence of Poland as a nation state.

The relations of nation states are determined primarily by their power to pursue their interests, and they usually conceive their interests in narrowly selfish terms. The influence of a British Labour Government in world affairs will in the first place depend on the power at its command and on the skill with which it used that power. What then is the most hopeful path towards a world society?

Orthodox Labour theory maintains that a world society can best be created by establishing the rule of law through a universal organisation like the League of Nations or the United Nations; within this general framework of international order nations can be brought into closer and more lasting co-operation through regional or functional institutions like OEEC or the Atlantic Pact.

At the present time international order is at once more necessary and more difficult to establish than ever before. Modern technology has both united and shrunk the world. Nation states are becoming ever stronger and closer to one another. Events in one part of the world immediately affect power relationships in all other parts. In particular, any local war in which new weapons of mass destruction threaten even the survival of the human race. All states have — and recognise — a powerful common interest in preventing war and economic crisis.

On the other hand, many parts of the world are undergoing revolutionary changes on a scale which occurs only once in a millennium. In non-communist Asia and Africa, the peoples are growing faster than their food production. They are demanding at once national independence, freedom from white control and a rapid rise in living standards. The rest of Asia and Eastern Europe is organised under a totalitarian regime which believes itself destined to rule the world. The United States of America, economically the most powerful of all countries, has leapt in a few years from isolationism to active participation in world affairs.

Socialists are by nature sensitive to these changes, as the Labour Government's policy in Asia has proved. Here too, however, the besetting sin of utopianism is always offering its temptations. Too often socialists tend to imagine that changes are morally or practically desirable simply because they are changes. Man reared in the doctrine of automatic progress cannot help feeling that everything that will be will be right. But most historical changes are morally neutral. It is difficult to maintain that the brotherhood of men is better realised in Eastern Europe under a 'people's democracy' than it was under the Austro-Hungarian Empire.

Moreover, those who imagine they are jumping on the bandwagon of history often find they have chosen the wrong vehicle. The world is going through profound changes, but it is difficult to interpret these changes rightly and impossible to predict their outcome. Many of the visible trends contradict one another. The century of the common man is also the era of the rape of the masses and of the managerial revolution. If economic man is dead in Europe he is deified in America. Most European interpretations are wrong because they use terms derived from Europe's own experience in the last hundred years. Not only the Webbs in 1935 but even Professor Carr in 1951 can describe Soviet Communism in terms of nineteenth-century European trends towards economic planning. But the striking thing about the world revolution is that everywhere the differences from European precedent are more important then the similarities. European categories crumble when applied to what is going on in Asia, Russia and America. The same slump which produced Hitler in Europe produced Roosevelt in the USA. Keynesian economics does not explain the problem of unemployment in India.

While these great changes are still in progress there is a danger in creating international institutions which attempt to set a rigid pattern for relations between the powers. Unless international institutions allow for major changes, they will not only break down, but will even increase the danger of world conflict. The juridical approach to international affairs is especially dangerous, since international law reflects a pattern of power which is changing daily. An international system must be founded on recognised common interests or a stable pattern of power — or both. It may then develop habits of co-operation which enable it to survive when the basis of interest or power has disappeared. But the development of common interests or the establishment of a stable power pattern must precede and not follow the creation of rigid legal or institutional forms.

The United Nations Assembly, for example, has assumed a universal authority, although decisions may be taken by a majority of states with little knowledge of or interest in the issues at stake and representing a minority both of people and of power. By its handling of the problems posed by Chinese intervention in the Korean war, the United Nations has already weakened its prestige throughout Asia. On the other hand, when Britain asked the Security Council to uphold her rights in Persia under international law, the majority of countries were not prepared to support international law in a case which seemed contrary to their sense of justice and history. By claiming a type of authority it is unable to exercise, the United Nations risks discrediting the very idea of international order.

One way out of the dilemma is to create regional institutions linking countries which are likely to have a continuing common interest however the major changes in the world develop. This is a wise course for small states which cannot hope separately to influence world affairs. But it carries dangers for a world power like Britain, which needs close co-operation with states in every region. For regional groups can exist only by discrimination against states outside their region. A regional federation does not necessarily contribute towards the creation of a world society. Indeed, the most dangerous conflicts in the world at present lie primarily between the two great continental federations, the United States of America and the USSR. The Commonwealth is the exception which proves this rule. Membership of the Commonwealth does not limit co-operation with states outside it precisely because the Commonwealth has no separate institutions.

Throughout its period of office, the Labour Government was severely handicapped by the absolute and relative decline in Britain's power. Peace found the ruins of Britain's nineteenth-century *imperium* strewn throughout a power vacuum which was flanked by two jealous continental super-states, each immensely stronger than before the war. But for the first few years Britain's weakness was masked by the prestige of victory, by the even greater decline of other European states, by Russia's exhaustion, and by America's readiness to accept Britain's advice until she found her feet. Thus, though even Britain's survival as an independent state was in jeopardy, the skill, patience and understanding of the Labour Government made British foreign policy the main constructive element in world affairs. And it was largely British statesmanship which not only carried the world through the emergencies of the post-war crisis, but also laid some foundations for a lasting world order . . .

. . . Germany remains the most dangerous problem for British policy in the future. Britain cannot ignore the possibility that Germany may seek national unity either by war with Russia or by alliance with Russia. It has been fashionable to see the answer in integrating Western Germany into some form of West European union. Britain herself has been unwilling to join such a union for fear of losing her independence outside Europe. But it is already obvious that if European unity is built without Britain it will be dominated by Germany. As Germany revives Britain may be compelled to integrate herself more deeply with Europe than is compatible with her other economic and political interests. Indeed, America is the only state with sufficient power to spare for correcting the balance in Western Europe. But many Americans believe that Germany's revival would justify their withdrawal from Europe instead of requiring them to play a more active part in Europe themselves.

Relations with the United States have thus become the central problem of British foreign policy. But material and moral factors severely limit the range of choice. Strategically Britain needs America even more than America needs Britain. Economically, though Britain might dispense with direct American aid at home, her plans for economic development abroad demand large-scale dollar aid. Politically, America's interests are far closer to those of Britain than the interests of any other present or potential ally; indeed, the Commonwealth would not survive a rupture between Britain and the USA. Morally, as a progressive democracy America is far closer to Britain than is Western Europe, southern Asia, or, of course, the Soviet Union. Anglo-American unity is indeed a condition of Britain's survival.

The final major change in the post-war pattern of power politics may come through a disruption of the Stalinist bloc. Tito's defection was premature in the sense that Russia has probably been able to eliminate the main sources of Titoism in the rest of Eastern Europe before the world situation gave them a chance of success. But the present alliance between the Soviet Union and Communist China is based on a very temporary congruence of interest. On the other hand, if China does separate herself from the Soviet Union a settlement in Eastern Asia will not necessarily become much simpler.

One thing at least is certain. The situation of 1945–50, in which the Labour Party's foreign policy came of age, has gone for good. Too many minds are still dominated by the picture of two continental super-states glowering at each other over a power vacuum in which Britain is the only strong state. The emergence of Germany, Japan and China as independent powers has already changed that picture. Within a few years southern Asia, the Middle East and Africa may also take the stage in their own right. Thus the vision of a world shaped almost exclusively by Anglo-Saxon policy is fading at the very moment when it seems most likely to become reality. It is much more probable that the future will bring a return to a world of many powers in which decisions are made by the methods of traditional power politics. If this is so, conventional diplomacy will come into its own again and the adjustment of national differences by negotiation and compromise will become more urgent than the construction of international institutions or the execution of moral blueprints.

These suggestions are offered without excessive confidence. The known facts are always so small a proportion of total reality that the fruits of scientific method should never be taken as rational grounds for defeatism or over-confidence. Three predictions at least are fairly safe. Britain's influence on world affairs in the immediate future will depend more than ever on her material power to help a friend or harm an enemy. Britain's fundamental interest in unity with the United States will remain supreme. And an understanding of power politics will be more than ever necessary to a successful socialist foreign policy.

C.A.R. Crosland — The Meaning of Socialism (1956)

Published in 1956, Crosland's The Future of Socialism *constituted the most articulate synthesis of social democratic thought in the post-war period, providing both a political analysis and strategy that has inspired successive generations.*

It too invited venomous accusations of heresy and betrayal. The Bevanites' Tribune *newspaper greeted* The Future of Socialism *with the headline 'Socialism? How Dare He Use the Word!' and concluded that a Labour Party taking Crosland seriously, 'will be set firmly and inexorably on the road to decline'.*

Crosland appeared to openly advocate two major divergences from party orthodoxy. The first was an assault on the traditional egalitarian case for nationalisation. The second involved restating the aims of socialism in ethical terms. But more than the intellectual champion of revisionism, Crosland emerged as a leading Labour politician of the 1960s and 1970s.

He was born in August 1918 in St Leonards-on-Sea, and educated at Highgate School followed by Trinity College, Oxford. Crosland saw active service in the Second World War as a member of the Royal Welsh Fusiliers, then in the Parachute Brigade, and returned to Oxford to complete his Politics, Philosophy and Economics (PPE) degree in 1946. He was briefly a Fellow of Trinity College where he taught economics. But Crosland's focus had already turned to Westminster, where his imminent rise owed much to being one of Hugh Dalton's most favoured protégés.

He was elected as the MP for South Gloucestershire in 1950, but following a boundary re-organisation before the 1955 election, unwisely moved constituencies and was defeated. In the late 1950s, he authored an influential report on the future of the Co-operative Society. In 1959, he was returned as MP for Grimsby by 101 votes, but subsequently held the seat in five successive elections.

Following the 1964 General Election victory, Crosland acted as George Brown's deputy at the Department of Economic Affairs, and was then appointed Secretary of State at the Department of Education in 1965 – where he ended the iniquitous eleven-plus. He also enshrined the binary principle that created thirty polytechnics, leading to the creation of mass higher education in Britain. He moved to the Board of Trade (1967), and again to the Department of Local Government and Regional Planning (1969). Following the 1970 defeat, Crosland returned to Government as Secretary of State for the Environment (1974–76), and Foreign Secretary (1976–77).

His main writings include Britain's Economic Problem *(1953),* The Future of Socialism *(1956),* The Conservative Enemy *(1962), and* Socialism Now *(1974).*

In a chapter from The Future of Socialism*, 'The meaning of Socialism', he sought to challenge Labour's ideological orthodoxy, arguing that 'social-*

ism' had no precise, descriptive meaning that could be empirically observed. Instead, socialism consisted of certain enduring ideals and aspirations — a belief in equality, a classless society, and the commitment to fraternity and co-operation. He sought to define a new egalitarian philosophy for the centre-left in terms of opportunity and outcome — in which public services and private enterprise would work together in harmony to bring about the ultimate goal of social equality.

Crosland's formulation laid the foundations for later revisionist thinking, and the emergence of 'New' Labour in the late 1980s and early 1990s owes much to The Future. Both displayed an attitude to public ownership that was pragmatic, instrumental and to a large extent sceptical. Both advocated selective state intervention within a mixed market economy. Both shared the commitment to sustained economic growth as the necessary basis for reducing economic inequalities and improving social welfare. Measures to improve Britain's rate of growth offered the surest route to sustainable redistribution, precisely the strategy adopted by 'New' Labour.

However, critics have argued that later revisionism, in contrast to Crosland, was not based on a systematic analysis of social and economic developments. It was according to David Marquand 'opinion-survey driven' rather than 'doctrine driven'. As a result, it is claimed, 'New' Labour lacks a coherent governing philosophy sufficient to steer it through the contingencies of power. For all the criticisms levelled at The Future of Socialism, and the subsequent impact of the fiscal and institutional crisis of the early 1970s, no one could sustain such a charge against Crosland's revisionist case.

Selected Text[2]

The Confusion Between Ends and Means

If we are to reformulate socialist doctrine, the first task is clearly to decide what precise meaning is to be attached to the word 'socialism'.

This is not any easy question to answer. The word does not describe any present or past society, which can be empirically observed, and so furnish unimpeachable evidence for what is or is not 'socialism'. Thus statements about socialism can never be definitely verified; and we cannot treat it as being an *exact descriptive*

---

[2]   Crosland, C.A.R., 'The meaning of socialism', in *The Future of Socialism*, London: Cape, 1956; rev. edn 1964. [Footnotes in this section are original.]

word at all. There is therefore no point in searching the encyclopaedias for a definitive meaning; it has none, and never could.

This can easily be seen by considering the numerous and often inconsistent meanings attached to the word by people who have called themselves 'socialists'. Marx, defining it as the 'nationalisation of the means of production, distribution, and exchange', meant something quite different from Proudhon, who defined it as consisting of 'every aspiration towards the amelioration of our society'. Sir William Harcourt, declaring in 1892 that 'we are all socialists now', evidently had a different version from his contemporary Bradlaugh, to whom socialism meant that 'the State should own all wealth, direct all labour, and compel the equal distribution of all produce.' And any history of socialist thought will provide dozens of different definitions, some in terms of ownership, some of co-operation, some of planning, some of income-distribution; and it soon becomes simply a matter of subjective preference which is chosen as the 'correct' one. Many definitions, moreover, are so vague as to be virtually meaningless; one can read almost anything, for example, into Sidney Webb's definition: 'the economic side of the democratic ideal'.

The confusion has become worse inasmuch as the word is also charged with a high degree of emotional content, and so has acquired a range of purely persuasive meanings. It is either used to denote or win approval, as in Hitler's National 'Socialism' and 'Socialism' in Eastern Europe, or when Left-wing weeklies attack a policy which they dislike as not being 'Socialist'; or pejoratively, as when Right-wing Americans speak of 'creeping Socialism'.

But the worst source of confusion is the tendency to use the word to describe, not a certain kind of society, or certain values which might be attributes of a society, but particular policies which are, or are thought to be, means of attaining this kind of society, or realising these attributes. To rescue the word from these confusions, and the debasement referred to above, one must begin by asking what, if anything, is common to the beliefs of all, or almost all, of those who have called themselves socialists. The only constant element, common to all the bewildering variety of different doctrines, consists of certain moral values and aspirations; and people have called themselves socialists because they shared these aspirations, which form the one connecting link between otherwise hopelessly divergent schools of thought.

Thus the world first came on the modern scene with the early nineteenth-century Owenites, whom Marx contemptuously termed 'Utopian' socialists.[3] They based their 'socialism' explicitly on an ethical view of society, a belief in a certain way of life and certain moral values. The means by which they thought this 'good society' could be attained are irrelevant today; and in fact they were quickly challenged by other socialist schools of thought, since when a continuous debate has proceeded, with no agreement, about what constituted the most suitable means. This debate would have no particular interest to day, but for the fact that all the protagonists tried to appropriate the word 'socialism' to describe the particular means which they themselves favoured.

Thus Marx appropriated it for the collective ownership of the means of production on the false assumption, that the pattern of ownership determined the character of the whole society, and that collective ownership was a sufficient condition to fulfilling the basic aspirations. And generally the word came to be applied to policies for the economic or institutional transformation of society, instead of to the ultimate social purposes which that transformation was intended to achieve; so one often hears socialism equated not only with the nationalisation of industry, but with government planning, or redistribution, or state collectivism. This of course is quite unhelpful, for although people may agree on ends, they may legitimately disagree about means. Moreover, the means most suitable in one generation may be wholly irrelevant in the next, and in any case (still more significant) a given means may lead to more than one possible end, as indeed has happened with each of the policies just mentioned.

Thus if, for example, socialism is defined as the nationalisation of the means of production, distribution and exchange, we produce conclusions which are impossible to reconcile with what the early socialists had in mind when they used the word: such as, that Soviet Russia is a completely socialist country (much more so, for instance, than Sweden) — even though it denies almost all the values which Western socialists have normally read into the word. Similarly, if socialism is defined as economic collectivism or State control of economic life, then Nazi Germany would correctly have been called a socialist country. But in neither case would the end-result be

[3]   To be precise, the word first occurs in *The Co-operative Magazine* in 1827, and was used to describe the views and demands of the original London 'Co-operators'.

described as socialism by most socialists; the means of nationalisation and planning have proved adaptable to more than one purpose, which shows how unwise it is to identify the means with the end.

Not only is it unwise, but it is also semantically and historically incorrect. The various schools of thought which have called themselves, and been called by others, 'socialist' — Owenites and Marxists, Fabians and Christian Socialists, Syndicalists and Guild Socialists — have differed profoundly over the right means; and no one means has a better title to the label 'socialist' than any other. The one single element common to all the schools of thought has been the basic aspirations, the underlying moral values. It follows that these embody the only logically and historically permissible meaning of the world socialism; and to this meaning we must now revert.

The Basic Socialist Aspirations

These ethical and emotional ideas have been partly negative — a protest against the visible results of capitalism — and partly positive, and related to definite views about the nature of the good society; though of course negative and positive strands are often inter-twined.

Perhaps one can list them roughly as follows. First, a protest against the material poverty and physical squalor which capitalism produced. Secondly, a wider concern for 'social welfare' — for the interests of those in need, or oppressed, or unfortunate, from whatever cause. Thirdly, a belief in equality and the 'classless society', and especially a desire to give the worker his 'just' rights and a responsible status at work. Fourthly, a rejection of competitive antagonism, and an ideal of fraternity and co-operation. Fifthly, a protest against the inefficiencies of capitalism as an economic system, and notably its tendency to mass unemployment. The first three formed the basis of socialism as 'a broad, human movement on behalf of the bottom dog'.[4] The first and last were censures on the material results of capitalism; while the other three stemmed from an idealistic desire for a just, co-operative and classless society. (I have listed only the social and economic aspirations. But of course underlying them, and taken for granted, was a passionate belief in liberty and democracy. It would never have occurred to most early socialists that socialism had any meaning except within a political

---

[4]   Cole, *A Short History of the British Working-Class Movement*, Vol III, p. 22.

framework of freedom for the individual. But since this political assumption is shared by British Conservatives as well as socialists, no further reference is made to it.)

As thus formulated, even these basic aspirations are not all equally relevant to present-day society. Some are expressed in language adapted to conditions that no longer exist, and in particular are too negative in character. This is natural, for they were, in large part, a reaction against the actual results of pre-war capitalism, and with two million unemployed, widespread poverty and malnutrition, and appalling slums set against a background of flamboyant wealth amongst the richer classes, it was natural that the negative desire to abolish evils should outweigh more positive and detailed aspirations.

But to the extent that evils are remedied and injustices removed, negative statements become less and less appropriate. And they are seen to be inappropriate by the electorate, a growing section of which has no recollection of unemployment, or poverty, or dole-queues, and finds Labour propaganda which plays on the themes and memories of the 1930s quite incomprehensible. To a population which has lost its fears, and now has every hope of a rapidly rising standard of living, a negative prospect against past wrongs is merely a bore.

Thus even when we go back to the basic aspirations, we still find the same, welcome, difficulty that the pace of change has overtaken the doctrine, and a re-formulation is needed. Of course if a Tory Government were to re-create all the old evils, matters would be simple. New thinking could be set aside 'for the duration', and negative statements would again suffice. But it is not likely that the Tories will act so recklessly, or that mere periodic counter-attacks to regain lost positions will remove the need for a map of the new terrain.

How should we re-formulate these aspirations to-day in such a way as to preserve their basic emotional and ethical content, yet discarding what is clearly not germane to present-day conditions? Of the original five, the first and last are rapidly losing their relevance in a British context. Such primary poverty as remains will disappear within a decade, given our present rate of economic growth; and the contemporary mixed economy is characterised by high levels both of employment and productivity and by a reasonable degree of stability. In other words, the aspirations relating to the economic consequences of capitalism are fast losing their relevance as capitalism itself becomes transformed.

But the remaining three more positive ideals, described above as stemming either from a concern with the 'bottom dog', or from a vision of a just, co-operative and classless society, have clearly not been fully realised. No doubt we should phrase them differently today, but their basic content is still perfectly relevant. We have plenty of less fortunate citizens still requiring aid; and we certainly have not got an equal or classless society, nor one characterised by 'co-operative' social relations.

Equality and Social Waste

The third objective to extreme social inequality is that it is wasteful and inefficient. If the divisions of class make deep incisions, and the space of free social movement is restricted, as is the case in Britain (mainly on account of the distinct layers traced by a segregated educational system), two undesirable consequences follow.

First, social intercourse between the classes is markedly inhibited, both by external differences in 'manners' and behaviour, and by subjective consciousness of class. One of the strong attractions of (for example) American society is the extraordinary social freedom, the relaxed, informal atmosphere, the easier contacts, the natural assumption of equality, the total absence of deference, and the relative absence of snobbery and of that faint, intangible but nonetheless insistent sense of class that permeates social attitudes in Britain. One does not ask that all Englishmen should suddenly take to calling each other 'Bud', or altogether abandon their well-known national posture of reserved hauteur; but it would be agreeable if they should intermingle rather more freely and with rather less restraint than they do to-day, and if our social system generally were less fragmented and sub-divided. But this is naturally a matter of personal taste and temperament; and possibly more reserved or inhibited Englishmen may not like the idea of a more mixed-up, egalitarian informal pattern of social life.

However, the British class system also involves a definite social waste, since it selects its leaders badly. If social mobility is low, as it must be in a stratified society, and people cannot easily move up from the lower or middle reaches to the top, then the ruling elite becomes hereditary and self-perpetuating; and whatever one may concede to inherited or family advantages, this must involve a waste of talent.

Opportunities for rising are, it is true, more ample than they used to be; and any really outstanding working-class child now can, with an effort, reach the top. But even on the simplest grounds of efficiency this is not enough. In our highly complex and professional industrial society, the problem of leadership is not one merely of finding the tiny minority of brilliant geniuses; for there are far more responsible top positions than geniuses to fill them. We cannot be content with correctly distributing all the (as it were) alpha material, but must make the best use of our beta resources also. And there matters are far from satisfactory. Clever working-class children are still denied access to the public schools, while the less clever but still potentially useful have only a rather uncertain access to the grammar schools; and there is certainly no perfect correspondence between natural talent and type of education. Moreover, as was observed above, inherited property, nepotism, and class favouritism all prevent a fair and effective competition, on merit alone, for the highest posts.

It follows that we are still not exacting the best from our population, or making the most exhaustive use of scarce resources of human ability. This is a definite social waste, and one directly related to a stratified social system which, by placing a premium on lineage, and barriers in the way of vertical mobility, prevents a genuine equality of opportunity.

How Much Equality?

How far towards equality do we wish to go? I do not regard this as either a sensible or pertinent question, to which one could possibly give, or should attempt to give, a precise reply. We need, I believe, more equality than we now have. We can therefore describe the direction of advance, and even discern the immediate landscape ahead; but the ultimate objective lies wrapped in complete uncertainty.

This must be the case unless one subscribes to the vulgar fallacy that some ideal society can be said to exist, of which blueprints can be drawn, and which will be ushered in as soon as certain specific reforms have been achieved. The apocalyptic view that we might one day wake up to find that something called 'socialism' had arrived was born of revolutionary theories of capitalist collapse. But in Western societies change is gradual and evolutionary, and not always either foreseeable or even under political control. It is therefore futile and dangerous to think in terms of an ideal society, the shape of which can already be descried, and which will be reached at some definite date in the future. Countries like Britain do not leap from one fully-fledged social system to another, but are, on the contrary, in a state of permanent transition.

Moreover, socialism is not an exact descriptive term, connoting a particular social structure, past, present, or even immanent in some sage's mind, which can be empirically observed or analysed. It simply describes a set of values, or aspirations, which socialists wish to see embodied in the organisation of society. One must confine oneself to saying, therefore, that society at any given moment either does or does not sufficiently embody these values; and if it does not, then further changes are required. But exactly what degree of equality will create a society which does sufficiently embody them, no one can possibly say. We must re-assess the matter in the light of each new situation.

We can thus only venture general statements of the objective. I feel clear that we need large egalitarian changes in our educational system, the distribution of property, the distribution of resources in periods of need, social manners and style of life, and the location of power within industry; and perhaps some, but certainly a smaller, change in respect of incomes from work. I think that these changes, taken together, will amount to a considerable social revolution.

On the other hand, I am sure that a definite limit exists to the degree of equality which is desirable. We do not want complete equality of incomes, since extra responsibility and exceptional talent require and deserve a differential reward. We are not hostile, as our opponents sometimes foolishly suggest, to 'detached residences in Bournemouth where some elderly woman has obviously more than a thousand a year'. I do not myself want to see *all* private education disappear: nor the Prime Minister denied an official car, as in one Scandinavian country: nor the Queen riding a bicycle: nor the House of Lords instantly abolished: nor the manufacture of Rolls-Royce banned: nor the Brigade of Guards, nor Oxford and Cambridge, nor Boodle's, nor (more doubtfully) the Royal Yacht Squadron, nor even, on a rather lower level, the Milroy Room, lose their present distinctive character: nor anything so dull and colourless as this.

But where en route, before we reach some drab extreme, we shall wish to stop, I have no idea. Our society will look quite different when we have carried through the changes mentioned earlier; and the whole argument will then need to be re-stated, and thought out afresh, by a younger generation than mine.

Liberty and Gaiety in Private Life:
The Need for a Reaction against the Fabian Tradition

Society's decisions impinge heavily on people's private lives as well as on their social or economic welfare; and they now impinge, in my view, in too restrictive and puritanical a manner. I should like to see action taken both to widen opportunities for enjoyment and relaxation, and to diminish existing restrictions on personal freedom.

The first of these requires, it is true, a change in cultural attitudes rather than government legislation. If this were to come about, much could be done to make Britain a more colourful and civilised country to live in. We need not only higher exports and old-age pensions, but more open-air cafes, brighter and gayer streets at night, later closing-hours for public houses, more local repertory theatres, better and more hospitable hoteliers and restaurateurs, brighter and cleaner eating-houses, more riverside cafes, more pleasure-gardens on the Battersea model, more murals and pictures in public places, better designs for furniture and pottery and women's clothes, statues in the centre of new housing-estates, better-designed street-lamps and telephone kiosks, and so on *ad infinitum*. The enemy in all this will often be in unexpected guise; it is not only dark Satanic things and people that now bar the road to the new Jerusalem, but also, if not mainly, hygienic, respectable, virtuous things and people, lacking only in grace and gaiety.

This becomes manifest when we turn to the more serious question of socially-imposed restrictions on the individual's private life and liberty. There come to mind at once the divorce laws, licensing laws, prehistoric (and flagrantly unfair) abortion laws, obsolete penalties for sexual abnormality, the illiterate censorship of books and plays, and remaining restriction of the equal rights of women. Most of these are intolerable, and should be highly offensive to socialists, in whose blood there should always run a trace of the anarchist and the libertarian, and not too much of the prig and the prude. If we really attach importance to the 'dignity of man', we must realise that this is as much affronted by a hypocritical divorce law which, as Matthew Arnold once wrote, neither makes divorce impossible nor makes it decent, as by refusal to establish a joint production council in a factory. A time will come, as material standards rise, when divorce-law reform will increase the sum of human welfare more than a rise in the food subsidies (though no doubt the party managers will be less enthusiastic for it). Socialists cannot go on indefinitely professing to be concerned with human happiness and the removal of injustice, and then, when the programmes are decided, permitting the National Executive, out of fear or certain vocal pressure-groups, to become more orthodox than the bench of bishops.

Much of this can at least claim the sanction of one powerful stream of socialist thought — that stemming from William Morris; though other, Nonconformist and Fabian, influences wear a bleaker and more forbidding air. For one brought up as a Fabian, in particular, this inevitably means a reaction against the Webb tradition. I do not wish to be misunderstood. All who knew the Webbs have testified to their personal kindliness, gentleness, tolerance, and humour; and no one who reads *Our Partnership* can fail to be intensely moved by the deep unaffected happiness of their mutual love. But many of their public virtues, so indispensable at the time, may not be as appropriate today. Reacting as they were against an unpractical, Utopian, sentimental, romantic, almost anarchist tradition on the Left, they were no doubt right to stress the solid virtues of hard work, self-discipline, efficiency, research, and abstinence: to sacrifice private pleasure to public duty, and expect that others should do the same: to put Blue Books before culture, and immunity from physical weakness above all other virtues.

And so they spent their honeymoon investigating Trade Societies in Dublin. And so Beatrice could write that 'owing to our concentration on research, municipal administration and Fabian propaganda, we had neither the time nor the energy, nor yet the means, to listen to music and the drama, to brood over classic literature, to visit picture galleries, or to view with an informed intelligence the wonders of architecture'. And so Sidney withheld approval from the Soviet experiment until workers' control had been suppressed, and Beatrice until the anti-abortion law had been enacted, and she could write with approval of the serious, youthful Comsomols with their passion for self-discipline and self-improvement: and of the emphasis on personal hygiene and self-control — 'there is no spooning in the Parks of Recreation and Rest'. And historically, without a doubt, this insistence on austerity was a vital service to a young and growing opposition movement.

But now we surely need a different set of values. Permeation has more than done its job. Today we are all incipient bureaucrats and practical administrators. We have all, so to speak, been trained at the LSE, are familiar with Blue Books and White Papers, and know our way around Whitehall. We realise that we must guard against romantic or Utopian notions; that hard work and research are virtues: that we must do nothing foolish or impulsive: and that Fabian pamphlets must be diligently studied. We know these things too well. Posthumously, the Webbs have won their battle, and converted a generation to their standards. Now the time has come for a reaction: for a greater emphasis on private life, on freedom and dissent, on culture, beauty, leisure, and even frivolity. Total abstinence and a good filing-system are not now the right signposts to the socialist Utopia: or at least, if they are, some of us will fall by the wayside.

Hugh Gaitskell — Socialism and Nationalisation (1956)

Hugh Gaitskell was a middle-class, public school-educated economist who became the leading social democratic politician of his generation. He chose to be a socialist because he resolved that it was right, rather than being born into it, and he believed that others could be persuaded of its virtues by force of rational argument. Gaitskell thus represented a new type of Labour politician, neither a carrier of the aspirations of the working-class majority of the labour movement, nor a resentful bourgeois in revolt against class or family, as Philip Williams's records in his incisive biography Hugh Gaitskell *(1979).*

He was born in April 1906 in Kensington, West London. After attending Winchester and New College, Oxford he lectured in economics at the Workers Educational Association in Nottingham, and University College, London. He served as a civil servant during the war at the Ministry for Economic Warfare and the Board of Trade under Hugh Dalton.

He was elected MP for South Leeds in 1945, and appointed as Minister for Fuel and Power (1947–49), Minister for Economic Affairs (1950), and then as Chancellor (1950–51), where his only budget was embroiled in controversy about the cost of rearmament for the Korean War, and the imposition of NHS charges on teeth and spectacles.

Gaitskell became Labour leader in 1955 at the age of 49, and for the next eight years led the Party with a zealous belief in its need to modernise. He inspired deeper loyalty from 'Gaitskellite' followers than any previous Labour leader, despite his reputation as a 'desiccated calculating machine'.

As a result, his leadership was dominated by a series of bruising internal disputes. He partly succeeded in harmonising his relationships with the left, co-operating with his archrival Nye Bevan over Suez in 1956, and initially won the support of key trade unions, notably the NUM, T&G, and GMBU. Yet his revisionist policies led to bitter confrontations with the party over public ownership and the proposal to reform Clause IV, equivalent as Harold Wilson put it, to 'taking Genesis out of the bible'.

However, while Gaitskell was convinced of the need to transcend nationalisation as the means of achieving greater equality, he remained dedicated to the ends of social justice. He did not believe that the historical Labour Party should be abandoned, nor should it be sacrificed as an independent political entity. Labour could secure a new progressive coalition alone, becoming the agent of moderate and responsible government. His sudden death in January 1963 robbed him of the opportunity to serve as the first Labour Prime Minister since Attlee.

Hugh Gaitskell's publications include Chartism *(1929),* In Defence of Politics *(1954), and* Recent Developments in British Socialist Thinking *(1956).*

The Fabian Pamphlet Socialism and Nationalisation *(Tract 300, 1956) reproduced for this collection helps to explain why revisionism acquired increasing prominence in the Labour Party of the 1950s. In part, it was a response to the failure of either party to reverse or even halt decline, and the steady worsening of Britain's economic problems. Three ideas animated it. People wanted freedom from restraint as much as an extension of state control. Full employment was the means to economic security. And the workplace itself should be transformed along democratic and co-operative lines.*

It also advanced a conception of socialism firmly rooted in the ethical commitment to equality that rejected wholesale nationalisation, and made a passionate appeal for a classless society of 'genuine equal opportunity for all'. It was highly sceptical of public ownership as an instrument for redistributing wealth.

The extract reflects the shock within Labour's ranks at the electoral defeats suffered by the party following the Attlee Government's demise in 1951, and sought to encourage Labour to adopt a more pragmatic position on nationalisation. This was compounded by a crushing defeat in the 1959 General Election. It led Gaitskell to conclude by 1959–60 that Labour had to finally repudiate public ownership as a socialist objective, if it was to construct a broader coalition absorbing the radical centre of British politics.

That was the revisionist message. Gaitskell put it into practice with greater tenacity and courage than any other Labour figure of the time.

Selected Text[5]

1. Socialist Ideals

Most recent writing on nationalisation has been about the way in which the newly nationalised industries are functioning, their achievements and weaknesses, the legislative and administrative framework in which they operate, their relationship to Ministers and Parliament, and similar issues.

Although I shall touch upon some of these matters in the course of this pamphlet, its scope is both wider and different. It is principally concerned with the relationship between nationalisation and public ownership and the broader, ultimate Socialist ideals for which the British Labour Party stands.

What are these ideals? We are not a doctrinaire party: we do not set out in great detail an exact declaration to every word of which every member must subscribe. The statement I make here represents only my own views, though I hope that it would also command fairly widespread assent among British Socialists.

Social Equality

First, we aim at social equality, which to us is substantially the same as social justice. We regard as unjust a class structure, in which a person's income, way of living, education, status and opportunities in life depend upon the class into which he is born. We reject a society in which one man is regarded as superior or inferior to another, regardless of personal qualities, again simply because of the section of society to which his parents happen to belong.

While we do not say that all should receive the same income, we hold that the differences should be related to generally accepted criteria of merit — such as the nature of the work — more being paid for dirty, harder, and more skilled, better performed, more responsible jobs. We say too that these differences should not be greater than are necessary to provide adequate incentives in the interest of economic progress. We believe in equal opportunity for all, and we claim that this is only possible if privately owned wealth is fairly evenly distributed, and if therefore a strict limit is placed on the extent to which it can be inherited.

---

[5]   Gaitskell, H., *Socialism and Nationalisation*, London: Fabian Society, 1956

But can there be equal opportunity? Does not the existence of natural differences between people make this an illusion?

Of course it is true that some children are cleverer, or more hardworking, or stronger or healthier than others: and of course it is true that these differences will play a large part in their lives. But firstly, this is no argument against providing equal opportunity at least to those with roughly the same abilities. Yet we are still a long way even from this.

And secondly, there is an obligation so society — not to make people alike — Heaven forbid! — but to help those who are less gifted to overcome their handicaps.

Equal Opportunity for What?

I must correct another misunderstanding. The phrase 'equal opportunity' is sometimes taken to mean a highly competitive and materialistic affair in which all start on the same line and proceed through life racing against each other to amass as much wealth as possible. This is not what I mean. While I certainly do not despise any desire to 'get on' and to enjoy higher living standards, I would not regard a society in which this becomes the sole motive of most people's lives as at all satisfactory. By 'equal opportunity' I mean equal opportunity for the pursuit of happiness, however people decide they can best achieve this.

I do not think it is the business of the State to lay down and to preach a set of rules. No doubt there have to be licensing and gambling laws — but these at least are negative. If the State were to direct ordinary people on how to pursue happiness, it would be intervening far too much with individual freedom. This is a matter which is best left to preachers, priests, teachers and poets — and I suppose one should add today, psychiatrists! And it is best done by persuasion, discussion and example, rather than by laws. It is surely true that people find happiness in different ways: some through artistic or intellectual development, some in more mundane and materialistic pursuits, some — perhaps the vast majority — in family life and relations with their friends.

There have been, and still are, some sincere and ardent reformers who do not take this view. They believe, not only that visiting an art gallery or listening to a concert of classical music is superior to watching a football match or reading a novel at home, but also that it is the business of the State to make people prefer the former to the latter. But to me the pursuit of happiness has always seemed such an individual and personal matter that it is in the main best left to people themselves to decide, though evidently their capacity for making wise decisions in these matters is limited, if they have never been given the chance to appreciate a concert as well as a football match. What the State should do is to provide a framework, the opportunities through which people have the best chance of finding happiness for themselves.

Full Employment

The second Socialist aim is economic security or full employment. This has always been a major item in Labour Party policy. And no wonder, when one considers the way in which unemployment itself, and the fear of it, have wrecked so many lives. Not many attempts have been made to give expression to full employment in exact quantitative terms. It has been recognised and made clear often enough that it cannot be taken to mean that everybody is guaranteed the same job for life. That would cause economic stagnation. But it has been interpreted as at least implying that there are more jobs available than persons seeking them.

This aim of full employment has usually been grouped with another — that of maximum productivity, of ensuring that all the natural and human resources available, all the most modern techniques, were so organised and applied as to produce the largest output of goods and services possible. Whether or not this is described as a separate aim, it must certainly be mentioned.

For despite constant propaganda to the contrary, the Labour Party is not simply concerned to share out more fairly an existing volume of production. It aims at a large output more fairly shared, not only so that living standards here may rise, but also in order that this country may play a greater part in helping the poorer, less developed countries of the world.

Industrial Democracy and Co-operation

Thirdly, we aim at industrial democracy, by which is meant a change of atmosphere and relationships in industry, which will give to the workers a better status, more power, more responsibility, and a true sense of participation. We want, in short, to see in people's working lives a reflection both of the political democracy we already enjoy, and of the greater economic equality which we intend to bring about.

We also want to see more 'co-operation' — better relationships between people whereby they work together more for the common good. In practice it is not easy to separate this ideal as an ultimate aim, on the one hand, from the ideal of social equality which we certainly expect to produce happier relations; and on the other hand from industrial democracy, in which the workers obtain a greater share of control and responsibility, and enjoy a greater sense of participation.

In short, the society we wish to create is one in which there are no social classes, equal opportunity in the sense described above, a high degree of economic equality, full employment, rapidly rising productivity, democracy in industry and a general spirit of co-operation between its members.

Furthermore, we intend to advance to these ideals by and through parliamentary democracy, the maintenance of which we regard as an aim of equal importance. This means that we have to proceed gradually, step by step, persuading our fellow citizens that our ends are just, and the means we choose will be adapted for the purpose.

2. The Traditional Case

But what means? This brings us to the question of nationalisation. Anybody who thinks about it for a moment will agree that nationalisation, which is an institutional change in the ownership and control of industry, must be treated as a means and not grouped with ultimate aims which I have just described. The fact that it is nevertheless often treated as an end, as, indeed more or less identical with Socialism, is because it has been regarded not as a means to achieve the ideals of Socialism but as the *only possible* means which *could not fail to produce the desired ends*. This applies both to nationalisation, which is generally understood to mean the taking over by the State of a complete industry so that it is owned by and managed and controlled for the Community, and public ownership which strictly speaking means the ownership by the community of any property whether individual or not, whether embracing the whole of an industry or only part of it. This is an important distinction to which I shall return later.

Why, however, was it supposed that these ultimate Socialist objectives were regarded as attainable only through the nationalisation of the means of production, distribution and exchange? To this vital question there are four answers, broadly corresponding to our four objectives. To begin with, I shall describe these without comment or criticism. Later I shall analyse them more fully.

Ending Unearned Income

The first is in essence a Marxist argument, based upon the Labour theory of value. The flow of unearned income — of rent, interest and profits — is the root evil of capitalism; it represents the toll laid upon the workers by the owners of capital, who thereby deprive them of their rightful earnings. The existence of unearned income is wrong in itself, irrespective of how it is distributed. In any case it all goes to one class — property owners — and not at all to the other — the workers — and, by a natural historical process, its distribution becomes more and more unequal.

Since this flow of unearned income to private persons by virtue of their ownership of capital or land is a major social evil, the transfer of their property to the State is obviously the necessary correction. In this way the toll levied on the workers will be brought to an end, and they will at least enjoy the full fruits of their labour. Thus public ownership brings social equality and the classless society.

Capitalism and Waste

The second main argument relates to the working of the capitalist system. Both in the light of experience and on theoretical grounds, it is claimed that the free individualist economy leads perpetually to the unnatural result of 'poverty in the midst of plenty'. Artificial scarcity is imposed through the existence of unemployed workers and unused factory space. Thus while consumers are left hungry, cold and poor, producers are complaining of gluts and surpluses. They are even driven into deliberately curtailing production, despite the vast unsatisfied needs of the world.

Unemployment, economic insecurity and waste are thus inevitable in a capitalist system. They can only be mastered by substituting a planned for and individualist economy, in which there will be no artificial scarcities but only such scarcities as are imposed by nature and are unavoidable. If the means of production are publicly owned and controlled, the State it is held, can ensure that they are fully used and to the best advantage. As in the case of an individual business, there will be a conscious purpose directing the efforts of all towards whatever objective are laid down in the Plan.

The Abuse of Power

Thirdly, it was argued that the private possession of capital inevitably gave too much power to those who own it, too much power over their employees, too much power to take, on their own, decisions of vital economic importance to the community, too much power and influence in society generally. This power ought to be exercised only by the community as a whole, which should therefore become the owner of the capital from which the power is derived. Only then could the workers enjoy greater power; only then would there be real industrial democracy.

Greed as the Spur

Fourthly, it was held that the capitalist system, based upon competition — the survival of the fittest, the desire to do down your neighbour, whether as a competitor or employee or consumer — was fundamentally unchristian, and would always prevent a real spirit of co-operation. Only in a co-operative economy, where men and women worked for the community, would the new spirit prevail. The rivalry between firms, the hostility between employer and worker, the greed for the maximum profit, would thus all be replaced by new and better relationships.

The Future of Nationalisation

We have examined both the traditional case for public ownership and control generally and the specific arguments put forward in favour of nationalising individual industries. We have seen that experience confirms the validity of these arguments but also reveals certain difficulties and weaknesses. There remains one other major question which is highly relevant to any discussion of the place of nationalisation in Socialist policy, and to which reference must be made. How far can the ideals of Socialism be achieved by means other than nationalisation? Or, to put it in slightly different words — how far can we advance towards these ideals without an extension of public ownership and nationalisation?

To answer these questions in full would involve a detailed and intricate discussion of fiscal policy, monetary policy, industrial relations, the use and abuse of physical controls, and much else beside. I must, therefore, content myself here with an outline reply only.

Applying Socialist Ideals

Let us take the Socialist ideals one by one.

First, the experience of the last fifteen years suggests that it may be possible to maintain full employment in a mixed economy without having to extend the scope of the nationalised sector. Although such an extension would be of value in any attempt at better economic planning, it cannot be said to provide either an automatic or unique solution. The real problem is how to maintain a very high degree of employment without inflation; and the answer in a democracy where free Trade Unions flourish, must be a combination of controls and voluntary restraints, which are not easy to maintain unless there is already a fair distribution of wealth and income.

Secondly, while a better framework may be constructed under nationalisation for the development of democracy in industry, its progress can certainly be carried very much further even within the private sector than now. Both the differences between different firms in Britain and more democratic practices in certain other countries suggest that this must be so.

Thirdly, as regards the closely associated question of economic power there can be no doubt that nationalisation does involve a significant transfer and diffusion of power; but we have seen that this is not such a simple issue as it is sometimes supposed, and that the gain to society of the transfer, though real, is not always obvious to all. Here again a more even distribution of wealth would make a big difference to the whole question.

Equality the Touchstone

One is, therefore, driven to the conclusion that the most vital question is how far greater social and economic equality can be achieved without more nationalisation and public ownership. So far greater equality has been brought about in Britain not so much by nationalisation as by the growth of social services, severe taxation on high incomes partly resulting from war, and an increase in the share of the national income enjoyed by wage and salary earners, resulting from the power of the Trade Unions exercised during a period of mild inflation. Can we expect a further advance on these same lines? And is such a further advance compatible with rising production if the greater part of the economy is still owned and controlled by private individuals? No doubt financial, monetary and physical controls will be available to the Government. But will these be enough, in circumstances where fiscal policy and the power of the Trade Unions are both used to redistribute wealth and income more evenly, to secure a steady increase in the national income, a mastery of the foreign trade problem and generally prosperous conditions?

The answers to these questions clearly depend upon which lines of policy it is proposed to adopt in order to produce social and economic equality and upon the repercussions on the economy which will follow from this adoption. Two such lines are of special importance. One is educational reform. I do not propose to discuss it here. But this at least can be said — that apart from the extra public expenditure involved in providing better schools, better teaching etc., there is no reason why advance on this particular front should lead to major economic difficulties.

The Dangers of Fiscal Methods

The second line of policy is a fairer distribution of wealth; it is this which presents by far the greater problem. I cannot describe in detail the various steps which will have to be taken to bring this about. But whatever fiscal or other measures are used, the dangers which they might involve in a still predominantly private enterprise economy (which is assumed here) really all converge at the same point. They all amount to the same danger of too little saving and too little investment. By too little saving I mean a disposition for the community as a whole to spend too much on consumption. In the short run and with a given level of spending on investment, this leads to inflation and balance of payments troubles; in the long run, if it persists, a shortage of saving must keep investments down as well.

By too little investment I mean not the consequences of too little saving to which I have just referred, but an unwillingness on the part of the business community to invest, i.e. to install new equipment, machinery and plant, to spend money in research, to do those very things which are in a large part the basis of rising productivity in the future. In the long run too little investment means a slower rate of economic advance; for one country in a competitive world this can have serious economic and political consequences.

Nationalisation and Saving

But how far can these two dangers which lie in the path of the advance to equality be averted by more nationalisation and public ownership? We must distinguish between them. First as to saving, it can be said that the larger the public sector the easier it would be for the government to insist upon a high rate of saving. It would simply direct the nationalised boards to fix their prices at such a level that they would make very large profits, all of which would be saved. There are good grounds for saying that up to now the nationalised industries have, if anything, been encouraged to do the opposite, and the policy should be deliberately changed so that they may finance more of their investment themselves. This would extend public ownership more rapidly as well as increasing saving.

But it is no use pretending that this would be very easy. The fact that since 1945 the public sector of industry, far from financing its development out of its own profits, has been borrowing extensively from private sources was not just accidental. While one reason for this is that the nationalised industries happened for the most part to be in a weak financial and physical condition when they were taken over, even more important are the economic and political obstacles in the way of higher prices and profits in these industries. One must be exceedingly careful not to ascribe to public ownership as such possibilities which really spring from a different *political* system which we have no intention of adopting. In a democracy it is not so easy for the nationalised undertakings to charge high prices in order to provide a large volume of saving. It is as difficult as it is for the Government to impose taxes, earn a budget surplus and thus reach the same objective — namely a rise in public saving — by a slightly different path.

Indeed of the two methods of increasing saving, by taxation and a budget surplus or by high prices, profits and reserves in the nationalised industries, the first is rather to be preferred. It is more certain — for the high profits in the nationalised industries will very probably invite higher wage claims. It is fairer — because the Government does not have to concentrate of the products of the nationalised industries only, or even on commodity taxation in raising the extra revenue; and it is less disturbing, because the wider choice available to the Government makes it possible to avoid increases in the prices of particular products which might cause demand to fall off too sharply, and create local unemployment.

We cannot therefore be sure that more nationalisation in itself will contribute very much to the problem of combining egalitarian policies with a high rate of saving, though undoubtedly it could, provided the appropriate policies were followed. Other devices will certainly also be important; they might include dividend limitation so as to ensure a high rate of company saving, and they will almost certainly have to involve fiscal measures of one kind or another.

The Rate of Investment

On the other hand if the danger to be expected arises more from unwillingness to invest, then the case for nationalisation as a counter measure is certainly much stronger. For though Nationalisation Boards may not always see eye to eye with a government proposal for higher investment expenditure and may take a more cautious or pessimistic view of a particular project, nevertheless the government does have much more prospect of speeding up investment in the public than in the private sector. In the last resort the government can insist and ride out any political storm that may arise through disagreement with the Board. This is simply not open to them in dealing with private firms.

The problem here is likely to be administrative and technical rather than political — the difficulty of the government having sufficiently experienced and expert advice to match the technical knowledge and judgment of the nationalised boards. But with a strong planning machine this is not an insuperable obstacle.

But which is likely to be the greater difficulty? Unwillingness to save or failure to invest sufficiently? A few years ago more stress would have been laid on the failure to invest. But recent experience suggests on the whole that partly because of the divorce between ownership and control in industry, partly because of fiscal incentives it may not be so difficult to ensure a continued readiness to invest by business executives even if the government is pursuing egalitarian policies. At the same time the problem of keeping down consumption so as to finance a high rate of investment is obviously not yet solved.

Altering the Distribution of Wealth

Can we then really envisage a continued further advance towards a more even distribution of wealth without a simultaneous sweeping extension of nationalisation and public ownership?

Here I believe we must draw a distinction to which I referred earlier between public ownership — the ownership by the community as assets and property of any kind — and the nationalisation of particular industries as this has been carried out in recent years. If it is nationalisation of which we speak, no definite answer can yet be given; but if it is the extension of public ownership then it seems to me that this is almost certainly necessary if we are to have a much more equal distribution of wealth.

The argument which leads up to this conclusion is simple enough. The distribution of privately owned wealth today is still very uneven — about three per cent of the population own two-thirds of it. Although distribution was even more unfair in the past, the effect of high death duties and income and surtax is slow in its operation chiefly because of a rise in the value of equity capital — a form of property which tends to be concentrated in the hands of wealthier people. If wealth is to be more fairly shared there are only two ways of doing it — either to arrange for the redistribution of the existing privately owned wealth among more people or to increase the proportion of wealth owned by the community, the income from which is also available for the use of the community.

Some steps towards the first could be taken by a change in the incidence of death duties, whereby the size of the tax was dependent on the wealth of the beneficiary instead of the value of the estate as a whole. But in practice the only effect of this would be to spread wealth a little more evenly among people who are already comfortably off. More drastic measures could, of course, be adopted to share out existing wealth. In theory there could be a capital levy with the proceeds distributed evenly among the whole population. From a Socialist angle such policies have two drawbacks. First, in the early stages at least, simple redistribution after a capital levy — quite apart from the political objections — would almost certainly increase consumption and reduce saving. Secondly, although for the time being such a move would profoundly affect the class structure, if the economy continued to be conducted on the lines of private ownership and inheritance a new class structure based on property ownership would before long emerge.

While, therefore, there is much to be said for privately owned property being widely spread, it is certainly not along this path alone that we can proceed. The second phase, a high proportion of publicly owned property — must also be adopted.

Alternative Forms of Public Ownership

As I have said this is not necessarily the same as nationalisation. There are several differences between them. Industries can be taken over and run by local authorities as well as by the nation through its central government, even if there are strict limits to the possibilities — especially with the existing structure of local government. But there is another and far more important distinction, which is especially important when the transfer to public ownership is gradual. The State may become the owner of industrial, commercial or agriculture property without necessarily exercising detailed control even over an individual firm — much less a whole industry. This can be done either by taking in death duties — not cash or bonds but equity shares and real estate — or, by using the proceeds of a budget surplus to purchase equity shares — or if political conditions allowed, by a capital levy which again could either be paid in shares or land and buildings, or if paid in cash could be used to purchase these assets.

One can envisage in this way a gradual extension of the public ownership of property, the income from which would be available for the community which might itself for a time be set aside for further purchases. This could undoubtedly be carried through without a great extension to the list of nationalised industries. It would no doubt be necessary to set up one or two new public Corporations which would in effect be large investment trusts — not so different in their operation from the insurance companies or some other financial institution. But they would be owned by the whole community to which their profits would accrue, and their operation would be ultimately subject to ministerial control. How far they would exercise control over the companies in which they held shares is not a matter on which it would be wise to be dogmatic now. Although as the process continued the possibilities of control in this way would become greater, this would be — as it were — a by-product of the operation, the fundamental purpose of which would be to produce more social justice. Another incidental advantage of developing institutions of this kind would be to make available a plentiful supply of risk capital and to make it easier to stimulate more investment.

Mixed Enterprises?

Here, I must add, more direct action might be necessary, different from either the complete nationalisation of a whole industry or the mere acquisition of equity shares. Such action might include either the establishment of 100 per cent State enterprises to carry out a project where private firms would not undertake the risk, or of some form of mixed enterprise involving a partnership between the State and private firms. There are other possibilities. One is the purchase by the State of certain selected firms and their grouping together under a holding company to form a single efficient unit within an industry; another is the extension of the activities of the existing nationalised industries into other fields. For example, the Coal Board might follow the example of the Dutch State Mines and operate chemical plants.

There is no need to elaborate further. The differences between these various forms of State ownership and control are matters of degree only. The point is that we need not conceive of public ownership as always a matter of taking over the whole industry, making a structural change within that one industry and setting up a single large organisation, but as embracing also many other types of change: in some of these the State will be a passive and in others an active participant; in some, completely new public or semi-public enterprises will be launched; in others, existing firms may come into public ownership and management.

In this way over the years, while more industries may be nationalised as circumstances require, we can envisage simultaneously the community becoming the owner, not of whole industries, but of many different shareholdings and other forms of property. It is already the owner of millions of houses, large forest areas, thousands of acres of land, valuable atomic energy plants, defence factories and dockyards and much besides, in addition to the nationalised industries. The Labour Party have proposed that it should also become the owner of some six million older rent-controlled tenanted houses. There is no reason why it should not become the owner of more and more industrial and commercial capital, replacing the passive shareholder, receiving dividends, and reaping the capital gains.

A New Alliance of Policies

The process of transition, during which the public ownership of property is thus gradually extended, will bring with it many difficulties, especially of fiscal policy. But as far as the working of the economy is concerned, the divorce of control from ownership in the private sector, and the change in the character of management will greatly facilitate progress on those lines. The fact that shareholders nowadays are purely passive and virtually without function, and that managements can manage without them so easily, means that the transfer of shares to public ownership will bring with it no serious administrative or economic problems comparable to those presented by the full nationalisation of a complete industry. If, as I believe, the major weaknesses of nationalisation be not the elimination of the profit incentive, but the creation of units which are too large to get the best response from those employed in them, and in the weakening of competitive attitudes in management, that is another argument for being careful about 'structural' changes which do just this. It is another argument for distinguishing between the transfer of land and capital to public ownership on the one hand, and the public control of management, industry by industry, on the other. Thus in the next phase, public ownership achieved by an alliance with fiscal policy, and not just nationalisation as conceived in these last twenty years, may well become a major instrument of Socialist policy.

Roy Jenkins — Is Britain Civilised? (1959)

Roy Jenkins' greatest contribution to post-war Labour politics was establishing the party as a guardian of libertarian values, and thus reclaiming from the centre-right the banner of personal freedom. He was an outstanding reformer as Home Secretary, and a formidable Chancellor of the Exchequer who would probably have succeeded Harold Wilson as Prime Minister had Labour not lost the 1970 General Election. Elected as Labour's Deputy Leader with an overwhelming majority in 1970, his fiercely pro-European

views began to alienate large sections of the party, leading to a humiliating defeat in the 1976 leadership contest.

Jenkins was born in November 1920 in Monmouthshire, the son of a Welsh Labour MP and former miner. He attended Abersychan Grammar School and Balliol College, Oxford as a contemporary of Anthony Crosland and Denis Healey.

Following war service in the Intelligence Corps at Bletchley Park, working in a secret team decoding German signals, he served briefly as an economist in a banking corporation. In 1948 he won a by-election for Labour at Southwark Central, a seat that was due to disappear in the 1950 election. He was duly selected for Birmingham Stechford, a seat he continued to represent from 1950 until 1976 when he was appointed President of the European Commission.

Jenkins was also a contributor to the New Fabian Essays *published in 1952. This collection advanced a pragmatic and instrumental approach to public ownership, with greater emphasis on socialist ideals and values, as a response to the defeat of the 1945–51 Attlee Government. Without exception, the contributors followed a similar line of argument: the nature of the British economy and the character of British society have changed, and the socialist alternative must therefore change too. The creation of strong public services on the basis of an efficient and profitable private sector was advocated as the best means of achieving socialist ends.*

Jenkins argued that any extension of public ownership should be justified on the grounds that it was, 'an essential prerequisite of equality of earned incomes and an inevitable concomitant of greater equality in the ownership of property'.

He was appointed Minister of Aviation in 1964, and Home Secretary in December 1965, despite Wilson's suspicious attitude to former Gaitskellites. In 1967, Wilson appointed Jenkins as Chancellor of the Exchequer instead of Anthony Crosland – following the resignation of Jim Callaghan in the devaluation crisis of that year. This was followed by a second period as Home Secretary (1974–76).

His publications include The Labour Case *(1959), and* What Matters Now *(1972). He was also a prolific biographer.*

In the essay 'Is Britain civilised?' Jenkins sets out the case for comprehensive liberalisation of Britain's restrictive legislation, and for the restoration of autonomy to consenting adults. It argued that the state should encourage the arts, and raise the quality of urban planning to 'improve human happiness' in a way government legislation itself was unlikely to achieve.

He proceeded as Home Secretary to implement a series of overdue reforms including abolition of the death penalty, homosexual law reform, the aboli-

tion of theatre censorship, divorce reform, and the decriminalisation of abortion.

Jenkins thus helped to establish Labour's revisionism as a response to a rapidly changing society – in part by recognising that with rising affluence, a social democratic party had to extend its programme to other fields beyond those issues that are conventionally defined as 'socialist'. Resolving economic questions was no longer sufficient for its appeal, another explicitly 'New' Labour theme.

In both Jenkins and Crosland there is an unusual streak of individualism and anarchism that has come to exemplify revisionist thought. Jenkins argued: 'let us be on the side of those who want people to be free to live their own lives'. A radical change in cultural attitudes was required, Jenkins believed, to make Britain a more civilised country in which to live.

Selected Text[6]

Is Britain Civilised?

This chapter is about the need to make this country a more civilized place in which to live. It concerns many subjects which are normally regarded as outside the scope of party politics. But they are nevertheless at least as important as many of the matters which are regularly chewed over by party propagandists.

There are three aspects to the discussion. First, there is the need for the State to do less to restrict personal freedom. Secondly, there is the need for the State to do more to encourage the arts, to create towns which are worth living in, and to preserve a countryside which is worth looking at. Thirdly, there is the need, independently of the State, to create a climate of opinion which is favourable to gaiety, tolerance, and beauty, and unfavourable to puritanical restriction, to petty-minded disapproval, to hypocrisy, and to a dreary, ugly pattern of life. A determined drive in these three directions would do as much to promote human happiness as all the 'political' legislation which any government is likely to introduce. It would also do something to break the paradox which this country presents to the world. Our standard of living is almost the highest in Western Europe, but our towns are the most dismal and the least well provided with amenities to be found in the region. It is not a combination of which we have any reason to be proud.

---

[6]   Jenkins, R., 'Is Britain civilised?' in *The Labour Case*, London: Penguin, 1959. [Footnotes in this section are editorial except where noted otherwise.]

Liberalizing the Home Office

The first aspect is concerned with what are often called Home Office questions. It may be thought that Mr Butler's[7] reforming zeal in this department has cleared most of them out of the way. As compared with his predecessors, Lords Kilmuir and Tenby, who were the most reactionary Home Secretaries since Lord Brentford in the twenties, he has certainly brought a mild breath of liberal air into this corner of Whitehall. But its effect should not be exaggerated. He has made a start with prison reform. He operates with moderate humanity the unsatisfactory Tenby compromise with the clearly expressed view of the House of Commons that hanging is a barbaric and useless penalty. After an effective political manoeuvre by Sir Alan Herbert he has overcome his colleagues' objection to a mild reform of the archaic and vague laws relating to the censorship of literature and has encouraged this to proceed as a private member's bill. And he had so far resisted the ardent desire of the Conservative Party militants that flogging should be reintroduced into our penal code.

All this is something. But it is certainly no equivalent to the whole-sale reform of which the Home Office is still in urgent need. The ghastly apparatus of the gallows continues to exist, and is used much more often than was thought likely when the Homicide Act was passing into law. Britain, despite our much-vaunted social and political maturity, still stands out as one of the few advanced countries which retains this presumptuously final penalty.

The law relating to homosexuality remains the brutal and unfair state in which the House of Commons almost accidentally placed it in 1885. This is despite the fact that Ministers have had before them for more than eighteen months the unanimous view of the Wolfenden Committee,[8] appointed by the Government itself, in favour of removing the penalty of the law from the private behaviour of consenting adults. Mr Butler has made it clear that no action can be expected from the Government here; instead he has taken the other part of the Wolfenden report, that dealing with prostitution,

[7]   The leading Conservative Minister R.A. Butler. Early in 1954, *The Economist* invented the mythical composite personality of 'Mr Butskell', a combination of the names of Butler and his Labour predecessor, Hugh Gaitskell, epitomising the consensus over post-war economic management. Gaitskell objected strongly to the term, claiming he was far more willing than Butler to use the budget as an instrument of economic control.

[8]   The Wolfenden Committee was established to examine the case for the legalisation of homosexuality and prostitution in Britain.

where the recommendations were a good deal less clear, and has legislated upon it in such a way as dangerously to increase police power. What is particularly hypocritical about the Government's refusal to act on homosexual laws reform is that none of its leading members (nor those of any other major institution) apply social disapproval to conduct which, for public consumption, they insist on keeping subject to the full rigours of the criminal law.

These are by no means all the gross restrictions on individual liberty which are in urgent need of removal. There is the fantastic position whereby the Lord Chamberlain, a Court official who may exceptionally have an intelligent playgoer's knowledge of the stage but never has anything more, possesses powers of absolute censorship over all the public theatres of London; and has frequently and recently used it to force some of the most intelligent presentations into the semi-obscurity of private theatre clubs. There are the ridiculous and (fortunately) largely unenforceable Sunday observance laws. There are the betting laws, which make off-course betting perfectly all right for anyone who has a credit account with a bookmaker, but a criminal offence for someone who has not. There are the licensing laws, which may have been necessary to cope with the mass drunkenness of the early part of this century, but which are today an unnecessary restriction and would not be tolerated by any other European country. There are the divorce laws, which involve both a great deal of unnecessary suffering and a great number of attempts (many of them successful) to deceive the courts. There are harsh and archaic abortion laws. There is the persistence in the treatment of suicide and (more importantly) attempted suicide as a criminal offence, which is hardly likely to prevent the former and makes rehabilitation after the latter more difficult. And there is the administration of the immigration laws (affecting foreigners, not Commonwealth citizens) which would often be more suitable to a police state, terrified of intellectual infection from the outside world, than to a Britain which is the traditional refuge of the oppressed.

The list is long, but it is not exhaustive. Many could no doubt make their own additions to it. But, it may be asked, are not these questions, just because they are outside the range of politics, irrelevant for discussion in a book of this sort? I don't think they are. In the first place, politics, whether conducted on a strictly party basis or not, ought to be much more concerned with these subjects than has recently been the case. Secondly, although debates on these issues have generally (but not always) been conducted without the aid of the Whips and with a certain amount of cross-voting, it would be a great mistake to imagine that there is here nothing to choose between the bulk of the two parties.

There is undoubtedly a libertarian fringe to the Conservative Party. In the long task of steering the Obscene Publications Bill through the House of Commons, in which I have recently been engaged, the cooperation of some Conservative members has been invaluable. Without their help it would have been impossible to have got through this modest measure of reform. Equally there are in the Labour Party a few members whose views on the libertarian issues are as obscurantist as are to be found anywhere in this country. But both groups are very much in the minority within their own parties.

The point is illustrated by the death penalty votes. In the key division on the second reading of the abolition bill (before either the Government Whips or the Conservative constituency associations had begun to apply their pressure) there were 288 votes for the bill and 264 against. The 288 favourable votes came from 5 Liberals, 47 Conservatives, and 236 Labour members. To get a completely fair picture, the number of Conservative votes for the bill should perhaps be increased by the 10 or 12 Ministers who deliberately abstained and who, had they enjoyed the comparative freedom of Opposition frontbenchers, would no doubt have voted for the bill. But the difference between the pattern of votes on the two sides remains enormous.

Two other examples, taken from the thin votes which are characteristic of Fridays, the day on which these issues are commonly debated, show the same trend. In 1951 a Private Member's Divorce Bill was given a second reading by a vote of 133 to 62. Despite the Labour Attorney-General's having spoken against the bill, the majority was made up of 108 Labour Members, 6 Liberals, and 19 Conservatives. The minority was made up of 47 Conservatives and 15 Labour Members. In 1958 a motion for a Select Committee to inquire into the Sunday observance laws (with a view to their relaxation) was brought before the House of Commons. It did not proceed further than a procedural vote, but at that stage 56 Members supported that motion and 33 opposed it. The 33 was made up of 20 Conservatives, 2 Liberals and 11 Labour Members. Both the Liberals and 5 of the Labour Members voting against the motion came from Welsh constituencies and no doubt reflected rather special local feeling.

It is therefore clear that on a wide variety of libertarian issues the balance of feeling within the Conservative Party is very different from that within the Labour Party. There is another point to be taken into account. The votes mentioned were all 'free' in the parliamentary sense that the Whips on both sides made no attempt to suggest that issues of party loyalty were involved. But the Conservative Party machine in the country is rapidly destroying the institution of 'free votes'. One of the major counts against Mr Nigel Nicolson in Bournemouth was that he had voted against hanging. This caused him almost as much trouble as the fact that he had abstained on Suez.

In North Belfast, moreover, Mr Montgomery Hyde, who has never differed from the Government on any strictly 'political' issues but who has been a notable libertarian, has recently been disowned by his constituency association. Neither Mr Nicolson nor Mr Montgomery Hyde will be in the next Parliament if their local Conservative associations have anything to do with the matter. This means not merely the likelihood of constant depletion of the libertarians in the Conservative Party; it also means that those who themselves escape the axe will have some very discouraging political corpses to reflect upon. There is not much advantage in being occasionally freed of the Whips, if this means being thrown on the mercies of the Major Grants of Bournemouth.[9]

Let nobody believe that Major Grant is a unique figure. He is no more illiberal than the many Conservative Associations officers who, until Suez gave them a really inspiring policy to support, found their political passions most fully engaged in insisting that hanging should continue and that Members of Parliament should not be paid enough; or than the delegates who bayed with such enthusiasm for the return of flogging at the last Conservative Conference; or even than those who at the same gathering assaulted a few interrupting members of the League of Empire Loyalists with a brutality which has not been seen in British politics since the decline of Sir Oswald Mosley and the British Union of Fascists.

The Labour Party is much better than this. It does not assault interrupters, however objectionable they may be; and on the narrow issue epitomized by Bournemouth or North Belfast it is impossible to recall a single instance of a Labour Member having got into seri-

---

[9]   Major Grant was a notorious right-wing Chairman of the Bournemouth Conservative Association.

ous difficulties with his constituency supporters, let alone being refused re-adoption, because he was too bold in advancing libertarian causes.[10] On the wider issues the case should not be overstated. A Labour majority would not automatically result in the achievement of all the reforms listed. A great deal would depend on the reforming zeal and liberal spirit of the man who became Home Secretary. And however well endowed he was with these qualities, he might still have difficulty on some points. There are many Labour Members who, despite the forthright speeches on the issue of their front-bench spokesmen, would at present be hostile to the implementation of the Wolfenden recommendations dealing with homosexuality. An attempt at licensing reform might encounter similar difficulties, particularly from the 'Celtic fringe'.

Nevertheless there is much that a strong Home Secretary could accomplish, even in these two difficult fields. And there is certainly far more to be hoped for from a Labour Home Secretary than from even the most liberal figure on the Conservative front-bench, and far better chance of effective parliamentary support for liberal causes the more the balance in the House of Commons is tilted towards the Labour Party.

Support for the Arts

The second aspect of the question concerns the duty of the State to encourage the arts and to preserve and promote the amenities of our towns and countryside. Government grants for the arts are at present exceedingly small. They amount in total to £6½ million a year — barely one-eighth of 1 per cent of Budget expenditure; and the greater part even of this tiny sum goes on the regular maintenance costs of national institutions like the British Museum and the Victoria and Albert or upon the upkeep of ancient monuments. As a result the great national collections have derisory sums available for new acquisitions. The National Gallery has been scraping along on a purchase grant of £12,500 a year, supplemented by occasional special

---

[10] The case of Mr Stanley Evans, which may occur to some readers' minds, provides no exception to this principle. Mr Evans, whose views on Home Office questions were in no way notably libertarian, quarrelled with his constituency Labour Party on a specific political issue. He immediately resigned and a by-election ensued. Had he been as pertinacious as Mr Nicolson or even Mr Hyde, it is extremely probable that an arrangement could have been reached by which he retained both his views and his seat. [Original footnote.]

grants. At a time when a single picture can cost £200,000 this sum is clearly inadequate for a planned programme of acquisition, such as is essential if the gallery is to maintain its position as a great representative collection and if the export of many outstanding works is to be prevented. Even the government has now recognized this, and the scale of grants has recently been somewhat improved. But much damage has already been done, and the new position still falls far short of the £150,000 a year which the trustees consider necessary for the proper fulfilment of their function.

The Tate Gallery has been even worse treated. Until recently it received no annual purchase grant at all. One of £10,000 — less than half the amount the London County Council spends on works of art for its schools, housing estates, and public buildings — was then authorized. This has recently been somewhat increased; but the gallery, making excellent use of its limited resources, has achieved high attendance figures and a world reputation in spite of, rather than because of, the attitude of the Government. Provincial museums and galleries receive virtually no Government assistance; and many of them, less helped by private benefaction than used to be the case, find it difficult to maintain their buildings and pay their curators, let alone to add to their collections.

The Arts Council receives a total grant of £1,100,000. For various reasons only about three-quarters of this is available for grants to specific institutions. Opera and ballet received £531,000 last year, of which £302,000 went to Covent Garden. The figure could hardly be less if the Royal Opera House is to carry on at all, for despite this assistance it has an accumulated deficit of £150,000 and very highly-priced seats. Nevertheless it makes a big hole in the total available to the Arts Council. It means that assistance in other directions much be spread very thin indeed. Last year only £70,000 was available for drama as a whole, with £20,000 going to the Old Vic. Symphony orchestras get almost nothing, and as a result the pay and conditions of work of the musicians are worse than those of their opposite numbers overseas. They have too little time for rehearsing new work because financial pressure makes it necessary for them to give more than twice as many concerts as most European orchestras.

The provinces inevitably do rather worse than London — the £302,000 for Covent Garden ensures that. But it is no use blaming the Arts Council for this and other deficiencies. It does the best it can with the wholly inadequate funds at its disposal. The only effective answer is not a reallocation but a big increase in the amount of money available. So long as we have a situation in which a single German town, such as Hamburg, makes half as much money available for opera and drama as we do in the whole of the country, so long as in this respect we limp behind Italy, France, even a small country like Denmark, and almost all our other neighbours, so long will this country offer totally inadequate facilities to its creative talent. The National Theatre is still a dream. So far from its being realized, theatres continue to close down all over the provinces. Over a hundred have gone in the past twenty-five years and almost the only example of a replacement is the strikingly well-designed municipal theatre in Coventry.

A switch to a new Government policy of moderate generosity would make the world of difference to the whole climate of our cultural life. The amount of money needed would not be enormous. Let us suppose the money available were increased to £15 million — which would make the Arts Council, the trustees of the Royal Opera House, those in charge of our national collections, and many other struggling bodies think they have awakened to a new millennium. We should still only be devoting 0.3 per cent of Budget expenditure or 0.1 per cent of national income to these ends. It would be money well spent, and provided the Government did not run away from a few newspaper speaks, I do not believe that it would be opposed by the main body of public opinion.

Some of the money might come, not from national, but from local sources. The 1948 Local Government Act, introduced by Mr Bevan when he was Minister for Health, empowered local authorities to spend up to a 2d rate on such purposes. It is central to our system of local government that the decision to use or not to use powers such as these should be left to the individual local authorities themselves; but if some of the £15 million could be used as an encouraging percentage grant to the local authorities (which they would only get to the extent that they provided some of their own resources as well), this would help to spread a cultural revival over the whole country. Even the best-intentioned national bodies are apt to be a little centralized and 'London-minded' in their approach.

Public generosity in the provision of leisure facilities should not be confined to the arts. As a nation we take great interest in sport. But the opportunity for active participation is for many people far too limited. More swimming baths, cricket pitches, running tracks, and playing fields of all sorts are all urgently necessary. In some cases much fuller use could be made of those which already exist. The

Labour Party has suggested that a Sports Council (analogous to the Arts Council) should be set up and charged with improving their facilities: but no piece of administrative machinery can do the job unless it is provided with adequate funds. A Labour Government must be generous in this field too.

Planning for Amenity

The local authorities have a still more important role to fulfil in improving the towns and preserving the countryside. They are the planning authorities and they are responsible for much of the new building. But their powers depend upon the framework laid down by central Government; and they are also influenced in the standards they apply by the lead which they get from Whitehall. Over the past few years the planning framework has been virtually destroyed. The Labour Government's Town and Country Planning Act had its faults. In some respects it was excessively complicated and it sometimes caused unnecessary inconvenience to private citizens. But it was immensely better than the present state of affairs. Planning powers have now been so emasculated that for urban sprawl, ribbon-development, the violation of green belts, the spoliation of attractive landscape, and the destruction of village homogeneity, we are back to the worst days of the thirties. Mr Macmillan, as Minister of Housing and Local Government, succeeded in building 300,000 houses a year. But he also succeeded, rather strangely for such a self-conscious representative of English traditional values, in doing more harm to the countryside than any Minister for at least twenty years.

This process cannot be allowed to continue. If the speculative builder is permitted to operate wherever he can find a convenient, undeveloped site, or even if individuals are allowed to build a house for themselves in any position which catches their fancy, there will, in twenty years' time, be no country worth looking at in either the Midlands or the South of England. This is a clear example of a conflict between individual selfishness (or thoughtlessness) and the general good. The man who is prevented from scarring an unspoilt landscape by erecting a gabled villa, set in its raw rectangle garden, upon the crest of a hill, will no doubt feel aggrieved. But the damage he might do for years to come to thousands of other people's enjoyment would be far greater than the inconvenience he himself would suffer through having to put his house in a less anti-social position.

Whether such a planning policy would on balance be popular is open to question; but, regardless of votes it is the duty of any party with a respect for the future amenities of life in the island to operate it.

A rough analogy is provided by the problem of smoke abatement. Superficially it is much more convenient for householders or factory owners to be allowed to burn what fuel they like and to belch as much pollution as they choose into the air. But smog kills thousands of people a year, means long periods of ill-health for tens of thousands more, and makes the lives of big city dwellers unnecessarily gloomy on up to thirty days a year. Is there not a case for a measure of social control here? Pittsburgh, which used to be a by-word for the squalor of its atmosphere, has completely transformed itself by smoke control and is now one of the most attractive industrial cities in the United States. Are we not capable of equally imaginative policies? It would be insane to frustrate them by extending the principle of consumer's choice, which I believe to have great value in its proper field, into areas where it is utterly meaningless.

Public authorities, as well as individuals and private concerns, are capable of acts of selfishness. The Central Electricity Authority and the Atomic Energy Authority have done their fair share of desecrating the countryside. It is important that they too should be checked. In some cases the Government can and should offer financial inducements for good planning. Local authorities, when they build outwards instead of upwards, are impelled by a variety of motives, but it is important that the much greater cost of high building should not be amongst them. It is worth a great deal of Government subsidy to ensure that when cities have to grow, they do so in the right direction.

On the whole, however, public authorities offend much less against the rules of planning and of good design than do private concerns. There have been very few buildings of architectural distinction erected in Britain since the war, but those that exist are mostly in the public sector. London Airport, the Festival Hall, new schools in Hertfordshire, London, and other go-ahead areas, and the Pimlico housing scheme are some of those which come to mind. Compare the LCC housing project at Roehampton, which is a positive addition to the skyline of London, with any private residential scheme, for houses or flats, which has been constructed or even envisaged.

It is not that private concerns have not had their chance. The rebuilding of the City of London gave them one of the greatest opportunities of the past three hundred years. A huge area was laid waste in the square mile where there is the highest concentration of commercial wealth to be found anywhere in England. Neither space nor money was lacking. Yet the result is an unimaginative and rather claustrophobic series of dismal rectangles. It is particularly ironical that the distinguished City newspaper of which the chairman of the Royal Opera House is managing director should just have completed one of the most hideous of these buildings. The TUC, not always thought of as a pillar of the aesthetic movement, has done incomparably better with its new offices in Great Russell Street. Private enterprise has some virtues, but in Britain (with a few very honourable exceptions) these do not comprise the wit to patronize good architects or the imagination to carry out a piece of effective town planning. If our countryside is to be preserved, if our cities are to be rescued from blight, and if the present age is to leave any monuments more inspiring than the National Farmers' Union building in Knightsbridge, it will depend upon public and not private authorities. Let us make sure that we give the public authorities the money, the powers, and the inspiration to do their jobs properly.

The third topic laid down for this chapter is the one with which it is most difficult to deal in a political book. It was defined as the need to campaign for a general climate of opinion favourable to gaiety and tolerance, and opposed to puritanical restriction and a drab, ugly pattern of life. It is not really a job for politicians, of course, although they, like any other leaders of opinion can do something to set the tone. Perhaps bodies like the Anti-Ugly Association, or the Council for the Preservation of Rural England, or the Society Against Racial Discrimination, or the Brighter Sunday Association can do much more. But the important thing is to encourage them all, and to recognize that one form of intolerance breeds another and one type of drabness makes another more likely. Let us be on the side of those who want people to be free to live their own lives, to make their own mistakes, and to decide, in an adult way and provided they do not infringe the rights of others, the code by which they wish to live; and on the side too of experiment and brightness, of better buildings and better food, of better music (jazz as well as Bach) and better books, of fuller lives and greater freedom. In the long run these things will be more important than even the most perfect economic policies.

Douglas Jay — Social Justice and Social Purpose (1962)

Douglas Jay was a forceful and rare intellect. The underlying power of his ideas helps to explain why revisionism gained such prominence as an ideo-

logical influence in the post-war Labour Party, with a conception of socialism firmly rooted in the ethical commitment to equality. Jay made the case for, 'not literally equality; but the minimum of equality that is workable if human beings are actively to use their talents; not equal shares, but fair shares; not equality but social justice'.

He was born in March 1907, educated at Winchester and won a scholarship to New College, Oxford where he achieved a First, and became a fellow of All Souls. Following a career in journalism that included the post of City Editor at The Daily Herald, he switched to the civil service at the advent of the Second World War where he served at the Ministry of Supply (1940–3) and the Board of Trade (1943–5). In 1945, he was appointed as Attlee's personal assistant on economic policy.

In 1946, he was elected as an MP, and ministerial responsibility followed quickly. Jay was appointed Economic Secretary in 1947, advancing to Financial Secretary in 1950, and, when Labour next came to power in 1964, as President of the Board of Trade until Harold Wilson dismissed him in 1967. He remained an active Member of Parliament until 1983.

Douglas Jay presented his socialism as a declaration of war on the deprivation and the distance of laissez-faire capitalism. He saw it as 'the cause of almost all other evils'. He believed that the redistribution of purchasing power was most likely to raise the sum total of happiness in society – unearned incomes were the main removable cause of poverty and inequality. He placed greater reliance on confiscation of inheritance duties than on higher personal income tax, and favoured family allowances, improved educational opportunities, and tax-remissions for commodities consumed disproportionately by the poor.

Jay advocated a 'case-by-case' approach to nationalisation. Public ownership was justified only on the basis of an unearned increment or market failure, and he argued of the knee-jerk nationalisers, 'control seems simply to have been confused with ownership'. He further inflamed traditionalists with an article published in the revisionist journal Forward after the 1959 election in which he described Labour's unmistakably working-class image, and 'the myth of nationalisation' as two 'fatal handicaps'. The party should change its name immediately to 'Labour and Radical'. The strictly limited role assigned by him to nationalisation, together with his presentation of *public ownership in purely pragmatic and reformist terms, appeared to threaten Labour's socialist identity and purpose.*

His publications include The Socialist Case *(1937),* Who is to Pay for the War and the Peace *(1941), and* Socialism in the New Society *(1962).*

In the essay 'Social justice and social purpose', Jay sets out the case for markets and choices as much as equalisation and empowerment. The price system was attractive to socialists both because it was effective in the allocation of outputs, and because it was tolerant of the individual's choices: a central principle of 'New' Labour. Having accomplished the redistribution of purchasing power through taxes and subsidies, freedom 'from' could take over from freedom 'to', ensuring the less well off were treated with dignity and respect.

This effort to reconcile the demands of equality with personal liberty was Jay's revisionist case. But this disdain for ideological orthodoxy led inevitably to deepening confrontation between revisionists and traditionalists in the Labour Party of the late 1950s.

Selected Text[11]

Social Justice and Social Purpose

Twentieth-century man has so far, despite all his vast technical and cultural achievements, failed to solve three major political problems. He has failed to devise a system which can stop international disputes from generating violence and war. He has failed to mobilize anything like fully all the world's human and physical resources for the production of wealth. And he has failed to share out what wealth is produced on any principle of justice which commands general approval and therefore promises contentment and stability. All these unresolved problems must threaten anarchy, bitterness and conflict; and the first, sooner or later, nuclear war. It is the argument of this book that only by the democratic Socialist solution, by the collective control of both economic and military forces according to generally accepted principles of justice, can this anarchy and conflict be prevented from deepening into catastrophe.

Socialism means the belief that every human being has an *equal* right to happiness and whatever else gives value to life; and that a world society enshrining this right can best be achieved, or

---

[11] Jay, D., 'Social justice and social purpose', in *Socialism in the New Society*, London: Longman, 1962. [Footnotes in this section are editorial.]

approached, by collective, 'social', and not just individualist, methods. There are thus two convictions that are fundamental to Socialism. The first concerns the ultimate aim: certain equal rights for all; and the second the basic method by which that can be attained, whether politically or economically.

The actual word 'Socialism' appeared in the debates among Owenite British Socialists and French followers of Saint-Simon in the first thirty years of the nineteenth century.[12] For those who confuse Socialism with Marxism it is perhaps worthwhile recording that the word 'Socialism' (in its modern sense) can first be traced as appearing in print in the Owenite *Co-operative Magazine* in 1827. It described the co-operative doctrines of the Owenites. In France it is first known to have appeared in print in 1832 in a paper, *The Globe*, edited by followers of Saint- Simon. The word was used in France to denote Saint-Simon's doctrine of a collectively planned society.

The new word 'Socialism' thus implied a belief in a 'social', as opposed to a Benthamite, *individualist*, method of guiding the new economic forces let loose by the Industrial Revolution. 'Social purpose', and not the blind forces of the market, should take a hand in controlling the production and distribution of wealth. Owen's deepest belief was that the new wealth made possible by the Industrial Revolution was being misused, because it was being directed by competition and blind market forces rather than by a social purpose. In this lay the basic disagreement between the 'liberal' believers in laissez-faire and the Socialists. It remains basic today. Indeed, if we argue by derivation, the 'fellowship of man' is the best expression of the original aim — equality of rights; for it is to the Latin word *socius* that the linguistic sequence leads back. Fellowship, it was believed, would naturally spring from recognizing that others had equal rights with oneself. When William Morris said 'Socialism is Fellowship', he was precisely right, linguistically as well as philosophically.[13]

Derivation apart, however, these were historically the essential ideas which inspired the first Socialists both in France and Britain. The notion of public ownership (rather than public control) as in

---

[12] Robert Owen was a nineteenth-century enlightened factory owner who pioneered an influential strand of community socialism. Saint-Simon was an advocate of an early form of collective planning and socialisation of the economy.

[13] William Morris was an influential socialist writer who believed that co-existence and co-operation were the natural order of human civilisation.

some sense of 'fundamental' means to the Socialist aim, instead of one important means among others, was a narrowing of the original conception, introduced much later largely by Marx. On the basis of some of the English Christian Socialists, he [Owen] thought and wrote many years before Marx evolved his theories.

Neither Saint-Simon nor Owen believed in wholesale State ownership of industrial property. Saint-Simon believed in collective organization by enlightened people, including bankers and industrialists, and Owen in co-operative 'community' ownership ('Villages of Co-operation') on a smaller scale. But nobody would deny that they were both great Socialists, and original reformers. Owen (born in 1771) acquired his new Lanark mills, where his first famous experiment in Socialism was established, in 1800, and left them in 1824. Marx was born in 1818. The Owenites officially described themselves as 'Socialists' from 1841 onwards. In 1844, four years before the publication of the Communist Manifesto by Marx and Engels, Owen's disciples and others (after at least twenty years of propaganda for the co-operative idea, and the setting up of co-operative societies in the 1820s) founded the Rochdale Pioneers Co-operative Society, from which the world Co-operative Movement largely sprang. In 1848 itself, a group of Englishmen, including Charles Kingsley, proclaimed themselves 'Christian Socialists', with economic co-operation rather than competition as their basic idea. Historically, therefore, the original ideals of Socialists were equality and co-operation for a social purpose. This does not prove that these are, morally or economically, valid. That must be proved or disproved on its merits, but it does show that the idea of State ownership cannot claim historical pedigree as the basic doctrine of Socialism.

What matters most, however, for the present and future is to determine what are the right aims for society, and by what means they can be achieved. Let us, therefore, start by clearly distinguishing between ends and means. Socialists believe equality rests not on dubious statements of fact such as 'Men are born equal'. Plainly they are not. They are born with an endless variety of character, intelligence, energy and ability. It rests on a moral judgement. Any and every human being has as much right as anyone else to whatever gives value to human life. If anyone questions this judgement, one can only reply: on what grounds should it not be so? Why should I have more right to happiness than you? Why should a white man have more right to a vote than a black? Or a Christian to freedom of speech than a Moslem? Or a man to equality before the law than a woman? Or a Communist to higher living standards than a non-Communist? Of course, any of these individuals may temporarily forfeit these rights by infringing the rights of others. But there cannot be any good reason for denying such rights, on any other ground, to any individual or group. To do this, whether on grounds of race, birth, religion, colour, politics, or any distinction other than the anti-social conduct of the individual, is the fundamental evil in society which Socialists condemn. Their belief in equality is not just limited to its economic form. It embraces all the political and personal rights which make happiness and civilized human life possible; and it is founded on the conviction that no man or woman has a naturally greater claim to these than any other.

Many secondary reasons for valuing equality can be, and often have been, advanced. Most of them are strictly arguments against inequality rather than in favour of equality. Matthew Arnold, who believed profoundly in equality as the essential foundation of any good society, thought excessive inequality incompatible with the spirit of humanity and sense of the dignity of man as man, and said that, 'on the one hand, in fact, inequality harms by pampering; on the other by vulgarising and depressing'. Professor Tawney, thirty years later in a slightly less unequal society, wrote of the, 'moral humiliation which gross contrasts of wealth and economic power necessarily produce'. Many since have deplored the resentment, envy or servility on the one hand, and snobbery and corruption on the other, which inequality brings. These arguments are all too obviously valid; have been often stated; and need not be repeated here. Yet, in the last resort, they are all secondary, and do not touch the basic case for equality. If we believe that all human beings have an equal right to happiness and civilized life, then it is for this reason that we should seek to establish a society in which these rights are embodied. The ultimate ground for condemning inequality is that it is unjust, not that it causes resentment or envy. It is the injustice which is the evil, not the resentment. Indeed, if the injustice were not evil, you could doubtless get rid of the resentment without getting rid of the inequality. But if the injustice is evil, the resentment is not evil but good; justifiable indignation against something which is wrong. The secondary consequences of a denial of equality, therefore, are highly important, but not fundamental. Many of them should be deplored and deflated. But they are not the root of the evil. The solid rock at the core of the argument for equality, and so in the modern world for Socialism, must remain the equal moral claim of all men to basic human rights.

Socialists believe in liberty, political and personal, as firmly as they believe in equality. But there are two reasons why this belief cannot be described as equally specific to Socialism. Liberals hold it too; or at any rate profess to. Secondly — and this is not so often realized — equality implies an equal right to freedom. A society in which only some people are free, or some are more free than others, is not a free society. Therefore you cannot have freedom in any real sense without equality. There have been all too many twentieth-century States in which coloured people, or Jews, or Communists, or non-Communists, or Arabs were denied political liberty. Liberty then becomes, as Professor Tawney has said, 'the privilege of a class, not the possession of a nation'. These cannot be called free societies. The existence of a group of second-class citizens is a denial of both freedom and equality; and experience shows that second-class citizens in the modern world are themselves so explosively conscious of this denial that such societies, happily, cannot survive for long. The time is passing when a nation can placidly remain 'half slave, half free'.

That is why Social Democracy is the only creed which can satisfy in practice the aspirations of twentieth-century man. You cannot have freedom without equality, because men and women today, in all countries and of all colours, feel themselves to have an equal right to be free. For this reason Liberalism is not enough. Its belief in liberty is not mistaken; Socialists share it wholly. Liberty can of course become a slogan invoked to defend palpable social injustices: freedom to profiteer, victimize, bully, cheat or pervert the public mind. But even if it is not, even if Liberals' belief in it is genuine, it is not enough, because unless it is extended to embrace a belief in equality, it denies itself by tolerating the 'half free, half slave' society. And if it is so extended, it must admit that the right to equality applies in the economic and social, as well as political, world. That, however, is to progress from Liberalism to Social Democracy.

Communism is also not enough, because, in the ostensible pursuit of economic equality, it denies political liberty to a large part of the society it rules. This is to fall into the same error as the Liberals, but to stand it on its head. If the leaders of the Communist State have more political freedom than others, that State is unequal as well as unfree. The principle of equality requires that people should have equal political, as well as economic, rights. To deprive them of the one for the sake of the other is to destroy equality in its own name. This would be an absurd and irrational exercise, even if it were performed in all good faith and sincerity. No doubt there have been devout Communists who believed that somehow political freedom would emerge necessarily out of greater social justice. But experience since 1917 has now proved, just what the fundamental argument would suggest, that the Communist dictatorship has a horrid tendency in practice to harden into oriental tyranny. It is not surprising, perhaps, that Communism has more appeal in Asia than in Europe or America. After a time, no doubt, rising standards of living in Communist countries may help to encourage a more liberal political system. But that is an argument for higher living standards, not for Communism.

So it is no accident that democratic Socialism alone can supply the answer to the twentieth-century political problem. This is not simply because the Socialist believes genuinely in both equality and freedom. It is due to the much more fundamental reason that you cannot have genuine freedom without equality, or genuine equality without freedom. Each implies the other in principle as well as in practice. The attempt, by either Liberals or Communists, to tear them apart is bound to create a politically or economically under-privileged class, and so sooner or later to provoke strain and conflict.

What is Equality?

Equality, therefore, is the specifically Socialist aim. But what does equality mean? The answer is not quite so obvious as may be imagined; although the question is curiously seldom asked, and the confusion seldom cleared up. Equality for Socialists has a different sense in the political and personal sphere on the one hand, and the economic on the other. Politically and personally, equality of rights means, literally, equality. If we are talking of the right to vote, to hold or express opinions, to enjoy liberty before the law, to engage in political activity, to criticize the Government; the Socialist believes that every individual should enjoy these rights with absolute equality regardless of personal distinction — other than those, as has been said, which the individual himself makes by breaking the laws that protect the right of others.

This principle, for me, was memorably expressed by a coloured schoolteacher in Atlanta, capital of the Southern US State of Georgia, in a recent conversation about the controversy over 'segregation' in

US state schools. I spoke in a room where everybody beside myself was coloured, and asked this schoolmaster what his answer was to the argument of the orthodox Southern whites that segregation was really better for the coloured people themselves, because it guaranteed them the same facilities and amenities, without the tensions caused by mixing races together in their daily lives.

'We want equality', he said. This seemed to me, and still seems, unanswerably valid. What the coloured people want is to enjoy precisely the same political and personal rights as the non-coloured. Why should they not? The principle of political and personal equality is at least gloriously simple. We can understand it without much difficulty, even if it is not quite so easy to practise.

But in the economic world, unfortunately, the issue of equality — even in principle — is rather more complex. Very few Socialists have ever advocated literal economic equality; an identical income, or even equal property. Bernard Shaw did for a time nominally advocate equality of income; though he ended his life grumbling, like any stockbroker, about the surtax. At any rate, no articulate British Socialist does today. The belief in 'differentials', higher earned incomes for skill, experience and merit, is extremely strongly held by industrial workers and throughout the organized trade union movement in Britain. There are at least three reasons why literal equality of incomes is not advocated as a serious aim. First it would be unenforceable. Even if it were achieved, it could not in any sort of free society be maintained. Second — and most important by far — many of those whose skill, character, knowledge or experience were above the lowest would not use their ability fully if they earned no more than those who contributed less. Therefore, the whole output of goods and services would be less, and society as a whole would be poorer. But there is surely also a third reason. Not merely would society not work very well if the more productive were paid no more than the less; but the great majority of mankind, including socialists, believe that the more skilful and the more diligent deserve some extra reward. It is certainly the general belief that the man or women who works more conscientiously or diligently, or bears more responsibility, deserves — other things being equal — a rather greater reward.

From these arguments two fundamental conclusions follow; the first of which is usually much better understood than the second. It follows, first, that in the economic world 'equality' is not literally the aim, as in the case of basic human and political rights. The aim is the minimum practicable inequality. It follows, secondly, that inequality is not justified beyond the point necessary to ensure that the productive abilities of the community are reasonably fully used. There is no justification for going beyond this. For nothing more than this follows from the argument that some differentials are necessary to get abilities used. Nor does there appear to be any reason to think that most people regard ability or character as deserving a higher differential than this. The skilful or diligent or responsible worker is felt to deserve more; but this perfectly valid moral judgement does not tell us how much more. The only rational answer to the question 'How much more?' is, therefore, this: that amount more which will ensure that their talents are exercised and that society benefits from them.

This then emerges as the basic *economic* aim for Socialists; not literally 'equality', but the *minimum of inequality that is workable if human beings are actively to use their talents; not equal shares, but fair shares; not equality, but social justice.* For the rest of this book 'social justice' is used in this sense, since it expresses the true aim far more accurately than 'equality' (which many people, strangely enough, interpret as actually meaning equality!). In the case of earned incomes, it means at least the differentials necessary to harness the services in question; in the case of property, only the individual ownership of property created by saving out of such earnings, and, in the case of income from the lending of savings or property, no more than is necessary to secure the use of the assets concerned.

We should not accept any other argument for economic inequality but this. Nor should we exaggerate what even this proves. It establishes, no doubt, that the active worker's earned income as an individual must vary according to the work he does, and how well he does it. But it does not in the least establish that his family's income need be wholly determined by his income as an individual. It is perfectly possible — within limits — to determine the earner's income according to the nature of his services, and his family's income according to their needs. It is one of the most extraordinary blind spots in much traditional economics, and indeed much general social thinking, that there is assumed to be some oral or economic reason why the incomes and living standards of non-earning members of a household should be made wholly dependent on the skill or diligence of the earner. But even if the scale of rewards to active earners thrown up by the process of free exchange were morally defensible, this would not follow at all.

Nor would it follow that those who are not earning by work — the old, young, infirm, unemployed, etc. — should get no incomes at all. Because those who work are entitled to rewards related to the nature of their work, it does not follow that those who are incapable of working should get none. The injustice of allowing no income to such people has indeed been longer admitted, because it is more glaring than the injustice of making the standards of children or other dependents wholly dependent on somebody else's earnings. Perhaps more human poverty and inequality have been caused by this latter confusion of social thinking than any other. For it is the dependents in large families with one earner of slight ability who have historically suffered most hardship. A great deal of social policy still ignores the fact that a child has no responsibility whatever for the incompetence or laziness or brilliance of its parents. That qualification has to be made at the start in laying down what we mean by the minimum of inequality as economically the basic Socialist aim.

The Party of the Future

When the rubbish and the undergrowth are cleared away, the immensity of the chance awaiting a modern British Labour Party must surely be plain to those with any vision at all. The nation wants a progressive Government, and will want a change all the more imperatively by the time the next election comes. For though the evolution of society sketched in this chapter is likely to last, the political mood summarized in the 1959 catch-words 'I'm all right, Jack', 'You've never had it so good', etc. may very well be fleeting. Material prosperity is entrancing for a time, but can pall. I once heard Mr Ernest Bevin say: 'A rise is all right — till you get used to it.' Idealism and social responsibility will still have their appeal in Britain, provided they are applied to real and contemporary issues.

What the Labour Party has to do is to present itself to the electorate as it really is, and not as it has allowed itself, partly through its own fault, to be painted. What it must not do is to deprive the nation of an alternative Government by failing to expound its principles in a fashion which is intelligible to the voters in the society it has itself created. That would be to inflict one-party rule on the electorate, and so not merely to fail Labour's own supporters, but to fail the nation. For if the Labour Party persists in making an out-of-date appeal, there is real danger of support being lost to the otherwise futile Liberal Party: and of the Tories retaining power through an electoral stalemate.

But, for all the reasons argued, nothing of the kind need happen. For Socialist principles, interpreted in the light of today, lay on us the duty to attack the very evils which large sections of the public are anxious to remedy. There is no dilemma whatever between Socialist principles and the mood of the public. It is presentation and interpretation of these principles which require to be brought up to date. Nor should we be very astonished that the conscious wants of the electorate should have some connection with the basic needs of the population. For they are one and the same thing seen from a different side.

Ordinary people want better public services, because housing, pensions, schools and medical care decisively affect their lives. It is possible to have them if the policies described in this book are carried through; and these are precisely the policies which Socialism means in contemporary society. People want to see social control and social responsibility asserted in the deployment of our national resources, in the planning of our towns and cities, and the restraint of arbitrary power. This again is the purpose of greater public control and ownership in a developing society. People want to see fair rewards, with reasonable differentials for active work and enterprise; and they do not think a moderate return on what a man saves from his own earnings is unreasonable. But they see no justification for huge gains from chancy capital appreciation, or great private fortunes handed on at death from one individual to another. Here again it should be a main task of democratic Socialism in the full-employment age to draw on the swelling stream of profit incomes and capital gains to sustain the communal public services which are still starved in all but a few countries. People want, passionately, not just a preservation but a growth, of personal freedom — the chance to do what the individual likes. Short only of infringing the rights and freedom of others. Socialists, should, therefore, strengthen the impulse towards industrial democracy, by intelligently encouraging it where a spontaneous demand exists. People welcome public enterprise and public ownership, where it is expansionist, competitive, efficient and pays its way. They are not too keen on compulsory State monopolies outside the field of public utilities and physical monopoly. Here again Socialists are very fortunate, though some still do not recognize how good and very fortunate, because the growth of public ownership in Britain has now reached the point where this public feeling broadly coincides with the economic and technical needs of the future. We have been saved from a very awkward dilemma which would have arisen if things had turned out the other way round.

Above all, ordinary human beings everywhere crave the peace, and do not wish to live indefinitely under the threat of nuclear war. But they have the sense to realize that no single nation can be trusted with nuclear supremacy; and they are coming to understand that there is no other way — certainly no short cut — to enduring peace other than through a steadily strengthened world authority empowered to settle disputes and in the end monopolize and control weapons of mass destruction. But this again is precisely the solution implied by the basic Socialist idea of collective control under the rule of law. People throughout the Western world want to see backward, once Colonial, countries given their independence and helped to raise their economic standards. This again is implied in the primary Socialist aim of equality. Therefore, the central aims of British Socialists, if they are intelligently thought out, coincide with the aspirations of the greater part of the nation.

It is indeed strange that, with all these tasks crying to be done, and wrongs to be righted, some people should still talk as if there were no targets for effort and idealism today. There is quite enough on which Radicals of all types can agree to occupy their energies for a generation, if they would turn their minds to action and desist from time-wasting trivialities. The only real traitors to the cause are those who do not genuinely seek to put their convictions into practice at all, but are content to remain in opposition, protesting and lamenting, and leaving the control of society to political reactionaries. A political party is not intended to be a debating society. But even this is not the conclusive reason why the neurosis of opposition for opposition's sake needs to be banished from the British Labour movement. The real reason is that there are things requiring to be done; old people to be helped; living standards to be raised; needier nations to be rescued; and peace to be maintained. To flag in the effort to achieve these things, not on paper but in the real world, is to be unworthy of the cause. The prime duty of any party in opposition in a democracy is to offer the public a practical alternative Government.

Therefore, a Radical political movement in Great Britain today needs both a determination to achieve its practical ends, and a national, and international, rather than sectional, spirit. It needs a spirit, as has been said, of 'conscience and reform'. If that is the theme of the British Labour Party henceforth, it will be faithful to the real basic principles of Socialism as they have developed from Owen onwards; it will answer the aspirations of the mass of the British public and the Commonwealth; and it will move in harmony with the most progressive and successful Social-Democratic Parties abroad.

It will have to express itself in three main ways. First, it must be a national party, based on conviction and principle, and not *tied* to any single section, group, 'class', faction or anything else. Even the notion of all the 'workers by hand and brain' is too narrow. People are bound together by conviction, not always by the way they spend their working hours; and many not actually working for a living — retired people, voluntary workers and numerous others — fully share Socialist beliefs and aspirations. They, like all who hold these beliefs, should be warmly welcomed in the great stream of progressive movement and not repelled. There are hundreds of thousands in Britain today, whether earning their living or not, who desire to support what should be the true aims of the greatest British progressive party, but would only be repelled by a narrow sectional outlook. Secondly, the Party must be up to date and recognize society to be what it is today, and not what it used to be thirty years ago. We all know in fact, every time we visit a railway station, a public park, a football match or a seaside resort, what the British public are really like. But some, for whatever reason, base their political ideas not on what they see around them, but on what they read in a book thirty or forty years ago.

Thirdly, the Labour Party must be a party of idealism. Despite the thick coating of snobbery and self-seeking smeared over the surface of life by ten years of Tory government since 1951, the deep tide of British idealism which pioneered Parliamentary democracy in the nineteenth century, piled up so many social reforms, and swelled to crests of achievement in 1906–12, and 1945–51, cannot really have just run underground for good. There must be, on the evidence of all history, a tremendous response waiting to be evoked by a party which champions the cause of the millions who are still needy and under-privileged in our own country, of political and social equality for the hundreds of millions in backward nations, and of the setting up of a civilised world Government once and for all. It would certainly be a cold heart as well as narrow mind which could not be roused by the magnitude of these opportunities, or was lacking in pride and hope that Great Britain, which has fought so often on the side of human freedom in the past two hundred years, should now

— however less strong militarily — spur on, if not lead, the civilised forces in the world today.

Nor should we under-rate the chances, or rewards, of success. It is no longer beyond the power of civilised man to establish a world system of law and order, or to expand immeasurably the production of wealth, or to distribute it fairly. We are nearer to achieving these things than ever before. Their achievement would unfold never yet imagined prospects of liberty and the pursuit of happiness. We are also nearer to catastrophe. Between these alternatives, neither possible in any previous age, we now have the power to choose.

Revisionism Revised: Disappointment and Defeat

J.P. Mackintosh —
Has Social Democracy Failed in Britain? (1978)

J.P Mackintosh was a steadfast opponent of Labour's fundamentalist left, who sought to modernise Croslandite social democracy following the institutional and fiscal crisis of the early 1970s. His critique of early revisionism was incisive and wide-ranging, and while he never succeeded in developing a new revisionist framework, his insights laid the foundations for Labour's modernisation in the late 1980s.

Born in Scotland in August 1929, he was educated at Melville College before securing a First in History from Edinburgh University in 1950.

Mackintosh was elected as the MP for Berwick and East Lothian in 1966 (with a brief interlude between February and October 1974) and served until his death of a heart tumour in 1978.

A consistent advocate of Scottish devolution and a passionate pro-European, he was reputedly one of the finest backbench orators of his generation. Other causes to which he gave passionate support included electoral and parliamentary reform, the creation of the Select Committee system, the reform of Scotland's arcane licensing laws, and the importance of raising standards in schools by setting children according to ability.

He combined active politics with a successful academic career. After post-graduate work at Princeton (1952–3), he was appointed as lecturer in History at Glasgow University, and then Edinburgh where he remained in post until his appointment as a Professor at Ibadan University, Nigeria. In 1965, Mackintosh became the first Professor of Politics at the University of Strathclyde, but was forced to abandon academic work on his election to parliament in 1966.

His publications include The British Cabinet *(1962),* The Government and Politics of Britain *(1970),* Nigerian Government and Politics *(1966), and* The British Prime Ministers *(1977), alongside numerous papers and articles.*

His essay 'Has Social Democracy failed in Britain?', published in the July 1978 edition of The Political Quarterly, *expounds a persistent theme in Mackintosh's writings: the fundamentally flawed nature of the Croslandite revisionist position. It lacked a coherent economic theory for a mixed economy that could stimulate growth within it he argued, and over-estimated the resilience of capitalism as the private sector lost its capacity for expansion and investment in the less favourable industrial climate of the late 1960s. This imperilled Labour's strategy for modernising the British economy – enabling it to compete more effectively – and therefore securing stronger public services.*

He argued Labour's first task was to evolve criteria for running a successful mixed economy where both public and private sectors could be energised to produce faster growth, rather than viewing it as a stage on the road back to complete public ownership. In addition, Mackintosh speculated that the original egalitarian revisionist project built around comprehensive education, redistributive taxation and high social expenditure, involved an overly ambitious commitment to 'social engineering'. This was designed to overcome entrenched problems such as lack of educational aspiration that were simply too deep-seated to be amenable to rapid political solutions.

Though Mackintosh was rather too pessimistic about the prospects for social democracy within the Labour party, he urged clarification of these thorny issues, and created the conditions for the subsequent revival of revisionist ideas in the 1990s.

Selected Text[1]

It has often been said that the Labour Party in recent years has lacked books, theories, ideas of what it should be seeking in politics. The

---

[1]   Mackintosh. J.P. 'Has Social Democracy failed in Britain?' *Political Quarterly*, July 1978. [Footnotes in this section are editorial.]

last major attempt to produce a theory of socialism appropriate to the post-war period was the late Tony Crosland's *The Future of Socialism* published in 1956. He shared these ideas with his close friend, Hugh Gaitskell. Although Gaitskell was replaced as leader of the Labour Party by an opponent from the Left, Harold Wilson, for practical purposes Crosland's ideas continued to be almost unchallenged and dominated the Labour Governments of 1964–1970. After the 1970 defeat, there were attacks from a revived Left, though apart from Stuart Holland's book *The Socialist Challenge* (1975), these lacked a theoretical base.[2] Much of the struggle was involved with pragmatic arguments over the Common Market. Yet despite this revival of a left-wing critique, the Labour Government which came into office in 1974 edged back towards a Croslandite position. By this time these views were being described as 'social democratic' in contrast to the unqualified socialism of the Left. When Mr Callaghan succeeded Mr Wilson in 1976, the social democrats felt discouraged and defeated. Their leader, Roy Jenkins, left British politics,[3] but at the same time if any ideas or policies could be said to have characterised Mr Callaghan's very matter-of-fact and cautious government, they were the continuation of an approach which Tony Crosland had set out in 1956. So any reappraisal of the theoretical basis in which the Labour Party has rested in the past 20 years must begin with and focus on a critique of Crosland's position.

Crosland had two objectives in his book, a negative and a positive. The negative one was to bring out the widespread but rather vague Marxist ideas which underlay much thinking in the Labour Party and to refute these ideas or rather to argue that they were totally out of date. The positive idea was to assert rather than demonstrate the moral objections to a class-divided society, to identify the root causes of these social evils and to indicate the kind of programme a Labour Government could pursue in order to remove these defects.

On the negative analysis, Crosland argued that the idea that capitalism was about to collapse was nonsense. He was writing at a

[2]   In *The Socialist Challenge*, Stuart Holland developed a major critique of the revisionist position on economic policy and strategy. This focussed on the dominant power within British industry of a small number of very large, multinational companies, eroding the capacity of national governments to maintain economic control. It attempted to expose the limitations of the Keynesian social democratic theory expounded most influentially by Anthony Crosland.

[3]   Roy Jenkins left British politics to become President of the European Commission in 1976.

time when the average annual growth rate was 3 per cent and when Mr R.A. Butler, speaking in 1954, could confidently forecast that the standard of living in Britian would double in 25 years.[4] He said that the Marxist doctrine that the rich would get richer and the bulk of the population poorer till a crisis took place was manifest rubbish. He pointed out that public ownership, which was supposed to cut down the number of those living on profits and thus diminish the class system, did not have this effect whatever its other merits. In general, capitalism no longer had the confidence and the political power it had enjoyed before the Second World War. The climate of opinion had altered. Keynes had shown how a mixed economy could be changed in the public interest, trade union power had grown at the expense of the management, and industry knew it had to justify its conduct in terms that the public could appreciate or it would be subjected to increasing public regulation. This was basically the old doctrine that political democracy gave the people enough power to ensure that private industry met public needs together with the point that public ownership of itself did not alter class attitudes and institutions.

So the achievements of the 1945–51 Labour Government had had real value because they had demonstrated the power of democracy, its capacity to overcome private capitalism and to set up welfare schemes, a national health service and other forms of redistribution which reduced poverty and increased equality of opportunity. But all this had not ended class divisions in Britain. The society, though more egalitarian and more inclined to produce social justice, still contained gaps in people's understanding of each other which did not occur in more social democratic societies such as those in Scandinavia or even in the United States. Crosland says relatively little about this, but his main objective was to produce a situation where professors and plumbers, bankers and bakers, lived on the same street, could mix freely and unselfconsciously and enjoy the same holidays and sports, and have the same pensions while their children mixed freely in the same schools.

When he turned to the reason why the Attlee Government's nationalisation measures had not produced bigger strides in this direction and why, even in the United States, class divisions were not pronounced, Crosland focused on social rather than economic causes. He concentrated on what he calls 'distance factors'. The four

---

[4]   R.A. Butler was Chancellor of the Exchequer during this period.

main ones were the education system in Britain, the differences in income and therefore in patterns of consumption, the unequal ownership of wealth and the different treatment of workers and of managers in industry. Of these, the most important was education. He wrote that 'the school system in Britain remains the most divisive, unjust and wasteful of all the aspects of social inequality'. Also he developed the old doctrine of marginal utility and pointed out that for a few to have cars and for the bulk of the community to be without creates much greater gaps than for all people to have cars but for some to have two cars. As he put it, 'the higher the level of average income, the more equal is the visible pattern of consumption' and this matters in societies where consumption is an indicator of social status and of personal happiness. Not only must visible consumption patterns be made more equal, but one of the root causes of differences which must be tackled is the unequal distribution of wealth. Crosland argues that further attempts to redistribute income from work will have relatively little effect in terms of well-being and could damage incentives, but there is no similar argument in favour of gross differences in the ownership of wealth. Finally, he focuses on differences of treatment in industry. He considers that this is not easily influenced by legislation but much more can be done by trade union action and he wants the unions to press for 'the equalisation of non-wage privileges, the spread of effective consultation, and high-level democracy at the national and industry level'.

This, then, is the revisionist or Croslandite programme for the Labour Party. Hugh Gaitskell carried it to an extreme and explicit level when he sought to cut Clause Four, the commitment to the public ownership of the means of production, distribution and exchange out of the Labour Party's constitution and when he even contemplated ending class war overtones by removing the word 'Labour' from the title of the Party. But the idea that public ownership, while a useful technique in particular cases, was no longer an effective overall solvent of both economic failings and of social divisions was, in effect, adopted by the Party. Harold Wilson lunching with John Janov of the *Daily Express* in the late 1950s said that Harold Macmillan was brilliant, for he talked about Empire while leading the Tories away from any commitment to imperial policies. Wilson said, 'It is my ambition to do the same for the Labour Party over public ownership'; and Labour went into the 1964 and 1966 General Elections with only one measure of nationalisation in its programme and that was the old one, left over from the Attlee Government, the commitment to take over the iron and steel industry.

So this philosophy produced the programme on which Labour fought the 1964 and 1966 elections. There was to be a small increase in public ownership but the attack on class injustices was to come from comprehensive schools, progressive attempts to equalise wealth, better working conditions and higher social usage. Here Professor Galbraith's work, *The Affluent Society*, added emphasis to Crosland's analysis that increased public expenditure could build up the social wage of the less privileged and make a major difference in reducing inequality. All this rested on the assumption that a successful mixed economy would produce a level of growth which would facilitate these changes in that increasing public expenditure and the real wages of the less well-off would be possible without acute tension involved in reducing the standard of living of other groups.

This, then, was the programme which the subsequent Labour Governments tried to carry through. Without going into elaborate details, it is clear that in some sense the programme was a failure. Fourteen years later, the kind of class divisions that Crosland objected to may have diminished a little but no more, and his ideal of a more egalitarian society is not markedly nearer. The Wilson administrations of 1964–70 and 1974–6 have not left behind a change in British society to match the achievements of the two previous left-of-centre governments of the century: the Liberal Government elected in 1906 and the Labour Government of 1945. The question is, why should this be? Was there a failing in Crosland's analysis?

The criticisms of his views have come from three directions. There has been a left-wing criticism of his position which argues that the original socialist or Marxist analysis was correct. Anthony Arblaster has set out this case in his article 'Anthony Crosland: Labour's Last Revisionist?'[5] and similar arguments are put in Stuart Holland's book. Then there is the right-wing attack, not so much on Crosland's objectives but on the possibility of carrying out his programme without crippling the economy or producing both a disastrous inflation and a lapse into authoritarian policies. Finally, there is the cogent criticism of the actual experience of recent years: that the programme does not appear to have worked. So, all in all, Crosland's adherents are on the defensive in the Labour Party, some

---

[5]   Arblaster (1977).

have left politics, and those who remain are unclear about which way to turn.

Taking the Marxist criticism first, the core of the case is that Crosland underestimated the power of capitalism. His thesis that it could be curbed and altered by the modern democratic state machine backed by public opinion was wrong. Stuart Holland argues that the multinational corporations bend governments to their will and make nonsense of their economic policies. Anthony Arblaster recalls that the 1965 National Plan did not *order* private firms to achieve certain targets but *asked* them to state their own targets. He cites the tenfold increase in assistance to private firms from £80 million a year in 1964–5 to £884 million in 1970–1, the offer of £100 million a year in the form of the Regional Employment Premium to go to the regions of higher unemployment, the 'abject collapse' in December 1975 in the 'negotiations' between Crosland and the Building Societies, all there as evidence that Labour Governments or any governments could not impose their will on the private corporation. 'The power of private enterprise — of capitalism in fact — remains far greater than Crosland was ever willing to admit, while the power of the state to control capitalism is correspondingly far less than he supposed.' Hence the need to abandon revisionism and return to a full-blooded policy of public ownership.

The problem about this critique is that facts mean different things to different people. The tenfold increase in government aid to industry is cited by Arblaster as evidence of industry's power over government, but it is the power of the drowning man to compel people to dive in to the waves to save him. If he can seriously believe that Upper Clyde Shipbuilders, British Leyland and Rolls Royce engineered their own bankruptcy in order to demonstrate resilience and capacity to control British government, then credulity knows no bounds. If he thinks governments can simply order private firms to invest or to move to certain parts of the country without providing any financial incentives, he is displaying the values and attributes of Stalinism in what is still a free society. It is one thing to prohibit by law. It is another thing to expect people to engage in positive activities just because a government wants them to do so. By these criteria, Labour and other governments have been defied and defeated by the trade unions far more often and more clearly than they have been defied by the forces of private capital, yet the Marxists are not prepared to accept this point. The whole history of the 1974 social contract and the recent revelations of Mrs Thatcher's inquiry as to whether a Conservative Government could survive a confrontation with the unions shows that British politicians fear union power far more than they fear the power of capitalism.

In reality, this critique is quite misguided. The great weakness of Crosland's position was not that he underestimated the resilience of capitalism but that he over-estimated it. Throughout his book he, like Marxists, classical economists and Keynesians, assumes that the urge driving private people is so strong that they will perform in the economic field whatever the state does to them and whatever the social atmosphere. Crosland did realise that steeply progressive taxation can have an effect on incentives and he wanted to reduce taxes on income and increase taxes of wealth. But he considered that while socialist governments might reduce and circumscribe the private sector, it would still have sufficient internal dynamic and desire to expand, to continue investing and growing. He realised that profits are not evil but are a source of investment and that they must be maintained at a reasonable level. Crosland was writing in the 1950s when the mixed economy was vigorous and it was accepted from extreme Left to extreme Right that all that was needed to achieve certain results was for governments to turn on and off the tap, to ease or restrict the incentives to certain kinds of expansion. In fact, the chief weakness in Crosland's whole position is that the mixed economy has not shown this resilience. The public sector has been demoralised by constant government intervention; and the private sector has lost all confidence because its rewards and reputation have diminished and managers have preferred to play safe, to cut production, to hold back investment, to accept union domination and restrictive practices not as part of a capitalist plot to beat Labour Governments but out of sheer doubt about the future. The one thing academic economists, including Crosland, never appreciated was that when it became clearly pleasanter and more remunerative to be a civil servant, a forecaster, an academic economist or a business consultant than to engage in actual production, then the mixed economy was in jeopardy.

The Right-wing attack mounted by writers such as Samuel Brittan and contributed to in a curious way by alleged Left-wingers such as Peter Jay in his days at *The Times* . . . concentrates on the weakness of Keynesian methods of controlling the economy and on the impact of trade unions on labour costs. They do not challenge Crosland's ideals in terms of an egalitarian society. They argue that the monopoly of power of the unions means that there will be a constant tendency to inflation. This can only be met by devaluation and the result, internally, must be an unacceptable redistribution of wealth from the weak to the strong, and, externally, a progressive decline in British standards of living compared with those of other industrial societies. One or two other critics then go on to say that the kind of public expenditure programmes advocated by Crosland are unsupportable and that the only remedy is a return to private purchase of services in large areas of health, education and housing which have so far been provided by the state.

Some of this criticism is clearly based on events, but it does not adequately consider the difference between British experience and that of other, similar countries. Just at the time when Gaitskell was taking Crosland's philosophy into the central policies of the Labour Party, the German SPD adopted much the same views in the Godesburg Programme. The question is why Germany under SPD leadership managed a 5 per cent growth rate and a relatively low level of inflation when neither were achieved by a Labour Government in Britain. Had there been this level of growth in the UK, the targets of the National Plan would have been met, the reductions in public expenditure enforced in 1966 and thereafter would have been unnecessary, the Labour Government would almost certainly have won the 1970 general election and the criticisms made of social democratic parties would have been mild or non-existent.

If, as Brittan argues, labour monopoly power must be met by monetarist policies or by what Peter Jay calls 'market socialism', this means running a level of unemployment sufficient to reduce the bargaining power of the public sector unions and of unions in key industries which would be barely acceptable in societies which believe (rightly) that governments can control the level of unemployment. It was one thing in the nineteenth century to allow the immutable laws of economics to create mass unemployment, it is another to do so deliberately simply to meet right-wing economists' distaste for the laborious and tricky task of negotiating and enforcing sensible wage policies.

Leaving aside the two criticisms from Left and Right and turning to the history of the period since 1964, why did these governments pursuing Croslandite policies fail? Why have they left no mark on British society comparable to that of the post-war Labour Government or the earlier Liberal Government elected in 1906? One point that must be noticed is that these two governments set out to achieve certain objectives that could be met by legislation. If, in the period before the First World War, a government decided to institute redistributive taxation, to finance old age pensions, sickness and unemployment insurance and to stop certain kinds of exploitation at work, all this could be done by legislation. Similarly, after 1945, the full Beveridge welfare plans, the National Health Service and the public ownership of certain industries were all open to enactment. The political opposition may have been bitter, the pressure groups may have resisted, but once the laws were carried through and complied with, the objective was achieved.

Crosland did not fully appreciate that his programme was different in proposing to alter social attitudes by means of economic and institutional changes when it is by no means clear that the latter will bring about the former. For instance, while a divided education system may intensify or feed class differences, it is not clear that a universal adoption of comprehensive schools will be regarded as better than others or perhaps a society with such discrimination built into it will then concentrate on differences of occupation or accent. To tax away all inherited wealth may remove the source of 'distance' in Crosland's terms, but this may only lead to a concentration on income differences when he accepts that these must be maintained. Crosland emphasised the value of the social wage, but if taxation has to rise to a level that hits workers with under-average wages, it is possible that providing such a social wage or benefits may exacerbate class feelings and lead to attacks on some groups as 'scroungers'. Putting workers on boards of management may lead to an easier relationship between the two sides in industry. Trade union pressure may produce a reduction in discriminatory work practices. But it is also possible that workers on boards may simply start behaving like managers and that trade union pressure for an end to blue collar–white collar distinctions may only lead to tension between the two sides in industry taking other forms.

A further and much more fundamental weakness of Crosland's policies was his assumption, typical of the 1950s, that growth could and would continue unabated. Significantly, he leaves the problem of running the economy to the last section of his book. He does not favour an incomes policy but thinks that the unions will usually behave with the necessary restraint. He considers the impact of higher taxation on wealth on the propensity to save, but concludes that institutional pressure to save will continue unabated; and also that similar corporate desires for higher output and better performance will keep up activity and investment in the private sector despite heavy taxation and the emphasis any Labour Government must place on public expenditure. In general, he thought that private industry was sufficiently confident and resilient to provide the motor power for innovation and growth; and he saw no great problem about the efficiency of the nationalised industries.

These basic assumptions have been proved wrong. But they also show how unsatisfactory the Left-wing criticism is and why it is driven to argue that capitalism has triumphed by pretending to drop dead. In reality, the building of a social atmosphere which regards profit as sordid and which suspects private enterprise has, over time, weakened and demoralised the private sector to the extent that it no longer provides the necessary growth to keep the whole economy moving. Private capital had preferred to go into property or overseas. The problem in regional and national investment policy was once thought to be a shortage of funds (hence the Development Agencies, IRC, NEB and so on). But this is not the case: it has been a shortage of projects, of industrialists with the confidence to expand. All this has led to a continued flow of talent into administration, academic life, the social services and media, anywhere but into productive industry. The old theory that men would relentlessly pursue their own economic self-interest may contain some truth; but if society so constrains the private sector that it makes sense to take up salaried posts in local or central government or the professions then these same motives will diminish that area of economic activity.

The real weakness of Crosland was that he did not realise that the balance between the public and the private sectors in a mixed economy cannot be left to natural forces. His whole theoretical position rested on growth and growth is only feasible if there are clear criteria for the distribution of resources within the public sector and incentives for it to operate well; and also if there is some clear legitimacy attached to the private sector so that it feels it is doing a useful job for the nation, that there is some point in the work load and the risks involved. For growth, it is necessary also to produce a proper theory of the relations that should prevail between the public and private sectors and of the role of an incomes policy. Should the state enforce a 'voluntary' policy by refusing discretionary grants and contracts to blacklisted firms? Should nationalised industries be allowed to move into ancillary forms of profitable activity (like the Coal Board going into North Sea Oil) and should private firms be allowed to offer services in competition with the public sector? Crosland did not realise that a theory of socialism must be based on an economic theory capable of producing and maintaining the rate of growth essential if the rest of his programme was to work.

The second major weakness of Crosland's philosophy was his simple assumption that all the changes he wanted would enhance freedom. He was not really interested in political philosophy but he took it for granted that a uniform system of comprehensive schools, by encouraging social contact and reducing class tensions, would do nothing but enhance freedom. He did not accept the need for an incomes policy, so he did not have to face the problem of the freedom to bargain for wages as opposed to the reductions in freedom caused by enhanced, enforced inflation. He assumed that with growth the balance between private and public sectors would remain roughly constant and that no problems would arise over closed shops, the existence in some sectors of a single employer, the state, and of the sort of problems that arise in small, working class towns where there is only one landlord, the local council.

In reality, this is a serious issue and there is a trade-off between some forms of enforced egalitarianism and freedom which those taking Crosland's position have to consider and resolve. For instance, does equality mean that all children from the same area must go to one school, or that they should have a choice of schools but one which does not depend on their parents' wealth? Does equality mean that within one comprehensive school there should be no streaming according to ability or even no examinations? If so, does there come a point where the lack of any indication of ability or effort militates against the working class child with no connections?

There are many such issues which Crosland did not consider. For instance, some wealth causes inequality; but if there is no inherited wealth and everyone depends on his or her job and if the bulk of well-paid jobs are in the hands of the state or its agencies, does this not produce a patronage state, the clientage system, with consequent reductions in independence and freedom? This whole question of freedom and independence as a positive value in a pluralist society was underplayed in the 1950s when both growth and personal liberty were assumed to be in no need of positive encouragement or preservation.

Does all this means that Crosland's ideas, now labelled as social democracy, have failed and that they must be abandoned? The interesting fact is that the moral ideas for which he was striving have not been challenged; the argument has been about means of achieving these ends.

The Future of Socialism sets out a programme which was both too deep and too superficial. It was too deep in that it sought to alter aspects of British society which can and are changing but which may be too entrenched to be open to quick political solutions: governments, at least in democratic societies, must not attempt social engineering which is beyond their means, for to set impossible targets only leads to defeat and frustration. It was too superficial in that he did not realise the need for an underpinning of economic theory which justified and maintained a mixed economy nor did he realise that some of his policies could endanger as well as enhance freedom or individual liberty.

The criticisms must be mitigated, however, in that Tony Crosland and Hugh Gaitskell were both men of the 1940s and 1950s. They had seen governments tackle the horrendous problems of war with success, they believed in the sovereignty and efficacy of political action and they had no reason to doubt that the post-war economic expansion of Britain would continue indefinitely. They were chiefly concerned with adapting the inherited left-wing views of the inter-war period to the realities of the 1950s. So it is perhaps hard to blame them for not foreseeing the full consequences of their policies in the changed circumstances of the 1960s and 1970s — though their policies helped to produce these changes.

So these flaws in their analysis remain. All that can be said is that their passion for social justice and their intellectual honesty still shine through their speeches and writings. If Crosland and Gaitskell were still alive today, they would have been the first to admit that their policies had not been fully successful. They would have struggled to rethink their case, to produce new programmes and to restore an element of idealism to Left-wing politics in Britain.

Evan Luard — Socialism at the Grassroots: Community Socialism (1979)

Evan Luard's project was to develop a critique of the centralising and corporatist tendencies immanent in state socialism. He sought to develop a libertarian, decentralist social democracy that could meet the changed economic and political circumstances of the late 1970s.

Luard has been in turn a diplomat, academic and politician. He resigned from the Foreign Service in 1956 over Britain's duplicity at the time of the Suez crisis, taking a fellowship at St Antony's College and becoming an Oxford City Councillor. He was elected as the MP for Oxford in 1964, serv-

ing as a Foreign Office Minister in the Wilson and Callaghan administrations, and defeated at the 1979 election.

He is the author of Conflict and Peace in the Modern International System, *and* Types of International Society.

In his work Socialism Without the State, *he elaborates with remarkable foresight a set of themes that closely informed 'second-stage revisionism' in the late 1980s. Notably, Labour needed to abandon the corporatist legacy of British state socialism. Luard's was a rare attempt to revise Labour's ideological stance in the turbulent years of 1974–9. Social democrats within the party concentrated on resisting the left's constitutional proposals, conceding defeat on major policy issues such as Europe, defence and economic strategy.*

This re-thinking took place against the struggle for power that had erupted by 1979. The reasons for the left-wing backlash, more severe than any since 1970, lay above all in the widespread disillusionment with the Labour Governments of 1974–9. The left's charge was that the parliamentary leadership had 'betrayed socialism' during those years, a recurrent theme underlying demands for policy and constitutional changes after 1979. This was reinforced by the increasing influence of a radical and youthful activist middle-class membership, and the continuing appeal of the left's alternative strategy and programme.

This led directly to the founding of the Social Democratic Party in 1981, with Labour's social democrats fragmenting into loyalist and secessionist factions in the most serious party split for fifty years. Prominent loyalists including Denis Healey, Roy Hattersley, and John Smith continued to fight a rearguard action under the organisational banner of the group Labour Solidarity. There is widespread agreement that had he lived, a figure such as Anthony Crosland would not have joined with those who left Labour to form the SDP.

This was not simply a matter of deep affection for the party, going back to his youth. It reflected his belief that Conservatism could only be effectively opposed by a broad-based Labour coalition, led by a leadership that that held the centre ground against the extremes of left and right in the party. The answer was not to abandon the ship, but to continue making the case from the inside for radical but sensible Labour policies.

Luard, along with twenty-five Labour MPs and 'the gang of four' (Jenkins, Williams, Owen, and Rodgers) nonetheless defected to the Social Democratic Party (SDP). Those who joined the SDP would dispute the claim, made by moderates such as Roy Hattersley who remained within Labour's ranks, that it was the defectors 'who exposed Britain to a full decade of Thatcherism'. The mould of British politics was not broken by the SDP, and Labour's retreat from the revisionist positions of the 1950s and 1960s was now almost complete.

Selected Text[6]

New Ends and New Means

We have been concerned with major changes within contemporary societies which have affected traditional ideas of socialism.

The first of these is the perpetual increase in the scale of organisation. This results at root from improvements in the system of communications. It affects every field of human existence. Even at the most basic level — the unit of habitation — villages are replaced by towns, and towns by large cities. In administration, the areas over which authority is exercised become greater all the time: local government areas are enlarged, more functions are taken over by the bigger authorities, above all, national governments take continually growing powers, intervening in an ever-wider range of ever more detailed and technical questions. In commerce and industry equally, mergers, take-overs and natural expansion lead toward larger and larger organisations, within which the individual worker feels himself an insignificant cog, without influence or status. And in both fields, the scale of organisation change in technology increases the size of every organisation in which men work and raises still further the remoteness and inflexibility of authority.

A parallel trend derives from the development of communications in a different sense: the growth of new means of transmitting ideas and influence, especially the mass media. The effect is that a far larger number of people are subjected to similar influences deriving from a very small number of sources. The role of parents and family in education and upbringing becomes less strong in relation to that of school and peer-groups. Upbringing increasingly becomes public

---

[6] Luard, E., 'Socialism at the grassroots: Community socialism', in *Socialism Without the State*, London: Macmillan, 1979.

rather than private. The development of state systems of education, and its extension over ten or twelve years, from early childhood to adulthood, has the effect of conditioning people more deeply and more consistently in the values, attitudes and even the opinions that are approved within that society. Moreover, and perhaps more important, the influences that mould children become similar not only within any given culture but even between them. The many diverse cultures and traditions which flourished even until the last fifty years are today increasingly submerged by a single universal culture of modern civilisation. While the total number of influences to which each person becomes subject may be larger than ever before, these influences themselves become increasingly similar to each other.

In considering the possibility of alternative forms of organisation, it is necessary to consider first, how far are those trends *inevitable* results from changes in communications and technology? How far in other words *can* they be counteracted, even if desired?

Since some of the trends we have noted result from changes in the communications system, the first question is whether the latter could be reversed. It is difficult to see how changes in the *capability* of communication could be undone, even if this was desired. There are virtually no cases in history of technical advances being reversed or forgotten, even deliberately. Moreover, there are many clear material benefits resulting from improved communication which many would be reluctant to forgo, even if it was accepted that they inevitably had adverse *social* consequences.

But the persistence of the present techniques of *communication* does not *necessarily* mean that the trend to large-scale organisation must continue. In certain fields, it is true, the trend towards increased co-ordination and control, at wider and wider levels, is almost certain to go on. At the world level, the common interest in peace and security, in spreading the benefits of economic development, and in reducing conflict and waste in many functional fields, will continue to promote this tendency and even to intensify it. Even within states the trend must be expected to continue in certain areas. In some fields, however, it may be that greater consciousness of the impoverishing effect of assimilation and centralisation may create countervailing forces: bring a greater concern to establish the maximum autonomy and independence for local units. For the key question is: even where increased scale, or increased co-ordination, or both, continue, how far need this in turn entail increased subordination, whether for groups or individuals? How far, conversely, are there some areas where the advantages to be gained in this way should be deliberately sacrificed to preserve greater diversity, independence and spontaneity? Which are the goals that are truly 'common' and to such an extent that men must be prepared to sacrifice independence of material convenience? And which are those where the social benefit from co-ordination is outweighed by the *individual's* interest in spontaneity and diversity?

One of the most widely pursued common goals of recent times has been economic growth, which is generally regarded as the most important ambition of states. These pressures to high rates of growth not only endanger the world's resources but do not even procure the material satisfactions they are intended to provide. For the effect of competition is that high rates of growth can be achieved only by high rates of investment designed to secure higher productivity. This secures equivalent production with more equipment but less labour. Thus more and more people are displaced from their jobs who cannot necessarily find alternative employment in service industries or elsewhere. All over the Western world, in shipbuilding, in steel, in motor manufacture, in textiles, in fishing, in agriculture and other industries, employment rapidly declines. So the total number of those unemployed increases in all industrial countries and remains high even in those where a relatively high rate of growth is being achieved. And the very fact of high unemployment, by reducing total demand, lowers the level of investment and growth for the future. Periods of growth become shorter and those of recession become longer. The relatively simple devices for stimulating growth in earlier times — lower interest rates, budgetary deficits, fiscal expansion and public works — are either not attempted through fear of inflation, or if attempted do not achieve their effect. Despite persistent recession inflation remains strong, partly because of the excessive increases in income obtained by those still at work, partly because of the large sections of the economy which are in public hands and are unaffected by anti-inflationary measures. Modern industrial societies, therefore in appearance so advanced, are yet characterised by the bizarre spectacle of a large section of the population being without work, while ever higher levels of investment are undertaken to reduce employment still further in the future, so ensuring that the benefits of high growth are enjoyed by fewer and fewer people. Only some form of disarmament in investment all over the world, designed to ensure that increased production is secured by higher employment rather than ever-increasing levels of productivity, could overcome this problem and create economies run for the sake of people rather than things.

So long as growth remains the most highly valued common goal in most societies a considerable degree of central planning, large scale organisation and restriction of individual freedom has to be accepted for the sake of achieving it. Similarly, for the sake of 'efficiency' in functional fields — ensuring that the principal administrative tasks, the running of the welfare state, the preservation of law and order, and other goals are fulfilled as economically as possible — the same price has been thought worth paying. Finally, as a means for securing a more 'just' society, with redistribution from more fortunate to less fortunate, the process of centralisation and authoritarian control has also been accepted: indeed, given the glaring injustices that remain, especially between states, it is likely that intervention for this purpose will increase rather than decline.

It may be that once a minimum achievement has been secured in each of these fields, they will cease to be the central aim of political endeavour. Men will concern themselves with new goals, relating to non-material rather than material satisfaction, the more intimate community rather than national states or world society. But even while the older aims remain dominant, some change in the *means* of attaining them could be pursued. For the question is not only *whether* they should still be sought: but *how* they should be sought with least infringement of the individuality, spontaneity and freedom of society's individual members. Even where the trends towards organisation and mass communications we have noted continue, how can we reduce the regulating, standardising, side-effects which they at present bring in their train?

The Reversal of the Spiral

What type of political or social action then could reverse the trends to centralisation?

Let us first be clear what are the aspects of centralisation and scale that are most damaging to human creativity and human satisfaction.

There is nothing in modern industrial technology as such, or even in large-scale administrative structures, which must inevitably crush all human satisfactions. The drudgery or monotony or unpleasantness of work is not *necessarily* greater in large administrative or economic structures than it is in small-scale ones. Large organisations can often provide pleasanter and freer working conditions. The modern office clerk in a large corporation, the worker in a large industrial enterprise, usually has at least a more attractive working environment than his contemporary in small organisations, or than his predecessors in less highly organised ages. Assembly-line work in industry can be *less* enslaving, *because* it is more repetitive, than older forms of manual work: anybody who has done it knows that one of its greatest merits is that it leaves the mind comparatively free for other things.

Moreover, its higher productive capacity means large-scale organisation and provides the means for more satisfying and richer existence than before: above all for far more leisure. To attempt to turn the clock back, to return to the spinning wheel and the ox, to abandon altogether modern industrial technique (as attempted so unsuccessfully by Ruskin, Tolstoy, Gandhi and other visionaries in earlier times) would only be a deluded and doomed attempt to hold back the future. Here history has a clear lesson: what works will win. Any technology which cheapens production is likely to prevail eventually. The immediate advantages such technology can afford are so manifest, the pressures of competition (national as well as commercial) in their favour so powerful, that Luddite creeds are no more likely to prevail today than in former times.

Thus to attribute the dissatisfactions of modern Western man, as do some contemporary writers, to 'industrial civilisation', or 'industrial technology', is a form of romanticism which conceals a faulty appreciation of the true source of discontent. This applies even more to currently fashionable denunciations of the 'consumer society', which have even less intellectual substance. So long as people have material needs or wants at all, they will be consumers. No-one is obliged in any society to consume more than he wishes. It is the pressure of advertising, which may lay undue emphasis on consumption and so increase wants, not the wants themselves, which may be justly condemned (for this reason there are strong grounds, on aesthetic as much as on economic and sociological grounds, for far heavier taxation of advertising expenditure than at present). If this is the objection, the denunciation should more logically be not of the 'consumer' society, but of the 'commercial society'.

It is not so much modern industry or technology that should be attacked but the *organisation* of modern industry and large-scale administration. What is really at fault is the lack of scope for spontaneity or originality in work, the oppressive character of the organisation's all-pervading influence, the remoteness of authority and its imperviousness to influence, the difficulty of obtaining promotion or recognition, the dependence of the worker on the organisation for welfare, pension, promotion and continued prospects, the moulding of attitudes by the ethos of the state or the firm, and other aspects. It is these that are dehumanising; it is these that can be said to degrade modern work when compared to that of the independent peasant proprietor tilling the fields, or the craftsman shaping his own products. The real problem for modern man therefore is how not to do away with large-scale organisation altogether, but how to enjoy some of its benefits without submitting to the slavery it can impose when allowed to rule unchecked.

If the danger of centralisation is that it creates excessive subordination, alienation and uniformity, one obvious remedy is deliberately to decentralise, to break up the organisation, to provide the maximum autonomy for its sub-units; and so to maintain, promote and encourage the maximum possible *diversity*. If large-scale organisation, political and economic, threatens to impose external goals on the individuals who are caught up in it, the clear solution is to provide the widest possible opportunity for sub-units to influence these goals. Finally, if the techniques of modern education, communications and child-rearing instil standardised and uniform attitudes, opinions and even personality, what is needed is deliberate effort to encourage diversity in all these fields to counteract these tendencies.

It is by these means therefore that the existing spiral may be reversed. It is equally by these means that the original ideals of socialism may be attained: a genuine sharing of ownership and control of the tools of work by those who use them, a true sense for the worker of control over his own destiny, a more free and democratic form of social organisation. If these ideals are to be achieved it will only be at a lower level of organisation: when socialism returns to where it belongs — to the community within which the human being lives and works.

Community Socialism

This aim — to encourage small-scale organisations, local units, community sentiments, to intensify the upward movements within society against the downwards — can be achieved only through a deliberate and determined effort. All the *natural* forces at present are in the reverse direction. The concentration of power at the top, and in the state in particular, which we noted in the early chapters of this book, mean that those who exercise power at this level have a built-in interest in maintaining the downwards movements, that they possess in their hands the means of maintaining them. They will not do this for selfish and personal ends, but to secure the goals and aspirations, the more efficient organisation of human affairs, that they believe necessary for society as a whole.

But even if they do believe it to be in the interests of society, rather than of themselves, what they do serves the interests of society only in the way that *they*, from their vantage points, at the apex of the organisation, believe to be desirable. They may well be applauded and supported in this view by large sections of the population indoctrinated with the same attitude. But that vision of society, seen from the term of the downward-moving initiatives required to order it still more minutely, is quite different from the vision from below, the view of what might seem desirable to *individual* persons and groups, taking the aspirations of their own small units or of individual human beings themselves as the measuring-rod.

This dilemma, the difficulty of promoting the upward movements against the downward ones, is particularly serious one for the socialist state. So long as socialist belief is tied to the concept of state socialism, of the state as the natural agent of all social goals, demanding the continual strengthening of state ownership, state social services and state institutions of every kind, it is committed to strengthening the downwards movement. The debasement of socialism which took place when it was tied to the concept of state power here takes its most costly toll. Only if socialism can be geared to new forms of social consciousness, social responsibility, social action and social ownership, based on the small-scale society, the genuine community, will socialist aspiration be allied once more to the upward-moving rather than the downward-moving forces.

The first requirement is to develop the concept of socialism at the *grass-roots*: of social ownership and socialist ownership and socialist organisation on a small scale, in the local unit; in the municipality rather than the state; the enterprise, or even the workshop, rather than the national industry; in the school, the housing association, the community centre, rather than in the society as a whole.

The concept of *sharing*, of common ownership, of common policies jointly agreed by all who participate, makes quite as much sense — indeed far more sense — in each of these contexts than it does in the framework of the state, where it has mainly been applied in recent

158   *New Labour's Old Roots*

years. The socialist city or small town, where a number of local undertakings, commercial or industrial, are run jointly, in the interests of the inhabitants as a whole, is more meaningful, in terms of achieving a sense of common aspiration, common ownership and common endeavour, than is the socialist state. Indeed, it is arguable that the neighbourhood is a more suitable unit even than the city for this purpose. The jointly run *neighbourhood* laundry, the neighbourhood bakery, the neighbourhood hairdresser, run not for profit but for the equal benefit of all who live within the neighbourhood, might give some *genuine* sense of participation, of sharing, such as has not been provided by most public undertakings until now. It is not impossible to conceive of neighbourhood meetings open to all residents, at which the policies of the neighbourhood cinema, laundry or village store (as much as the cemetery or cricket team) are discussed. Ownership in this form would give a more meaningful share of control to the public, said to be the owners, and would more genuinely correspond with social sentiments and loyalties, than public ownership of the traditional kind under which the local bakery is one unit in a vast national chain. It is even possible that many would be willing to pay 2p a loaf more for real, crisp, locally-baked bread, sold close to hand, in their own bakery, than for soggy, nationally manufactured, steam baked bread, sold at the city supermarket. 'Efficiency' would, in such society, cease to be the sole criterion of organisation.

Similarly, in industry, when the individual small-scale enterprise is the autonomous unit, owned by, and ultimately controlled by, those who work within it, the sense of sharing, the sense of common ownership, the sense of joint participation, which were once at the very root of the idea of socialism, might begin to have some reality once more. And here too the real grass roots are one degree lower still. Even *within* each enterprise, some decisions can be reached jointly in the individual workshop or shop-floor, by those directly involved. As in parts of Swedish industry today, the maximum autonomy and independence can be given, even within an integrated factory, to an individual group of workers, given their own production targets, to be reached by whatever methods they themselves decide, perhaps practising a form of socialism among themselves. Craft workshops can more easily share control.

Finally, equally far down in the grass-roots, in the school, the community centre, the housing estate, there is scope for autonomy, for individual, shared decision making. In the school, parents, teachers, and even older pupils, can join together in running the establishment, according to methods and principles they themselves have jointly decided; with far greater freedom in the choice of curriculum and of disciplinary methods, far less controlled by the rules and regulations laid down by local and national authorities, than is the case today. In the housing estate, whether public or private, the residents could be given authority to reach decisions together, within a set annual budget, concerning amenities and improvements and common undertakings, at little additional cost (but here again scale is important — decisions for a council estate of 5000 people will evoke far less sense of participation and far less interest than decisions reached in each street, or in an individual block of flats). Finally, in the community centre, providing it serves a genuine community, a living neighbourhood, as does a village hall, rather than a vast and amorphous borough, joint decisions can be reached about genuinely local affairs, community activities, youth clubs, recreation, welfare services, so long as councils at a higher level are prepared to relinquish some of their existing powers. So long as genuinely local bodies are allowed to consider nothing but footpaths and graveyards it is scarcely surprising if interest flags.

The goal of 'participation', so much discussed in recent years depends totally on a breaking down into units of this kind. Where large numbers are involved, decision making cannot truly be shared. At a meeting of many hundreds, few have the opportunity to speak, and they will not necessarily be representative. Even in purely mathematical terms, a share of a twenty thousandth in a decision is clearly worth less that a share of a hundredth or of a tenth. Only if decisions are taken at a genuinely local level, genuinely at the grass-roots, therefore, can the goal of social participation, social control and social ownership have much meaning.

Only if a sense of belonging can once more be mobilised, only if ordinary men and women can be given the opportunity to control their own lives by sharing in decision-making, only therefore at the genuinely grass-roots level, can the ideals of socialism today be adequately realised, and the sense of community that has largely disappeared from modern societies be once more revived.

The Revival of Diversity

Equally important with the rediscovery of community is the revival of diversity: the reawakening of the variety and differences within mankind which the centralising force of modern society has tended to stifle.

To some extent the revival of the community, of small-scale units of organisation, will automatically have this effect. The more the local unit, the individual enterprise, housing estate or school can organise its own affairs in its own way, the more they will gradually come to diverge: in the policies they favour, in the patterns of existence they provide, the value-system each seeks to express. If the downward-moving forces from the top, the demands of organisation, which are the main standardising influences at the present time, can be gradually reduced, the scope and freedom for greater diversity will to some extent be automatically enhanced.

But here too there will be needed a *conscious* effort to stimulate that process, the *deliberate* encouragement of diversity, if the standardising forces of modern mass communications are to be counteracted. The existence of mass media can scarcely be undone, any more than the existence of better communications of other kinds. There can however be deliberate effort to promote diversity among those media: to make available the widest possible choice of content and editorial policy among newspapers, of programme-content in television programmes, of the style and character of plays and films on show. But this can be achieved only if there is some resistance to the almost irresistible: to the overwhelming and standardising influence of the box-office, the desire to attract the largest possible number of viewers, readers, or cinema-goers, and so to reproduce endless marginal variations on the lowest common multiple of popular taste.

At present the trend in these fields is in the opposite direction. In most countries the number of newspapers is declining. The readership of those remaining is increasing and competition between them intensifying. Their dependence on advertising revenue, and the pursuit of ever-larger circulation for advertisers, further promotes the trend towards increasing sameness. Each must publish precisely the same stories about the same scandals concerning the same celebrities, the same conventional centre-right political attitudes, the same number of nude photographs, if they are to be able to compete. For the same reason, however many different television channels may exist, they are obliged under a commercial or competitive system to show precisely similar programmes, the same comedians, pop-groups and variety shows, the same quiz programmes and party-games, in precisely similar proportions: because only this will retain the mass audience.

The result is that, though each programme possibly appeals to more people than any alternative might, virtually no group or individual is satisfied. For everybody belongs to a minority of one kind or another, and no minorities of any kind are satisfied by programmes that are exclusively directed to the majority. The majority can only be fully satisfied, therefore, by greater not less, diversity, by more attention devoted to appealing to minority tastes. Entire pages, or entire newspapers, could be given to presenting the type of material and discussion which appeals to readers numbered in hundreds or even tens of thousands, instead of only in millions as today. Minority groups could be invited to produce their own programmes, or write their own columns. And governments and other authorities could provide subsidies that would enable such a variety of tastes to be adequately catered for. Public support could be given to television channels designed to provide for minority rather than majority audiences, for example by covering many or all of the overheads. Governments might spread advertising among the widest possible range of journals and newspapers. They could give adequate subsidies for the operation of radio and television stations to ensure that more adequate time is given to serious discussion of controversial topics, and to the expression of minority views. Libraries, public and private, could support minority journals which might otherwise be unable to survive.

Another important way of promoting diversity is by assisting, encouraging and even promoting voluntary associations for those with particular interests or to promote particular causes. These may provide alternative channels for the expression of views, to counterbalance, or to influence, those expressed by more powerful organisations, political parties and other bodies. They may keep alive causes and creeds that might otherwise die. Community associations and clubs and societies may sustain interests and activities the individual alone could not maintain. Local authorities may help such associations, for example by subsidising the activities of minority groups, and providing facilities for them in community centres. Voluntary associations may then provide some counterweight to the official organisations which otherwise dominate most areas of life today.

Perhaps even more important, if the standardising influences are to be overcome, is the need for more diversity in education. For it is here above all that basically similar methods of instruction in similar types of school by similarly trained teachers is in danger of instilling a nationwide uniformity of knowledge, belief and attitude. Teachers themselves may not wish this. They may consciously stress creativity and originality of their work. But in practice the pressures of supervision and inspection, national qualifications both for teachers and pupils, national examinations and national syllabuses, make it almost impossible for any worthwhile degree of variety, either in subject-matters or method, to be introduced. The pressure to establish exact equality in education has the same effect. In consequence the school runs the risk of becoming a sausage-machine, producing ever-increasing numbers of products that are uniformly well-stuffed, but also equally undistinguished (in the exact sense).

Only decentralisation of the control of education will encourage the development of unorthodox methods and syllabuses and so reduce standardisation. We have already suggested that teachers and parents should largely control each school, with the least possible interference from above. The establishment of a wide variety of schools experimenting in their own methods and syllabuses (for example, for the specially religious, the specially athletic, the specially artistic, the specially scientific, the specially academic, the specially mechanical or inventive) could help to create divergent personalities and talents. Parents could choose the type of school suited to their child's special talents; and the headmasters should normally accept all applicants. The need for equality presupposes equal *opportunities* for all in education (which can certainly not be provided through selection to privileged schools at an early age, still less by the purchase of educational opportunities for money); but it does not logically presuppose an exactly similar education for all, regardless of interests or aptitudes. Indeed to provide identical education for children who by their nature are unlike, to seek to make non-academic children academic, or vice versa, is in itself a form of injustice (as well as of inefficiency).

What needs to be ensured, therefore, is that parents are provided with the maximum possible *choice* of school. This should be limited as little as possible by geographical, and not at all by financial, considerations. While first schools should perhaps remain essentially community schools to which all children of a locality go, and so become a form of community focus, secondary schools should be open to all over a wide area, according to the *style* of education they provide. And local authorities would need to pursue a deliberate policy of encouraging such diversity among them. In this way schools may be chosen increasingly according to the basic values, methods of teaching and subject-matter they favour, rather than according to the age-range, district, or intelligence quotient they cater for. Some would be especially concerned with creativity, some with discipline and self-control, some with inventiveness, some with science, some with music and the arts, and so on.

One of the main reasons why diversity in education has become more important today is the increase in leisure-time in the modern world. In a rational system the greater part of education should be directly designed to equip people for leisure, since this will constitute by far the greater part of their lives. By providing greater knowledge and training in the arts, for example, schools can provide an inexhaustible resource which will last pupils through-out their days. The capacity to draw, to paint, or for handicrafts, a knowledge of flowers and birds, an appreciation of the theatre and cinema, an interest in the history of coins or stamps or motor-cars, may serve as a far more important support in future life than a smattering, in precisely equal proportions, and regardless of natural interest, of mathematics, science, geography or scripture is likely to do. Similarly, if consciousness of the leisure revolution had percolated, government investment, government legislation and government activities would be devoted as much or more to providing satisfying and enriching spare-time activities as in providing means of producing more and more commodities people have less and less need or desire to consume. If leisure is to be effectively used, the study and promotion of enjoyment perhaps today needs as much study as that of learning.

The deliberate effort to promote diversity, spontaneity and independence could be made in these ways the primary aim of policy, even at the expense of functional goals. The pursuit of 'growth' at all costs remains a rational political goal for countries in which poverty remains widespread. It is questionable whether, in a world whose natural resources are rapidly being exhausted, it should remain the supreme object of policy for nations that have achieved the prosperity of most modern Western societies; still less that it should occupy their governments and parliamentarians to the exclusion of virtually all else as today. The ultimate concern must be the quality of life society can make available to its citizens: not 'the good life', but the good lives, the many different forms of good life that may be chosen by different individuals. And for that end the type of community organisation adopted is far more important than economic growth.

This demands far more thought that hitherto among politicians and political thinkers about the relationship of particular kinds of social or political institution to particular human satisfactions. For though the dangers that men confront from their own political institutions may be greater today that at any previous time, so also are the opportunities they present. The fact that man has now attained self-consciousness in a social as well as an individual sense, transforms his capacities as a political animal. Until today the type of political order men have created has been the effect mainly of the hazard of history, of mutual competition for power, whether individual or collective, of passive inheritance from the past, or of the blind forces of integration and organisation, rather than of conscious *choice* of socially desirable types of political system.

Though all these factors retain some weight, today more than ever men have the opportunity deliberately to choose, or even to *create* the types of order — economic, political, legal and social — which they believe can provide for them the satisfactions they value most highly. More than at any previous time it has become possible for men to free themselves, from the prison of the present and the shackles of the past; to analyse which are those forms of society best equipped to provide particular types of human satisfaction; and to construct the political constitutions and the social institutions required to procure those values most cherished. In this they will need to create both more diverse institutions, and more small-scale forms of organisation, appropriate to the variety of humankind and human aspirations. Only this will counteract the overwhelming pressures to conformity and uniformity; make possible creative evolution rather than mechanical role-performance. Only this, likewise, will make possible the full achievement of the ideals of socialism, by allowing the individual to build his own community according to his own beliefs; to share, in willing participation and mutual assistance, within a living and organic human community.

David Marquand — The Unprincipled Society (1988)

In common with his friend and mentor J.P. Mackintosh, Marquand sought a full-scale re-assessment of social democratic theory. The Labour leadership, he argued, had clung to an outdated, bureaucratic form of social democracy instead of revising its assumptions along libertarian lines. Because Labour Governments of the 1960s and 1970s had been largely con-

cerned with extending the frontiers of the state, too little progress had been made in reforming the constitutional and parliamentary system.

Marquand's contribution was to argue, probably more forcefully than any other theorist of his generation that revisionism itself needed to be revised, 'because it could no longer speak to the needs of the time'. He drew an explicit parallel between the crisis of revisionist social democracy in the 1970s, the malaise of the British state, and Britain's relative decline. A new social democratic commitment was needed he argued, participative and decentralist, informed by the ideal of civic morality founded on republican virtue.

Marquand was born in September 1934, and educated at Emanuel School, and Magdalen College, Oxford where he gained first-class honours in Modern History. Following post-graduate study, he was appointed as a leader-writer on The Guardian *(1959–62), but returned to academic work at St Antony's College, Oxford (1962–4), and the University of Sussex (1964–6).*

In the 1966 General Election he was elected as Labour MP for Ashfield. Marquand was appointed as Parliamentary Private Secretary at the Department for Overseas Development (1967–9), and as opposition spokesman on Economic Affairs following Labour's defeat (1971–2). But he was, 'singularly ill-suited to the feverish inconsequence of parliamentary life'. In 1977, he left British politics to join Roy Jenkins' Cabinet at the European Commission, returning as Professor of Contemporary History and Politics at the University of Salford (1978–91), Professor of Politics at the University of Sheffield (1991–6), and subsequently as Principal of Mansfield College, Oxford (1996–2002).

He was a founder member of the SDP in 1981, having helped Roy Jenkins to develop his notion of 'the radical centre' in the 1979 Dimbleby lecture, advocating an end to the 'tyranny' of the 'two-party' party system.

His published works include the biography of Ramsay MacDonald (1977), The Progressive Dilemma *(1991),* The Ideas that Shaped Post-War Britain *(1996, with Anthony Seldon), and* The New Reckoning *(1997).*

The Unprincipled Society *(1988) had three essential themes. It provided a critique of neo-liberalism and the historiography of the New Right.*

It proposed an alternative account of the rise and fall of the post-war social democratic consensus. And it tentatively outlined a new synthesis founded on a communitarian public philosophy — 'a politics of mutual education'.

In particular, Marquand asserted that the adjustment problems plaguing the post-war British economy were as much to do with politics as economics. The Croslandite model had collapsed because, 'it had no philosophy of public intervention or of what might be called the public realm'. Social democracy could no longer act through public institutions whose legitimacy had finally been destroyed by the fiscal crisis of the early 1970s. Its only future lies in abandoning technocracy and 'imposed reforms' in favour of, 'the slow process of argument and negotiation'.

By the end of the 1970s, Marquand had begun to question whether the task of revising social democracy could even be achieved within 'the formal framework of the Labour Party'. In this sense, his argument amounts to an abandonment of the post-war revisionist model as much as a revision of it. He was later to criticise the 'opinion survey driven' nature of Neil Kinnock's modernisation project for its failure to develop a coherent governing philosophy.

Nonetheless, Marquand's analysis has assisted Labour, to some extent unwittingly, in coming to terms with the centralising tendency in its traditions. In urging the left to abandon the 'mechanistic' route to social justice, and in making community central to the ethical re-statement of social democratic values, he pre-figured defining 'New' Labour themes for the 1990s.

Selected Text[7]

Doctrine and Reality

> It is a commonplace that the characteristic virtue of Englishmen is their power of sustained practical activity, and their characteristic vice a reluctance to test the quality of that activity by reference to principles. They are incurious as to theory, take fundamentals for granted, and are more interested in the state of the roads than in their place on the map.[8]

Tawney wrote at a time of upheaval and confusion, unprecedented in the lives of most of his readers. The First World War had destroyed the Hohenzollern, Hapsburg, Ottoman and Romanov empires; the whole mechanism of international trade was in disar-

---

[7]   Marquand, D., *The Unprincipled Society*, London: Heinemann, 1988. [Footnotes in this section are original references.]

[8]   Tawney (1921).

ray; a seismic shift was taking place in British domestic politics, as Labour replaced the Liberals as the main anti-Conservative party in the state.

Disruptive though they were, however, the changes of that time were in some ways less disorientating than those of our own. Since the long post-war boom petered out in the early 1970s, increasingly interdependent national economies have been weighed down by a worldwide bias towards deflation, from which no single medium-sized nation state can escape alone. Big shifts are taking place in the international division of labour, as the newly industrialising countries of the Third World become progressively more competitive in standardised, mass-production manufacturing. International competition is in any case becoming more intense, as communications become faster and technology transfer easier. Above all, the 'information revolution' generated by recent advances in micro-electronics, fibre optics, software engineering, communications and computer technology has begun to re-shape industrial society, much as the industrial revolution re-shaped agrarian society in the late-eighteenth and nineteenth centuries.

Doctrine, however, has lagged behind reality. Between them, these changes have overturned the guiding principles of the post-war economic order. Naturally, they have affected different countries in different ways, but almost all industrial societies have faced acute problems of social, political and, above all, intellectual adjustment. Yet, in spite of prolonged searching, no one has discovered a new set of guiding principles to take the place of the old ones. The governments of the industrial world are adrift, unable to steer with the instruments they used in the past, but uncertain what instruments to use instead.

This book looks at the ways in which the upheavals in the world economy have impinged on Britain and on the doctrines over which her politicians dispute, tries to identify the sources of her adjustment problems and explores the implications for the future. But it goes wider than the familiar story of stubborn unemployment, declining manufacturing and lagging competitiveness. Its object is to identify the social and intellectual factors which lie behind the economic record, and to tease out the lessons for the political economy, not to rehearse it yet again. It is based on the assumption that, even in a time of rapid change, behaviour cannot be studied fruitfully in isolation from beliefs and traditions; that people respond to change as they do partly because they think as they do, and that they think what they do partly because they have been brought up to think it. Thus, it is concerned with values and assumptions as much as with policies and actions, and with the legacy of the past as much as with the present and future.

It starts from three related propositions. The first is that, in Britain, doctrine and reality are unusually far apart. From the mid-1940s until the mid-1970s, most of her political class shared a tacit governing philosophy which might be called 'Keynesian social democracy'. It did not cover the whole spectrum of political opinion, of course; nor did it prevent vigorous party conflict. The two great parties often differed fiercely about the details of policy; on a deeper level, their conceptions of political authority and social justice differed even more. They differed, however, within a structure of generally accepted values and assumptions. For most of the post-war period, most senior civil servants, most of the leaders of the most powerful trade unions, most nationalised industry chairmen, most heads of large private-sector companies and most commentators in the quality press shared a common experience and a broadly similar set of aspirations. They were determined to banish the hardships of the pre-wars years, and to make sure that the conflicts which those hardships had caused did not return. Thus, both front benches accepted a three-fold commitment to full employment, to the welfare state and to the coexistence of large public and private sectors in the economy — in short, to the settlement which had brought the inter-war conflicts to an end.

The Keynesian social democrats had many achievements to their credit, but they could not cope with the adjustment problems of the 1970s. The post-war consensus collapsed under the Wilson-Callaghan government of 1974–9, amid mounting inflation, swelling balance of payments deficits, unprecedented currency depreciation, rising unemployment, bitter industrial conflicts and what seemed to many to be ebbing governability. The Conservative leadership turned towards a new version of the classical market liberalism of the nineteenth century. Though the Labour leadership stuck to the tacit 'revisionism' of the 1950s and 1960s, large sections of the rank and file turned towards a more inchoate mixture of neo-Marxism and the 'fundamentalist' socialism of the 1920s and 1930s. But these successor-doctrines are no better suited to the world of the late-1970s and 1980s than was the Keynesian social democracy of the post-war period. At the centre of the neo-liberals' moral universe lies the idealised Market of the rising manufacturers of the first Industrial

Revolution. At the centre of the neo-socialists' lies the epic struggle between expropriators and expropriated, whose most compelling hymnodist was Marx. Though their intellectual foundations were laid by men of genius, whose insights can still enrich our understanding, neither doctrine addresses the complex, self-reinforcing network of interests, institutions, assumptions and values from which Britain's adjustment problems stem.

The neo-liberal approach to the problems of change and adjustment to change is, at bottom, simple. Adjustment comes through the 'undistorted' competitive market, for the undistorted market automatically rewards those who have the wit and will to adjust, while punishing those who lack them. Governments should therefore leave it to the market to determine how adjustment is to take place. This market-liberal approach contains an important germ of truth. It is true that, in a competitive market, the adaptable will prosper while the unadaptable go under. It is also true that governments cannot indefinitely shield the unadaptable from the consequences of their failure to adapt. But the economic theories underlying the neo-liberal approach cannot encompass the complexities of the adjustment process. They explain − or purport to explain − how resources are most efficiently allocated at a given level of adaptability. They have nothing to say about the cultural, institutional or political factors which help to make some societies − or some groups within a society − more adaptable than others. Yet these factors hold one of the keys to performance in the market. Adaptation depends on innovation; and innovation is not an autonomous force, working in a cultural vacuum. Innovations are sterile unless they are applied, and the men and woman who decide whether and how to apply them are shaped by the inherited values, assumptions and institutions of the societies in which they live. These values, assumptions and institutions are not all equally hospitable to innovation, and market forces alone cannot make them so. In the early-nineteenth century, England and Ireland were both parts of the United Kingdom, and governed according to the same market-liberal principles. England had the most productive and innovative economy in the world. Most of Ireland remained poverty-stricken and backward, and her economy fell further behind England's than it had been before.

There is no reason to think that things are different today. Information technology is at one and the same time capital-saving, labour-saving and energy-saving; to societies which exploit it fully, it offers the prospect of enormous gains in productivity and wealth. But the proviso is crucial. It will be exploited fully only if radical changes take place in the pattern of employment, the level of skill, the organisation of industry and the attitudes of managers and workers. Market forces alone cannot ensure that these changes take place, any more than they could ensure that equivalent changes took place in early-nineteenth-century Kerry or Donegal. Still less can they ensure that the gains will spread evenly or fairly. Technological and economic revolutions of this sort bring benefits, but they also have costs; in a market economy, there can be no assurance that those who bear the costs will get the benefits. The children of the handloom weavers whose livelihoods were destroyed by steam-powered textile manufacturing may well have been better off materially than their grandfathers had been before the factories came. In the meantime, the handloom weavers starved. No one is likely to starve as a result of the information revolution, but in the absence of countervailing policies, the poor, the unskilled, the old and the unemployed may well lose more than they gain.

Much the same applies in the international sphere. Only innovative and adaptable societies can take full advantage of technological revolutions; sluggish and unadaptable ones fall behind. Competitive pressures alone cannot force the latter to mend their ways. Late-nineteenth-century Britain is one of the most striking cases in point. Britain had been the pacemaker of the industrial revolution, but in the long upswing of the 1890s and 1900s she fell behind the new pacemakers, who were better adapted to the advanced technologies of the period than she was. Yet she had stuck to market-liberal principles more faithfully than they had done. As the Prussians realised in the nineteenth century, and the Japanese in the twentieth, market-liberalism is a doctrine for those who are already well-equipped for the market. It is no friend for those who need to equip themselves.

The neo-socialist approach is more confused and, in an odd way, more gingerly. At the core of the socialist tradition is the vision of a stable state, in which men will somehow contrive to enjoy the fruits of economic abundance without suffering the pains of economic change. Perhaps because of this inheritance, neo-socialists are mostly ill attuned to the problems of adjustment. Their critique of the existing system is directed to different issues, and their solutions spring from different preoccupations. In practice, most of them have been more anxious to shelter from the changes of the last fifteen years than to adapt to them. All the same, most depict the crisis of the 1970s and 1980s as a crisis of capitalism. If only by implication, most conclude that it can be resolved only by socialism. Socialism need not mean state socialism, of course. Many neo-socialists look forward to a decentralised economy, socially owned, but based on some form or other of workers control. But, as a technique for achieving economic adjustment, what is sometimes called 'market socialism' suffers from the same disadvantages as market liberalism. Adjustment would still come through the market; and market forces would still be powerless, by themselves, to overcome the social and cultural handicaps which the weak and unadaptable bring with them to the market.

As the Soviet Union and Eastern Europe show, however, there is no reason to believe that state socialism is a satisfactory alternative. The market may not always know better then the state, but it does sometimes know better. In Charles Lindblom's phrase, state direction is a matter of 'strong thumbs, no fingers'. No better way has been found to mobilise society's resources for war or for some great collective purpose like the building of the pyramids or the exploration of space; significantly, even societies in which state intervention is suspect have relied on it for activities of this sort. By the same token, however, no one has discovered a more efficient device than the market for co-ordinating the multifarious private purposes of a heterogeneous peacetime society.

The second proposition is more complicated. It is that we can understand the adjustment problems with which these doctrines cannot cope only against the background of two centuries of British history. The British economy was beginning to lag behind other advanced economies in investment, growth and competitiveness by the last quarter of the nineteenth century. Though the curve of relative decline since then has been jagged and irregular, the forces behind it have been in operation throughout. Britain has had to face the worldwide upheavals of the last fifteen years from the position of a chronic invalid exposed to a snowstorm. If we want to come to grips with her predicament, and close the gap between doctrine and reality, it is not enough to examine her behaviour during the storm. It is also necessary to explain the long years of invalidity which preceded it.

That is, of course, one of the most complex and controversial questions in modern British history. It would be absurd to offer a simple, unicausal answer. All the same, certain themes emerge fairly clearly from the mass of detail which surrounds it. In at least three related respects, twentieth-century Britain has been the prisoner of her nineteenth-century past. She was the first industrial society in history, the pathfinder to the modern world. The values and assumptions of her elites, the doctrines disseminated in her universities and newspapers, the attitudes and patterns of behaviour of her entrepreneurs and workers were stamped indelibly by this experience. But because she was a pathfinder — because she made the passage to industrialism early, at a time when the technology was still primitive, when the skills it required were still rudimentary and when it could still be managed efficiently by the small-scale, fragmented structures of liberal capitalism — the experience taught the wrong lessons.

Britain had become the pathfinder in the first place because she had broken more decisively than any other country in the world with the values and assumptions of what Harold Perkin has called the 'Old Society'.[9] The notions that property has duties as well as rights, that consumers owe producers a just price while producers owe consumers just dealing, that the community is a whole greater than the sum of its parts, that high and low are bound together by a chain of reciprocal obligation, that man is placed on earth by God to serve greater ends than the satisfaction of his own wants — all these were victims of a cultural revolution, which preceded and made possible the industrial revolution. More thoroughly than any other country in Europe, Britain's culture was permeated with the individualism which her intellectuals codified and justified, and to which the astounding growth of her economy gave the sanction of success. To the British, it seemed almost self-evident that industrialism must be the child of individualism. 'Progress' could come only through setting individuals free to pursue their own interests and to make what use they wished of their own property, without reference to society or interference from the state. But although these attitudes suited the conditions of primitive industrialism, they did not suit the sophisticated, science-based and organised industrialism which slowly superseded it. With suitable modifications, the communal ethic of the 'Old Society' has turned out to be better adapted to the capital- and skill-intensive industrialism of the twentieth century than the individualistic ethic of the industrial revolution; and it is in societies where something of the old ethic survived the transition to

[9]   Perkin (1989).

modernity that sophisticated industrialism has flourished most. Having made one cultural revolution in the seventeenth and eighteenth centuries, however, Britain has been unable to make another in the twentieth. In the age of the industrial laboratory, the chemical plant, and later of the computer, she stuck to the mental furniture of the age of steam.

Most of that furniture was arranged around her extra-ordinary role in the outside world. Not only was she the first industrial society in history, she was also the first world power in history, the guarantor as well as the midwife of the worldwide trading system which the guns of the Royal Navy had made possible. But she was a world power of a very odd kind. In Andrew Gamble's phrase, she was the 'World Island': the centre of an informal network of trading relationships and capital movements, of which her formal empire was merely a part. This network was permeated with the same individualism that permeated her economy. It was not managed from London, in the interests of the imperial state. In an important sense, it was not managed at all. It depended on the spontaneous, unplanned activities of private entrepreneurs and investors, looking for profit wherever they could find it. They were not agents of some overarching imperial mission; they pursued their own private interests, not the interests of the empire in general or of the mother country in particular. Here too, what had been an asset in the days of Britain's industrial supremacy became a handicap as others overtook her. British entrepreneurs failed to compete with the Germans and Americans in the new technologies of the late-nineteenth and early-twentieth centuries because, in the short term, they could survive and prosper by selling more of their existing products in their traditional markets in Latin America and the colonies. Meanwhile, capital which might have been invested in modernising British industry flowed abroad instead. The same theme sounded repeatedly between the wars and after 1945. This external network, moreover created a powerful nexus of internal interests with a stake in its survival. Partly because of this, successive governments gave higher priority to the world role, financial or military, than to the home economy. Examples include the return to the gold standard in 1925, the high expenditure on overseas military bases in the 1950s and 1960s and the sacrifice of the National Plan to the $2.80 sterling parity in 1966. And although the long post-script to world power ended with Britain's belated entry into the European Community in the early 1970s, it was plain that her political class found it exceptionally hard to adjust to membership.

The legacy of the nineteenth century does not end there. One reason why British politicians and officials cannot easily adapt to EEC membership is that the 'Westminster Model' of parliamentary government rests on the doctrine — heavily influenced by the utilitarian individualism of Jeremy Bentham and his followers who thought that sovereignty was inherently unlimited and who dismissed the notion of fundamental rights as 'nonsense on stilts' — that the Crown-in-Parliament must be absolutely and inalienably sovereign. An obvious corollary is that British governments cannot share power with other tiers of government, sub-national or supra national. In its day, the 'Westminster Model' was a remarkable example of successful adaptation. The accommodations and concessions which gave birth to it made possible Britain's peaceful transition to democracy, and the peaceful incorporation of the Labour Movement into the political order. Here too, however, assumptions born of successful adaptation in the past impede adaptation to more recent changes. Not only do we live in an interdependent world, in which absolute national sovereignty is an illusion and transnational power sharing inevitable, we also live in an interdependent society, dense with organised and unorganised groups, whose co-operation in the productive process is essential to the smooth running of the economy. In practice, governments have either to break the power of these groups — a costly and uncertain business, itself inimical to the health of the economy — or to share power with them.

Thus, in fact even if not in form, they too have ended the Westminster monopoly of sovereignty. Buttressing the doctrine of absolute parliamentary supremacy, moreover, are the twin assumptions that the courts should not limit the freedom of action of the sovereign Parliament, and that there is in any case no need to limit it since informal restraints and political processes provide adequate safeguards against the abuse of power. Yet, in an increasingly diverse society, in which deference to customary authority is waning, these assumptions have become recipes for mistrust and alienation.

Half a century of social change has, in short, invalidated the doctrines which are supposed to underpin the political order. This, in turn, has undermined public confidence in its equity, and made it more difficult for governments to mobilise consent for the changes without which economic adjustment is impossible.

This leads on to the third proposition: that Britain's adjustment problems have as much to do with politics as with economics, and with tacit political understandings as with political institutions. If we reject market liberalism and state socialism, we are left, in practice, with some variant or other of the mixed economy — of an economy in which resources are largely allocated through the market, but in which public power intervenes on a significant scale to supplement, constrain, manipulate, or direct market forces for public ends. That sentence, however, raises as many questions as it answers. Public intervention implies a public purpose: otherwise, those who do the intervening cannot know what they are trying to achieve. But in a political culture shaped by the assumption that society is made up of separate, atomistic individuals, pursuing only their own private purposes, the notion of a public purpose which is more than the sum of private purposes is apt to seem dangerous, or meaningless, or both.

The result is an intellectual and moral vacuum at the heart of the political economy. Since the war, at the latest, Britain has had a substantial public sector and a large capacity for public intervention. But because the notion of a public purpose is alien to it, her political class has had no philosophy of public intervention or of what might be called the public realm. There are no agreed criteria for determining the ends which public intervention is supposed to serve, and no agreed procedures for deciding what the criteria should be; and the suggestion that there should be seems quaint, if not utopian. So does the suggestion that the public sector should be seen as the instrument of a public good, which the members of the public have agreed in common, and to the pursuit of which they therefore have a common obligation. Yet, without such a philosophy, it is hard to see how a political economy which depends on public intervention can command the support which it needs to function properly. In its absence, the public sector is apt to become a battleground for warring private interests, while its 'outputs' appear increasingly arbitrary and capricious. In good times, no obvious damage need result. Hard choices can be avoided, and predatory interests bought off. In default of active support, the system can make do with passive acquiescence. But in bad times, when passive acquiescence is no longer enough and when all decisions hurt, arbitrary ones are likely to undermine support for the system, at the very point when it is most needed. It would be wrong to suggest that this is a complete summary of the recent history of Britain's political economy, but few would deny that it summarises a good deal of it.

This has obvious implications for the problems we have been discussing. The questions of how to halt the decline in Britain's international competitiveness, of how to devise a satisfactory form of transnational power sharing and of how to respond to the growth of group power and the decay of traditional authority all pose hard choices. Except in the shortest of short terms, the answers cannot be imposed successfully from the top down. Yet none of the doctrines around which post-war British politics have revolved offers anything other than imposed answers, for none of them provides the moral basis for the sense of community and mutual obligation which would make it possible to look for answers in a different way.

By the same token, however, solitary speculation is unlikely to produce a satisfactory alternative. The notion that social problems can be solved by a Wise Man's cerebrations is only slightly less pernicious than the notion that salvation lies in a Great Man's will. The hope that, if only a new Marx or a new Keynes or a new Freud arose among us he would be able to tell us what to do, rests on a dangerous misunderstanding of the relationship between social thought and social change. Usable doctrines do not spring, fully armed, from a theorist's brow. They have to be hammered out in the give and take of a debate, provoked and shaped by the lived experience of particular societies at particular times. Because of this, the debate is unlikely to yield worthwhile results if it takes place in a historical vacuum. Men are made by their histories, and start their journeys to the future from the point where past history has left them. Ahistorial theorising, based on the implicit assumption that the awesome complexity of real-world behaviour can be reduced to simplified models, which apply in all societies at all times, may sometimes yield useful insights into the human condition, but it is a perilous guide to action. One reason why so many discussions of Britain's current political and economic problems lead nowhere is that they are based on over-simplified interpretations of the recent past. Like a beach whose old contours have been partially — but only partially — reshaped by a storm at sea, the political landscape of today still bears the double impress, first of the long hegemony of post-war Keynesian social democracy and secondly of the crises which destroyed it. We cannot hope to pick our way across it unless we understand the nature and origins of those crises and of the governing philosophy which failed to cope with them.

This book is intended as a contribution to the search for a new governing philosophy which has been the dominant theme in British politics since the post-war consensus broke down. Its object is to help clear the ground of the obstacles which have so far held up the search and, if possible, to point towards a more promising direction. Rather than proposing a new doctrine, it sketches out an approach through which a new doctrine might be sought.

Against that background, the relationships between politics as mutual education and the failures of adaptation which we have been discussing in this book is clear enough. For a common theme runs through all these failures. It can be detected most easily in the disarray of the Westminster Model, and in the dwindling legitimacy of its institutions and conventions. This disarray has come about because the Schumpeterian assumption that democratic politics revolve around a competitive struggle for the people's vote — and the corresponding, essentially Benthamite, assumption that the victors in that struggle are entitled to make what use they wish of the power placed in their hands — can no longer provide the basis for a legitimate political order. The institutions and procedures which depend upon these assumptions still exist, and for the most part the decisions which emanate from them are still obeyed. But they are plainly losing authority; and are no longer trusted. Trust is ebbing partly because the conventions and assumptions of club government are no longer respected by the members of the club themselves, but even more because an increasingly sceptical public no longer believe that they provide adequate safeguards against the abuse of power.

The result is a paradox. As we have seen, the conception of power and authority summed up in Dicey's famous notion of the 'absolute legislative sovereignty or despotism of the King in Parliament', and the cluster of attitudes and assumptions which has grown up around that conception, have traditionally lain at the heart of Britain's political culture. Indeed, they have gone well beyond politics: current obsessions with the right of industrial management to manage almost certainly spring from the same emotional sources. For those who hold these attitudes, power is, in some sense, unshareable: something finite, which one has or does not have. To share it is to lose it: to divide it is to diminish it, and in doing so, to diminish its holders. The whole notion of federalism — the notion that state power should be divided between different tiers of government, each supreme in its own sphere — is alien. So is the central European view of democratic government as a process of consensus-building, based on power sharing between different social and political interests: the 'consociational', as opposed to majoritarian, conception of democracy. The same applies to the suggestion that private bodies should share in public decision-making, and, for that matter, to the suggestion that workers should share in the government of the firms that employ them. On one level, the traditional conception still holds the field. Governments still conduct themselves in accordance with it; and it still gives them an enormous capacity to make outward changes of form and structure. Yet on a deeper level, it is in retreat. The institutions and practices which it has underpinned for so long are losing legitimacy; and, because of this, the powers it gives are becoming, in certain crucial respects, illusory. They still make 'mechanical' change easy — perhaps all too easy. They make it more difficult to win consent for the deeper changes of attitude and custom without which a backward political economy cannot expect to adjust to the current upheavals in the outside world.

The same theme runs through the complex story of Britain's failure to become a developmental state. Almost by definition, political institutions which have lost legitimacy cannot sustain state-led adjustment on the Japanese or Gaullist pattern. In any case, negotiated adjustment on the central European pattern is more likely to work in a highly industrialised society, with a strong Labour Movement and only a tiny agricultural sector. Negotiated adjustment depends upon consensus building, and that in turn depends upon a form of power sharing. Instead of the secretive, collusive and transitory quasi-corporatism of the 1930s and the post-war Keynesian social democracy, government and the organised producer groups would have to establish British equivalents of the explicit, stable neo-corporatist institutions of the Scandinavian and central European social democracies. One possibility would be to adopt John Mackintosh's proposal to replace the House of Lords with an 'Upper House' representing the unions, the employers and other organised interest groups which already have systematic relationships with Whitehall. Another would be to extend the NEDC and give it a voice in policy making. A third would be to set up a 'house of industry', on the lines recently proposed by Sir Ian Gilmour. A fourth, complementary rather than alternative to the others, would be to create neo-corporatist institutions in the regions, and to devolve developmental functions down to them — implying the emergence of a number of developmental states, region by region. It is, after all, worth noting that the countries where the negotiated approach works best are the small nation-states of northern and central Europe, perhaps because they have a stronger sense of community than big ones. Other things being equal, moreover, regional bodies are more likely than national ones to display the flexibility which is even more essential in a time of rapid technological change than at other times. As well as, and more important than, any changes of structure, however, this sort of power sharing would require changes of attitude and belief. Politicians and public would have to accept that, in complex industrial societies, parliamentary election should not be the sole channel of representation: that, in their capacities as producers, 'the people' are likely to be represented better by groups organised on functional lines than by members of parliament elected on a territorial basis; and that it is therefore right, as well as expedient, for governments emerging from territorial elections to share power with functionally based producer groups. And such changes of attitude and belief are, of course incompatible with the current British conception of parliamentary sovereignty, and with the assumptions underlying it.

The patent inability of recent British governments to follow an independent economic policy in an increasingly interdependent world points to similar conclusions. In this respect at any rate, the classical European nation-state is obsolescent. Plainly, national governments can overcome the consequences of their obsolescence only by sharing power with international or supranational authorities. If the world economy is to escape from the present deflationary impasse, economic decision-making must somehow transcend national boundaries. The experience of the 1970s and 1980s suggests, however, that the mere co-ordination of national policies is not enough: as Michael Stewart has shown the temptation to exploit the gains accruing to the free rider is likely to be too strong. Since national economic sovereignty stands in the way of recovery, the world needs an international economic sovereign. The trouble is that no such sovereign is in sight. The days have passed when the United States was strong enough to assume the burdens of sovereignty, at any rate in the western world, and there are no new candidates for the post. In the case of European countries, however, the logic of inter-dependence points towards further devolution upwards to the EEC, which alone can cope with the macro issues for which the nation state is too small. For, in default of an international economic sovereign, the most likely development is a world of mercantilist trading blocs; if this happens 'Europe's' chances of weathering the transition now taking place in the world economy will partly depend on its ability to turn itself into one of these blocs. The logic is, in fact, remarkably similar to the logic which led the founding fathers of the EEC to reject intergovernmental co-operation *à l'anglaise* in favour of the 'Community method' and the Jenkins Commission to relaunch the concept of monetary union in the late-1970s: with all its faults, the EEC is still the best available prototype of the sort of transnational power sharing the times demand. From the perspective set out earlier in this chapter, it is true, this raises all sorts of problems. The EEC is, in some ways, a monument to the technocratic fallacy that politics can be equated with management, and its opaque, only dubiously accountable decision-making processes are far removed from the ideals of double-loop learning and politics as mutual education. But that is an argument for strengthening the European Parliament, and making the other Community Institutions accountable to it. And here again, the absolutist view of power which permeates Britain's political culture stands in the way.

In a rather more complicated fashion, much the same applies to the fundamental distributional question which lies at the heart of the politics of adjustment. As we saw in Part Two, there are two ways of approaching it. One is to try to negotiate a settlement, socialising the pains of adjustment and allocating its costs and benefits in a way in which the undistorted market would not have done. The other is to try to push the losers out of the way. As we also saw, neither approach has worked in Britain since the late-nineteenth century. The losers have been too strong to push aside, but successive attempts to construct a cross-class coalition, based on a distributional consensus of some sort, have come to nothing. The reasons include the suspicions and resentments partly engendered by the late-nineteenth-century switch from 'active' to 'passive' property and the fractured, non-encompassing character of the British Labour Movement — none of which is likely to disappear in a hurry. But although no one could pretend that it would be easy to reach a consensus in any circumstances, it is more likely to come through power sharing and negotiation than in any other way. Certainly, approaches based on reductionist individualism have repeatedly failed. The proclaimed egalitarianism of the revisionist Labour politicians of the 1960s and 1970s turned out to be of little use. Equality of outcome conflicts with an intuitive sense that risk, enterprise, self-sacrifice, skill and deferred gratification deserve some reward. Equality of opportunity, on the other hand, is in practice vacuous. Yet devil-take-the-hindmost reliance on the market cannot generate a consensus either. Losers and potential losers will not accept it, in any case. Much more importantly, it too conflicts with an intuitive sense of what is fair: why *should* the losers have to bear the brunt of changes in the environment, which cannot possibly be their fault? Negotiation and power sharing would work, however, only if government abandoned its exclusive control over such sensitive matters as tax policy, welfare policy and perhaps even macro-economic policy and treated them as items in the bargaining agenda. It hardly needs saying that this would entail at least as profound a break with the traditional British approach to politics as would any of the others.

In all these spheres, the conception of power and authority which has underpinned Britain's political order since the eighteenth century has become an obstacle to successful adjustment. The notion of politics as mutual education is not only alien to the conception; it is also subversive of it. If it were adopted, the traditional conception would have to be abandoned, and the practices and institutions which it has fostered would have to be changed. Of course, this does not guarantee that the communitarian, power-sharing and participatory approaches which politics as mutual education implied would be any more successful. Guaranteed success belongs to Utopia. The only certainty is that the approaches of the last hundred years and more have failed. If the argument set out here is right, they have done so because the view of man and society on which they rest narrows horizons; restricts opportunities for moral growth and inhibits individual and social learning.

The alternative rests on a richer, more complex and in some ways more generous view of human nature and human possibilities, but it is not, for that reason, easier or more comfortable. On the contrary, it is more demanding. It rules out manipulative short cuts to change, imposed 'reforms', technocratic fixes. Its style is humdrum, not heroic: collegial, not charismatic: consensual, not ideological: controversial, not declaratory. It depends on the slow processes of argument and negotiation. It requires patience, open-mindedness and, above all, humility before the astonishing and sometimes exasperating diversity of others. At its core lies the belief that men and women may learn if they are stretched; that they can discover how to govern themselves if they win self-government. But the key words in that sentence are 'may' and 'can'. No one who has lived through any of this century would be foolish enough to replace them with 'will'. To substitute the politics of mutual education for the politics of command and exchange would be to gamble — not, it is true, on the altruism or moral excellence of others, but on their sociability and capacity for growth.

No doubt, some will flinch from the risks involved. Yet that has been man's gamble since he descended from the trees.

Revisionism Re-born: Labour's Years of Recovery

Bernard Crick — Socialist Values and Time (1984)

Bernard Crick would not conventionally be regarded within the canon of revisionist thought. He has made an outstanding contribution to political theory and practice in the last thirty years. But there are few common threads to link him intellectually or politically with the authors featured in this volume.

Yet there are two important senses in which Crick should be regarded — at the very least — as a 'neo-revisionist'. First, he argued strongly for the Labour Party to regard itself as a fluid coalition of interests and ideologies, rather than as a wholly 'socialist' movement. Second, he understood that for the party to rescue itself from oblivion in the 1980s, it had to formulate a coherent public philosophy instead of relying on a pragmatic appeal and 'muddling through'. In an article on socialist literature published in 1960, Crick had praised Crosland's The Future of Socialism *as the most comprehensive and important work of the decade, as he denounced the 'denunciation and sectarian polemic' of the New Left.*[1]

Crick was born in December 1929, educated at Whitgift School and University College, London. After spells at Harvard, McGill, and Berkeley

---

[1]   Crick (1960).

Universities, he was appointed lecturer in politics at LSE in 1957. He was then appointed Professor of Political Theory and Institutions at the University of Sheffield (1965–71), and Professor of Politics at Birkbeck College (1971–84). He also edited the influential journal Political Quarterly *(1966–80).*

His most important contribution to political theory is In Defence of Politics *(1962; revised edition, 2001). Politics is not about management or diplomacy he argues, but deals fundamentally with the conflicts that arise in a free society. In this sense, it is essential to liberty. This formed the backdrop to Crick's extensive work on citizenship in the school curriculum.*

His other publications include The Reform of Parliament *(1964), and the authoritative biography of George Orwell (1980).*

After Labour's General Election defeat in 1983, Crick gave a highly influential Fabian Society lecture in which he argued that the party must develop a 'public doctrine', a set of linked principles and ideas that could inform its policies. This would not be a fully worked out ideology or a philosophy. But it would move Labour away from the instrumental pragmatism that seemed the only alternative to the fundamentalist left in that period. Crick was no doubt influenced by Orwell's suspicion of doctrinaire socialism, and his literary appreciation of social changes underway in Britain.

This contribution was published as a Fabian pamphlet Socialist Values and Time *(1984). Central to Labour's public doctrine had to be a conception of personal liberty, Crick argued. Freedom had not been hopelessly tainted by capitalism as both Marxists and neo-liberals such as Hayek believed. Individualism was about more than private gain through the competitive market economy. It was concerned with self-actualisation, creativity, and freedom, and thus should be embraced by the left, not handed over freely to the Conservative right.*

Crick also recognised that if public ownership constituted a fundamental principle of the party from its very foundation, this involved ascribing to Labour a distinctively socialist character. Instead, he saw Labour as a loose coalition of ideas and interests and, 'socialism itself, except in a very broad sense, is only one element in this coalition . . . certainly subsidiary, in both electoral and historical terms, to the Labour Party as the representative of organised labour'. To revive itself, the party had to rediscover the disparate traditions of political thought that were early influences on the Labour Party — among them radical social liberalism, Victorian ethical reformism, and the evolutionary socialist ideas of the Fabian Society and the Independent Labour Party. In common with later revisionists, Crick called for a re-fashioned concept of democratic socialism.

Selected Text[2]

This pamphlet is an attempt to show that the beliefs of democratic socialists can be restated in modern terms: that we possess both a theory and a doctrine which, while not dogmatic, nor derived from sacred books, such as are available to followers of both Marx and Adam Smith, yet can be stated more simply than some believe. The beliefs have common ground with much libertarian Marxism (still more with much of Marx's Marxism), but the common ground can be expressed in common language and common sense. The tradition associated with the early Fabians, with early Shaw and Wells, with G.D.H. Cole, R.H. Tawney, Harold Laski and both Anthony Crosland and Dick Crossman, is still very much alive and should stand up and speak for itself as a public philosophy, as the ideology of a public political party not of a private socialist debating society — as it seemed that some of the Far Left, not too long ago, wished the Labour Party to become.

We need thought, thinking and rethinking, reviewing and re-forming old thoughts as well as forming new, quite as much as we need research groups on policies — perhaps at the moment more. Research needs a sense of direction unless we are to recreate a parody of the Fabian tradition: the suspicion that research was for the sake of research. I think the new spirit of the Fabian Society can be the main, though far from the only, forum for such thinking; even though, as will emerge, I dislike the excessive centralism and the trust in benign, permeated bureaucracy of the old Fabian tradition. I like the old phrase 'inevitability of gradualism' — despite the fact that nothing is inevitable. For the 'gradualism' of old Fabianism spoke of the persistent means towards a far from 'gradual' end. Any social theory, as well as elementary common sense, will see how long is the time-scale towards the radical social transformations that are needed to make life more decent, just and prosperous for all, not just for the favoured and favouring few. But the electoral defeats were so grievous and our loss of our old public philosophy so profound, that we have to start *almost* as if from the beginning again.

Evolution and Revolution

I think that all socialist ends are revolutionary but because they do aim at a new society they can only be pursued by political and gradu-

[2]   Crick, B., *Socialist Values and Time*, London: Fabian Society, 1984.

alist means — as fast and no faster then we can persuade all those who, despite the obvious failure of Thatcherism, are not persuaded. Even in 1918 Rosa Luxembourg warned Lenin, just as she had warned him thirteen years before, that freedom must be the means not the eventual end of the party's strategy; and though the time traveller, H.G. Wells, visited Russia in 1920 and at first had good words to say for the Bolsheviks, he was under no illusion that Lenin's 'dictatorship of the proletariat' was either temporary (as the Roman origin of the office of Dictator was meant to suggest) or anything other than the rule by a small party oligarchy.

George Orwell wrote in *The Lion and the Unicorn* (probably with both Lenin and the Webbs in mind) that:

> Centralised ownership has very little meaning unless the mass of people are living roughly upon an equal level, and have some kind of control over the government. 'The State' may come to mean no more than a self-elected political party, and oligarchy and privilege can return, based on power rather than on money.

His 'Fairy Story' or fable written in 1944, *Animal Farm*, was not so much untimely as something that created an astonishingly belated popular recognition that the revolution, based on cries of 'Liberty, Equality, Fraternity', had, once again, been betrayed. Yet he did not argue that the fault lay in any inevitable growth of power hungry elites (the 'pigs'), but rather in the excessive credulity and trust of the other animals in their leaders: 'all animals' must be the basic power behind long revolutionary changes as well as the objects of 'the revolution' led by those who unhappily become 'more equal than others'. Beaumarchais once remarked melodramatically that, 'Slaves are as guilty as tyrants'.

Great confusion has arisen between the myth of the 'revolution' as a climactic *event* and the reality of the 'the revolutionary *process*'. The opportunity for reshaping societies towards greater social justice may only come either through the sudden overthrow or more often the breakdown of repressive autocracies, but the revolutionary opportunity does not guarantee the revolutionary outcome: a benign outcome needs restraint and tolerance, as well as skill and will, exercised through decades and generations. If the classical Marxist critique of capitalism was broadly correct, its theory of inevitable stages was wrong: for it failed to reckon with and guard against nationalism, bureaucratisation and above all the pure power-hunger and desire for self-perpetuation among new as much as among old elites. At the least, the theory of stages needs re-stating in terms of possibilities; and even diluting to allow for the overlapping stages. This could yield a less misleading model of the post-revolutionary world, one more open to variation and to influence by popular debate, rather than depending on belief in laws of history wholly determined by social structure or modes of production. Such laws (or rather tendencies) always condition but they never determine human action.

Thus the debate in the first part of the century between 'true Marxist' revolutionaries and revisionist evolutionary Austrian and German Marxist 'Social Democrats' (in the sense then current) was perhaps never as contradictory and unbridgeable in theory as it seemed to the passionate protagonists. They did, however, differ about progress through either evolution or gradualness, such as German socialists and British Fabians used to argue for in the 1900s and 1920s; but the essential point was that they both then thought that by governing with the right values and deliberate stages of economic and social planning, a socialist society could be achieved. In this they differ from the new Social Democratic Party, who, whether from wisdom, class-interest, exhaustion or fear, no longer believe that an egalitarian society can be achieved or should be achieved, even: only perhaps equality of opportunity. They hope more modestly, if somewhat vaguely, simply to manage a mixed economy benignly with the interest of the welfare of the disadvantaged strongly in mind. They aspire to civilise, perhaps to inject a few socialist values into, not to replace, the economic dynamic of that competitive, individualistic ethic of Western capitalism which intrudes so systematically and unasked into so many aspects of social, cultural and personal life.

The Social Democrats are right about the primacy of liberty, but they are wrong to think that it is always threatened by equality and to believe that a proper sense of individualism must always be linked to the competitive acquisition of private property. Their own project is perfectly possible, given favourable economic growth such as Anthony Crosland assumed in the 1950s and 1960s in his book, *The Future of Socialism*. The philosopher should lament and not mock that their hour of electoral opportunity seemed to come at a time of unique difficulty for their theory; whereas it is the decline of the economy in Great Britain that could also give opportunity to the left of the Labour Party, as now seems to happen in France and Greece. Some social democrats could have remained social democrats within the Labour Party — theirs was not a difference in theory or doctrine, but political misjudgement and failure of nerve at a crucial moment.

I would boldly but simply claim that there is no *necessary* incompatibility between revolutionary and evolutionary varieties of socialism: if socialism is to occur at all, it must be pursued and consolidated through political means. Ralph Miliband, a Marxist who will not join (or rejoin) the Labour Party, has written in *Marxism and Politics*:

> Regimes which depend on the suppression of all opposition and the stifling of all civic freedoms must be taken to represent a disastrous regression in political terms from bourgeois democracy ... But the civic freedoms which, however inadequately and precariously, form part of bourgeois democracy are the product of centuries of unremitting popular struggles. The task of Marxist politics is to defend these freedoms; and to make possible their extension and enlargement by the removal of their class boundaries.

His views on this point are not untypical of many modern Marxist intellectuals in the West, the Third World and even in Eastern Europe. In an earlier book on *Parliamentary Socialism*, he argued that the acceptance of parliamentary conventions and evolutionary socialism emasculated the alleged revolutionary spirit of the early British Labour movement. Apart from the fact that this no longer seems to be true (if ever it was historically), his thesis can at best only apply to specific contexts. It would be a massive *non sequitur* to say that because of some past experiences, socialism cannot proceed by parliamentary means; or to identify all forms of republican assemblies with the specific conservative conventions of a particular phase of the British parliamentary tradition.

Determined democratic socialists, however revolutionary their long-term aims, have to build up *popular* support if their measures are to work. When they resort, as in Eastern Europe after the Second World War, or in many contemporary states in Africa and Asia, to dictatorial coercion and control, not merely is liberty destroyed, which is obvious enough, but even sheer welfare is grievously limited. The evidence is now overwhelming in the Soviet world that productivity suffers both through the sheer inefficiency and often corruption of unchallengeable centralised bureaucracies and through a massive indifference, sullenness and propensity to go slow when workers can neither change their jobs, form free trade unions, strike, nor even — if driven to that pitch — hope to revolt with any chance of success. The very working masses whose productive power is essential to any kind of progress are rendered impotent.

George Orwell in 1944 reviewed F.A. Hayek's *The Road to Serfdom*:

> Professor Hayek is probably right in saying that in this country the intellectuals are probably more totalitarian-minded that the common people. But he does not see, or will not admit, that a return to 'free' competition means for the great mass of people a tyranny probably worse, because more irresponsible, than the state. The trouble with competitions is that somebody wins them. Professor Hayek denies that free capitalism necessarily leads to monopoly, but in practice that is where it has led, and since the vast number of people would rather have state regimentation then slumps and unemployment, the drift towards collectivism is bound to continue ... Such is our present predicament. Capitalism leads to dole queues, the scramble for markets, and war. Collectivism leads to concentration camps, leader worship and war. There is no way out of this unless a planned economy can somehow be combined with freedom for the intellect . . .

Consider the many one-party States in the Third World who claim to be socialist but whose dominant ideology is, in fact, nationalism. This nationalism often enables rulers to take the support of the masses for granted. But there is a world of difference between such States which can, like Tanzania, at least tolerate criticism and public debate about policies among the ruling elite and intelligentsia, and those more common one-party States in which no public dissent is tolerated. The moral differences are the most important today because of the growing number of developing countries claiming to be 'Socialist'. Their claims will become ever more strident the further back into history the original struggle for national liberation fades: nationalism cannot remain forever an off-the-peg justification for each and every arbitrary act of party, leader or President. The differences in economic efficiency may be less obvious and may be affected by a hundred and one contingent factors; but in theory (that is in long-term tendency), other things being equal, it is unlikely that uncriticised planning can be more effective than plans that are open to public debate and which may even have arisen from debate. Plans that can be criticised can be modified. People who tolerate criticism are more likely to change their minds. If the plan may neither be criticised nor modified and it does not work as expected, then little is left but to impose it with coercion, suppress evidence of failure and discontent, and imprison all those who say that the Emperor has no

clothes. Such desperate anti-political measures have even been dig-
nified by a name: 'permanent revolution'.

In multi-party regimes there may well be consensus, indeed,
which can hinder or delay the realisation of socialist goals. But
socialists, like anyone else, must realise that great enterprises take
much time. Rome was not built in a day. There is no answer but
patience and skill in persuasion. The building of socialism is the
work of generations and to do this we need, once again, to do things
that matter to people immediately and then carry them with us,
slowly, patiently, definitely, step-by-step towards greater future
betterment. Socialists must distinguish between a consensus of values (which is rare in any society) and the need to reach a consensus
about procedures (which is common in parliamentary democracies).
These rules or conventions of the political game may be biased, quite
naturally, in support of the existing system. But socialists cannot
hope to modify these rules except by the rules, by persuasion or by
demonstrating good fruits from political power gained by socialist
parties observing these very rules. Socialists should not be surprised
if their criticism of these rules is sometimes taken as a threat to ignore
them; and thus if the very people we want to reach and uplift, often
reject us and suspect us of being not merely anti-establishment — as
we are or should be — but anti-political. Even such a mild and democratic business as the British Labour Party's plan to abolish an
appointed and hereditary House of Lords, needs balancing simultaneously with measures which appear to ordinary people to check
the powers of the Government in other ways. Intellectual socialists
cannot have it both ways; to hold that the mass of the people have
been 'socialised' into conservative constitutional beliefs is not to
ignore such constraints, but to demonstrate that it is in these terms
that the argument has to begin and has to be won. All politics,
indeed, must deal with people as they are.

The potential political and the actual productive power of the people is, indeed, more essential to socialist theory than it is to contemporary capitalist theory: this is the minimal core of truth in the
original labour theory of value. While popular capitalist doctrine
still preaches the individual work ethic, that workers should work as
hard as they can for necessarily disproportionate rewards and that
there are jobs to be had for those who *really* want to work, liberal
economists favour a more technical argument about the inevitability
of capital-intensive industry and uncontrolled 'free trade' in finance
and international investment, whatever the cost in unemployment.

Full employment is no longer seen as economically possible or as politically crucial: free market theorists now gamble on the passivity of the masses if the marginal rate of mere subsistence can be found and funded, coupled with investment in a type of mass-communications designed, quite literally, both to take people's minds off things that matter to create unfree illusions of helplessness (which was the satiric intent of Orwell's 'prolefeed' in *Nineteen Eighty-Four*, aimed at the contemporary mass media not at a distant future). 'True Conservatives', or old fashioned Tories, however, while believing deeply in natural hierarchy and in maintaining inequality, yet are genuinely paternalistic: they have a sense of community and would draw the line, if they knew how, at any economic doctrines that result in mass unemployment.

The 'new conservative' faith in the universality of the market mechanism could well founder on the bitter, dehumanising effect of mass unemployment. But equally socialist leaders must show sensitivity to a complex industrial world in which the workers and managers, if not persuaded freely and given time to adjust, simply will not work or will not work well, will prove unwilling to adjust themselves to new technologies and changing social priorities. Even an advanced industrial power which attempted genuine socialist programmes all at once, too quickly and without a broad prior base of support stretching far beyond party activists, could face some of the same problems as in African and Asian socialism: the danger of alienating elites from the masses. Chairman Mao Tse-tung's 'Cultural Revolution' was no answer to such a problem, but equally the move towards a managerial bureaucracy in China is neither socialism nor the glimmering of liberalism that some Western observers imagine.

Coercive government by party bureaucracy all too often is the crowning achievement of revolutions pursued by non-political means. The Apostle Paul was right to say that, 'every man that striveth for the mastery is temperate in all things', if he is serious about the 'mastery'. And in Western industrial societies coercion by mass unemployment also marks the failure of 'mastery', not its typical or most efficient mode. 'Mastery' involves patience with men and women as they are, as well as an ability to persuade them of what they or their children could become.

Put in simple terms, one does not, as I *think* Miliband now agrees, throw out the baby with the bathwater. Liberty is not hopelessly tainted by capitalism, nor is the idea of liberty as we know it 'purely bourgeois', a product of the rise of capitalism as both Marx and Hayek have argued; the one rejoicing, the other lamenting, but agreeing on this essential point. On the contrary the tradition of free politics and of republican government long preceded the capitalist era: it was both an ideal vision and an occasional imperfect practice from the time of European classical antiquity, the memory of which, among scholars and humanists, even among fearful tyrants, never died. We do not quarrel with J.S. Mill's views on representative government nor on liberty: we simply work to realise them in a way open to all, not just a few.

There could come in time a revolutionary 'transformation of values', certainly of the priorities we give to our many different values; humanity could discover 'the dignity of work' as William Morris hoped, and reject its alienation, and a common culture could arise in place of an impersonal division of labour which both separates and cripples culture and citizenship; but all this will not, except in religious myths and their ideological substitutes, come suddenly or at once. The ideas and the sense of direction already exist, but the recruitment has hardly begun, detailed maps and plans for provision along the route are not to be found, nor has thought been given to how to keep up the spirits of the army on the march — still less to what should happen if it decided to stop or turn round. Transitions are never easy. Deliberate ones have been rare. But enterprise is possible, if conducted by free men in a freely chosen way. Personally I am a 'moderate Socialist', but no longer a 'moderate' in newspaper senses: my goals are extreme and therefore I moderate and measure my means. The 'march of the common people' depends on the people wanting to march.

Roy Hattersley — Choose Equality (1987)

Roy Hattersley was an essential figure in the re-birth of revisionism in the Labour Party. His open espousal of the market economy in the seminal revisionist text, Choose Freedom *(1987) caused little controversy at the time. Yet as Peter Kellner subsequently noted, 'a subtle but vital shift in*

Labour's ideology had been completed. Instead of being a party which found the market guilty until proved innocent, it was now a party that regarded the market as innocent until found guilty'.

Hattersley was born in December 1932, educated at Sheffield City Grammar School and Hull University. A WEA organiser in 1957-59, he served as a Sheffield City Councillor from 1957 to 1965, and was elected MP for Birmingham Sparkbrook in 1964. He remained on the revisionist wing of the Labour Party throughout his career, and was a close ally of both Anthony Crosland and Roy Jenkins.

In 1967, Hattersley was appointed Under-Secretary of State at the Department of Employment and Productivity, and Minister of State at the Ministry of Defence in 1969. He joined the Cabinet in 1976 as Secretary of State for Prices and Consumer Protection where he served until Labour's defeat in 1979.

In 1981, Hattersley watched many of his closest political allies desert Labour for the Social Democratic Party (SDP), but chose to remain in the party retaining the fighting spirit he had so admired in Hugh Gaitskell twenty years earlier. He was elected Deputy Leader in 1983 as the other half of the Neil Kinnock 'dream ticket'. Hattersley published Choose Freedom *in 1987 as an attempt to create for Labour a socialist ideology that could combat Thatcherism while defeating Bennite extremism. 'Socialism' he declared, 'exists to provide — for the largest number of people — the ability to exercise effective liberty'. Tracing the historical roots of this viewpoint back through Tawney, Hobhouse and T.H Green to the radical utilitarianism of John Stuart Mill, Hattersley argued in line with that tradition, both that liberty and equality were indissolubly linked, and that the enabling democratic state could be deployed in pursuit of these twin ideals.*

He was also a prolific writer and journalist, publishing a Victorian trilogy based on his own ancestors, The Makers Mark, In that Quiet Earth, *and* Skylark Song.

The essay 'Choose equality' sets out Hattersley's proposition that democratic socialism is in his view, 'about an extension of freedom brought about by a more equal distribution of resources'. Socialism is a means of practical freedom for individuals. Its ultimate aim, therefore, was, 'the real — as distinct from the theoretical — emancipation of previously powerless citizens'.

The paper also reveals the extent to which revisionist thought, in its steadfast commitment to social and economic equality, was prepared to challenge market liberal principles. Real freedom for the individual could only be sustained by 'co-operative action' and 'collective provision'.

A socialist government would need to intervene selectively in order to prevent market abuse and unfair exploitation of market dominance. The extent to which a revisionist is prepared to detach the ethical values of social-ism from an underlying moral critique of capitalism therefore has limits. Policies should implement social democratic, rather than Conservative or Liberal, values. Equally, the end must not be lost sight of in debating the means. Fraud busting in the welfare state is not a right-wing policy. But stigmatising the poor and undermining the social consensus for their sup-port is an omnipresent danger.

The ideological transition from traditional socialism to social democracy in the Labour Party had also been painful. This helps to explain the eventual break between Hattersley and 'New' Labour, despite his formative ideologi-cal role in its birth during the 1990s. It has − to some − been an unfortu-nate, even tragic, breach.

Selected Text[3]

That the pursuit of liberty through equality has sometimes failed is not in dispute. But the pursuit of liberty through the unregulated economy and the promotion of freedom by the state simply aban-doning restraint over weak and powerful alike have failed continu-ally and conspicuously. Socialists take it for granted that a society in which monopolies are allowed to flourish and where wealth is allowed to extend its power without restraint cannot be a genuinely free society. Much of the first half [of this book] was devoted to criti-cism of the arbitrary − indeed artificial − distinction which is made between social freedom, political liberty and economic equality: the three conditions are inseparable and the aim of all three is individual emancipation. And it is worth spending a moment considering why, in the past, the pursuit of that aim has sometimes been side-tracked into policies which actually reduce the liberties which they are sup-posed to enhance.

Part of the problem is the paradox of the relationship between our overriding principle and the practice by which that principle is applied. Socialism requires the use of collective power to increase individual rights and to extend individual freedom.

Until power and wealth are evenly distributed, the only way in which the weak and poor can pursue their aims is by concerted action for a common goal. But the collective action is not an end in itself. Once the victorious army has liberated the oppressed people,

---

[3] Hattersley, R., 'Choose equality', in *Choose Freedom: The Future for Democratic Socialism*, London: Penguin, 1987.

the temptation to worship both the military ethic and the military technique becomes almost irresistible. The confusion of means and ends is often more sentimental than sinister. Surely, the rhetorical question runs, we can do more together? And so we can. But what we can do by common action ought to be directed to the extension of individual freedom. There is no reason, apart from linguistic confusion, to believe that collective action should result in a collectivist society. Power, once attained, is certainly difficult to relinquish. But — to extend the military analogy — socialists rarely retain power like liberating armies which forget, once the tyrant is defeated, that one tyranny is very much like another. When socialists retain for the government rights which should be passed out to the people, there is usually a genuine belief that the suffocating hand of state bureaucracy will provide the greatest good for the greatest number. That may be because some socialists do not understand that the greatest good is the greatest freedom and that the only argument of consequence is how it can be extended to the greatest number. It may be the product of misplaced paternalism and the presumptuous notion that those who are elected always can judge what is best for those by whom they are elected. Those, comparatively common, errors need closer examination. But much of the problem stems from the willingness to argue the case within the terms set down by our opponents. When freedom is defined as the absence of restraint, socialists know that it does little or nothing to liberate the generality of men and women. If socialists insisted on defining freedom in a way which is related to the reality of making people free, two benefits would result. First, at least one side of the political argument would have taken up an intellectually defensible position. Second, democratic socialism would be seen as primarily concerned with freedom — and democratic socialists would take greater care both to observe that article of faith and to avoid a reputation for heretical disregard for that canon of belief.

The intellectual confusion about the meaning of freedom (and the abduction of the word by the political right) is undoubtedly the principal reason why it is popularly supposed that socialists do not care about liberty. There is something in our nature which encourages the British to believe that denial of the rich's right to send their sons to the private school of their choice in an infringement of liberty whilst the denial of the poor's ability to send their children to a decent school of any sort is not. But socialists in Britain, and radicals before them, must take some of the blame for not tackling the freedom argument head on. The other major social failing has been either weak-minded belief or meek acceptance of the propaganda that socialism involves a directed economy, governed by state monopolies through the bureaucratic allocation of resources. Two minor obstacles to the understanding of freedom's inalienable connection with socialism are worth a moment's examination before we discuss that particular liability; for by examining them it is possible to illustrate avoidable confusions and help construct a description of what a society committed to the freedom that equality of outcome brings is like. The two detriments are a popular misunderstanding about the role and responsibility of trades unions and a widely held misconception about the record of local government. In both cases it would be disingenuous not to admit that socialists, operating in both areas, have from time to time seemed hell-bent on proving their critics right . . .

. . . The subject of primary incomes — and therefore the contentious clichés about 'incomes policy' and 'free collective bargaining' — is dealt with at length in the final chapter. But it is worth observing here that whatever the arguments may be against some form of income planning (and those arguments are formidable) we should dismiss, with at best embarrassment, the complaint that it leaves too many trades unionists unoccupied and too many branch agendas deprived of any interesting items of business. The trades unions do not exist in order to exist; they are there to do their best for their members. Were it to be proved that the members did better under some other system of wage determination, it would be the clear duty of the trades unions to step aside.

In much the same way, it is imperative for local authorities — particularly socialist local authorities — constantly to recall that their existence is not an end in itself. The contribution made by town and county councils to the achievement of a more civilised and more compassionate society is immense. They have certainly moved Britain further along the road to democratic socialism that anything which national governments can boast. And those general encomia are appropriate to many — though not all — of the much maligned Labour councils of the 1980s. The GLC, for example, although indulging in all sorts of trivial absurdities, principally concerned itself with the provision of major benefits. The problems of local government — at least in terms of their role as agencies for promoting individual rights — most frequently occurred under a previous generation of councillors and aldermen. It was they who sometimes fell into the error of believing, or acting as if they believed, that municipal government was an end in itself. It would be easy to offer the resistance to council-home sales as the prime example of recent attempts to elevate the importance of the corporation over the desires and interests of its ratepayers. No doubt there were some housing-committee chairmen whose objection to the 'right to buy' was based on their reluctance to see a reduction in the size of the corporate estate which they managed and felt they owned. But most of the resistance to the sale of municipal property was a product of the principle with which this book attempts to deal. Socialist councillors saw the right of one family to buy cheaply the house in which they lived as the denial of another family's right to live in a decent house at all. General opposition to council-house sales was misconceived, but it was misconceived for honourable reasons. The consideration which prompted the rejection of one set of rights was an attempt to protect another. At least the councillors were asking the right questions, even though they gave the answer which — on any considered view — was likely to reduce rather than increase the sum of liberty. The same defence cannot be advanced for those councillors who insist on regulations which, whilst masquerading as protection for the whole community, are really no more than the preservation of municipal uniformity or bureaucratic convenience. There was a time when pigeon-keeping was prohibited on Sheffield council estates and when, in the same city, it was an offence (punishable with eviction) to paint a front door in anything except the stipulated colour, while to fence in pieces of garden which were adjacent to individual houses but designated collective property, would have been unhesitatingly designated as improvements. Even today — in many great cities — allocation policy, repair procedures and rent-collection schedules are more to the convenience of housing officers than of help to their tenants. They are perhaps minor sins, but they are sins to be avoided, and they help us to draw up the operating rules of the socialist society. The operating rules which should govern its social and bureaucratic organisation are those which produce the freedom that comes from real equality. That requires those who pursue that end constantly to measure their policy decisions against the fundamental question: does it increase equality, and in doing so does it increase the sum of human freedom?

Some of the policies which provide an affirmative answer to that question can easily be described. A socialist government committed to real equality will clearly embark on a massive programme of redistribution, confident that it is more likely to improve overall economic performance than to depress it and certain that it will produce a more efficient rather than a less effective use of resources. Equality of outcome is a close relation of utilitarianism. To redistribute the Duke of Westminster's millions amongst the tenants of the Peabody Trust flats which stand on his land would clearly increase the prospect of human happiness. It is difficult to imagine what it is that the Duke does with his countless millions since they amount to more than a man can count — let alone spend — in a single lifetime. It is not, however, difficult to conceive how the fortune would be spent if it were spread between several thousands of comparatively poor families. Of course, some of it would go on beer and tobacco. But we ought not to be too sanctimonious about that — particularly if we are supporters of the view that a real extension in individual choice is the object of policy. But much of it would clearly be used for purposes which were undeniably desirable, even by the most sanctimonious standards. More important, it would offer the economic basis for emancipation: the material ability to make more of the choices which society theoretically provides. Were the Duke of Westminster's fortune to be reduced by draconian action to a minimal part of what it is today — leaving him, let us say, with more than £5–£10 million — the deprivation would not, in the real meaning of the term, reduce his ability to make the choices which determine the pattern and quality of life. However, were the money distributed amongst the poor, there would be a major increase in their freedom. New opportunities would open up before them — material, aesthetic, even spiritual. Freedom is closely related to purchasing power. If you doubt it, ask the Duke of Westminster. By a conscious policy of redistribution we increase purchasing power and the freedom of those to whom the resources are given without a corresponding reduction in the purchasing power and freedom of those from whom it is taken away. *Equality of outcome is really an extension of marginal utility.*

The fundamental question — much more difficult to answer than the so-called dilemma of redistribution itself — is the form which the redistribution should take. For those who believe in freedom, it is clearly better to redistribute in cash rather than kind, income (primary and secondary) rather than the social wage. For a redistribution which takes the form of goods and services provided by the state inevitably imposes consumption patterns on those who receive it. Often the consumption patterns are wholly desirable and uncontentiously beneficial. Often it is necessary to ensure that those patterns are repeated in order to avoid the social consequences with would flow from their abandonment. There are no circumstances in which we could leave participation in the health service to voluntary decision. The health service is an instrument of collective protection. Socialists will profoundly disagree with those neo liberals who defend the right of men and women to neglect medical care for themselves and to die of whatever diseases they choose to neglect. But only idiots will support a collapse in general medical provision and the consequent contamination of society as a whole. The necessity for generalised medical cover has been accepted since the introduction of compulsory vaccination. And the health service is, in part, a continuation and extension of that principle. In part it was intended to provide — by redistribution — an essential service which the poor had been unable to afford. But the intention was not to offer them choices which they had previously been denied. Medicine was free at the point of use so that patients should take it, not take or leave it. The subsidy was intended to influence, perhaps even determine, conduct.

The government was deciding the nature of the good, and healthy, life. And in this particular, the government was quite right. In other areas, government subsidy is not so much concerned with setting a pattern of national conduct as providing individuals on low income with the chance to enjoy services and opportunities which more prosperous citizens are able to finance out of their own resources. The subsidised bus fares of the metropolitan counties were meant to encourage travel by public transport and thereby reduce road congestion. Pensioners' bus passes are intended to help pensioners with their travel costs. General subsidies are not intended to supplement income so much as to change behaviour. Specific subsidies are meant to increase purchasing power. But they may do it in a way which, given a free choice, would not be the first priority of the recipient. Thus pensioners may choose to travel (free) to the park when, if they were given the cost of their bus fare, they would choose to buy a newspaper and read it at home. Of course, the cost of buying the Guardian may be, in real terms, higher than allowing the occupation of a seat which would otherwise be empty. But the principle is clearly demonstrated. Until there is a far greater equality of income, personal subsides are essential. But one crucial advantage of moving towards a more equal income level is the opportunity which it provides to allow more citizens to make their own choices.

For those choices to be effective, the men and women who make them have to be provided with a maximum amount of information about the alternatives from which they may choose. That, of course, includes information about government — not simply accounts of what the government has done, offered for retrospective examination and possible criticism, but descriptions of the current options open to government and explanations of why the chosen path was followed. Britain remains the most secretive society in Western Europe. Indeed, Professor Ralf Dahrendorf suggested in his Reith Lectures that it was by preserving the monopoly on information that the British establishment maintained its authority. That authority will not be eroded by House of Commons select committees which examine departmental ministers and senior civil servants but do not possess the power to push and probe, which is the hallmark of the Congressional Committees which they so unsuccessfully attempt to imitate. The select committee system is simply a recent example of the establishment allowing the system to bend a little in order that it should not break. Faced with a specific decision to reveal or not to reveal, it is the instinct of British government, and the reflex response of British civil servants, to keep the information within a magic circle. That passionate prejudice will be overcome only be the creation of a legislative obligation to make everything public — only compelling reasons of uncontestable national interest justify an exemption to the statutory rule. British history is littered with examples, from the invasion of Suez to the attempted sale of British Leyland, of policy which the government endeavoured to pursue in private because they knew that its decision would not command public support. Such conduct has little to do with democracy and is only obliquely related to the governance of truly free people.

But socialists believe that the people must be protected against private as well as public tyranny, and the power that comes from knowledge must be given to consumers in their inevitable battles against manufacturers and retailers and to workers in their long struggle for fair wages, decent conditions and proper representation. It is preposterous that a car manufacturer can sell a customer £10,000 worth of complicated equipment without being explicit about the durability of its parts and the opportunities, which the design engineers ignored, to increase the working life of expensive components. It is unreasonable to expect trades unions to strike reasonable bargains unless they possess the knowledge on which reason can be based. And if . . . socialists should aim to make the economy more efficient (as well as make society more equal and more free) by extending workers' management rights over the companies which employ them, it is essential that the new 'owners' and 'managers' be supplied with the information which enables them to discharge their new responsibilities with judgment based on knowledge. To make Britain a truly free and equal society, we have to break down the barriers of secrecy which divide society into complicated hierarchies of ignorance and knowledge.

The wider dissemination of information is part of the freedom and equality argument which it is easiest to advance. Though there are, no doubt, some members of the new libertarian right who believe that the knowledge that their product was 'unsafe at any speed' was the exclusive possession of American motor-car manufacturers and could not be removed from their ownership without an infraction of natural rights. And it is comparatively easy to explain the case for extending material equality by redistribution, even in the language of the new liberals. A high level of taxation levied on the capital and income of the rich clearly is an infraction of their rights to spend their money as they choose. But if it sustains a level of child benefit which liberates inner-city children from sickness and deprivation, the totality of freedom has clearly been increased. For those children — healthier, better educated and more self-confident — are clearly enabled to enjoy theoretical rights which were previously beyond their practical attainment.

'Taxing people is wrong,' said S.E. Finer, the Gladstone Professor of Government in the University of Oxford. But he did not go on to explain whether or not in his view it was equally immoral to deny people the basic necessities of a decent house, an adequate school, the prospects of permanent employment — all aspects of the civilised society which taxes provide. Every increase in public expenditure is, according to the new liberal definition, a denial of freedom to the subscribing taxpayer. But what it provides for the recipient of government expenditure is very often a greater freedom than that denied by the taxation. There are, however, more difficult questions to be answered about more complicated issues. They involve the organisation of society and the socialist belief that inevitable natural differences should not be extended by the structure of the state into gross inequalities. It is easy to say that such a situation is avoided by a combination of progressive taxation and high levels of welfare, education and social security provision. That is certainly the beginning of the process, for it allows the concentration of compensating resources on the areas of greatest need. The best (and most easily accessible) pre-school provision should be in the areas where the children of nursery-school age live in circumstances which reduce their educational prospects. At present, quite the opposite is likely to happen, and medical treatment is more easily available to the congenitally healthy middle classes than to the sickness prone children of first-generation immigrants. The case for helping them can be advanced in terms of pure compassion — adding the socialists' ideological commitment to equality (or not) according to circumstances and according to taste.

The argument for changing the structure of society so as to make it work, in favour rather than against its less privileged members, is more difficult to popularise. That is, in very large part, because the state would have to set the new rules and the state is neither popular nor trusted. For many people it is difficult to imagine the state working for individuals rather than against individualism. There is in the public mind an instinctive suspicion that the state must be an instrument of authority rather than of liberation. It is the agency of regulation, and regulations are thought to be, by definition, the negation of rights. Some regulation — determined, monitored and enforced by democratic will — is essential to the protection of individual rights. Indeed, it is necessary for a well ordered society. It is Margaret Thatcher who, in advocating extensions of police power, says that she is protecting the right not to be burgled, the freedom not be to assaulted and the liberty to avoid sexual abuse. Even the neo liberals of the far right believe in the state's duty to protect itself from external aggression and internal disorder. That requires coercive organisation. Milton Friedman did not, to my knowledge, demonstrate against conscription during the war in Vietnam; nor does he audibly complain against the constant increase in his tax bill which results from the escalating arms budget. Nor do many new liberals feel an irresistible liberal urge to oppose extensions of those authoritarian ordinances which preserve the privileges of the prosperous and the advantages of the financially secure. The new right does not oppose zoning regulations which prevent desirable residences from being overlooked. It only opposes extensions of public-sector housing which protect the poor from being overcrowded. We all believe in the power of the state when the state acts to protect our interests. There is no difference in principle between the state levying extra taxes and imposing new laws in order to defeat the menace of invasion and the state behaving in exactly the same way in order to combat the threat of poverty, sickness and civil commotion. We may argue that in 1940 invasion was more of a real and tangible prospect than was social disintegration in 1979; and we may go on to insist that the state could defeat Nazi Germany but cannot beat poverty. But, in both cases, the argument is about something other than the *propriety* of state action. In the first argument the reservation concerned *necessity*. In the second, the doubts related to the likelihood of success. But in both cases the same underlying principle applies. If the crisis is sufficiently desperate, and if collective action will solve it, then we are neither so nihilistic nor so self-sacrificial as to oppose the power of the state being employed. To embrace state action to solve the security crisis of 1940 but to reject it as a solution to the potential poverty crisis of 1945 is merely to put our crises in order of personal preference.

Few people are opposed to the state power which achieves their chosen aims and when (for the purpose of our present examination a more important qualification) its exercise seems likely to achieve the stated object rather than becoming defused into a miasma of pointless bureaucratic regulation. To the followers of Friedman and Hayek who say, in effect, that the state must be employed rigidly to hold the ring within which the roughest and best-trained boxers thrash their opponents, there is little to be said except that it is possible to construct a nobler description of the state's duties. A more difficult argument to answer comes from the well-intentioned and compassionate who claim that whilst the state may initially be employed for purposes which are desirable in themselves and achieved by actions which are within the states' competence, the process, so honourably begun, always ends with bureaucratic interference in matters best left to the individual. From that has developed the notion that any development of state power is, by its nature, certain to limit the sum of individual freedom. It is as if there is a total amount of power within any community and when the state extends its authority the power available to individuals is automatically diminishes. But power is not finite; it is capable of extension. The rule of the state ought to include the taking of those powers which enable it to increase the power of the individuals within it. The state can perform that role. The cynics who insist that it may intend to make men and women free, but by interference only further enslaves them, are wrong. The error has been encouraged by the mistakes and misconceptions of individual politicians both national and local.

It is no good for socialists simply to argue that next time round they can be trusted, that given another chance they will always use the apparatus of the state to enhance freedom and never to limit it: more persuasive proof is needed of such good intentions. The importance of making our intention clear, though bearing witness will not, in itself, be enough, should not be underrated. It is not surprising that British socialists are thought to undervalue liberty; they do not talk about it sufficiently to give a credible impression of concern. But more tangible proof is also needed; sureties have to be given. One is the increasing liberalisation of socialism's own institutions, the Labour Party and the trades unions. But something more certain than that will be needed too. The best and surest way of demonstrating that the state will not exploit the people is to pass the state's power into the people's hands. Socialists — suffering from the paternalistic legacy of Burke's doctrine on representative government — are inclined to argue that if they do what the people want, they may be forced into doing the wrong things. It therefore follows that extending the opportunities for direct democracy will lead to all manner of legislative and administrative tragedies.

Hayek judged the people better. He said that democracy led inevitably to equality — since it benefited the masses against the classes and the masses have most votes. That judgment was confirmed by the British experience of educational reorganisation — once the truth about the selective system was revealed. It is certainly endorsed by the desire to defend the health service and reduce unemployment — if necessary at the cost of postponing tax cuts. That does not mean that every vote in every forum will always and invariably be a choice of the equality and freedom alternative. The likelihood is that the smaller the unit of choice, the more likely are the participants to vote for their own rather than the general interest; and there will be some areas in which it is necessary to take special precautions to protect minorities against the tyranny that majorities would impose. If — as we should — we give municipal tenants the power over the management of their estates, it will be necessary to retain allocation policy within the responsibility of a central authority — or to lay down national guidelines which prohibit by law discrimination against ethnic minorities, religious or racial groups. Similar precautions will have to be taken in areas where elected local authorities are now free to exploit sections of their communities in the interest of more powerful groups. It is, for example, intolerable that the distribution of pre-school places should be determined by the activities of pressure groups which — being largely made up of middle-class activists — argue most strongly for extra facilities in their own middle-class areas. The imposition by national government of minimum standards of provision or an obligation to operate policies which do not discriminate against women or minority groups does not, in itself, prohibit the extension of democratic control. Democratic socialists do not pretend that the state will or should wither away, but they do believe that it should be kept in its proper place. Opposition to the intrusive state does not require the withdrawal of the state from these functions which are necessary for it to perform in the interests of greater equality and freedom. We could not allow tenant management committees to prohibit the allocation of houses within their areas to black or Asian families or to set up the segregated ghettos for designated problem families which have been demanded on some corporation estates. But that does not mean that the tenants' committees cannot take responsibility for the organisation of repairs or the specification of management rules governing the use of open spaces, the care and maintenance of communal property and the designation of traffic-free roads and parking areas. If national and local government simply retained the powers which were necessary for the economies of scale to be enjoyed and the objects of greater equality and freedom to be pursued, the corporation tenant would enjoy far greater freedom and responsibility than he does today.

The same rule applies to the government and management of schools. If 'parent power' — currently espoused by the social democrats — is a concept which has any real meaning, it is a notion which needs careful examination by both the real libertarian and genuine egalitarian. For, whilst in one of its manifestations it can diffuse and devolve power towards the recipients and away from the providers of education, in other forms it can become no more than a vehicle for middle-class hegemony over secondary schools. 'Parent power' is, by its nature, bound to favour the articulate, self-confident, success-orientated middle class. If those talents and energies are harnessed to improve the education system in part or in whole the result is obviously to be welcomed. But what appears to be an extension of choice can easily become a system by which the strongest groups are able to acquire a disproportionate share of available resources. The 'voucher scheme' (designated unworkable rather than undesirable by Sir Keith Joseph in 1985) illustrates the problem exactly; though, since vouchers are 'parent power' at its most dangerous extreme, it naturally over-emphasises the dangers inherent in less divisive schemes.

Supposing that in a segment of a great city parents were issued with pieces of paper which acted as passports to places in the school of their choice, the result can be easily described. A league table of schools would be created. The middle classes would be the first to know which the 'good schools' were and would become the most determined campaigners in the battle to obtain places within them. The 'good schools' attracting the most highly motivated pupils and the most qualified teachers — would improve. The 'worst schools' would deteriorate, suffer public excoriation and become populated only by pupils who cannot find places in superior establishments. If, in addition to taking complete control over allocation policy, parents were able to decide the curriculum and distribute resources within the education region, the distinctions and divisions would be emphasised. The 'sink schools' would be regarded as unworthy of investment. The school which topped the table would be rewarded by special allowances and posts of special responsibility — a situation not fundamentally different from the way in which funds were allocated between the old grammar schools and the secondary moderns which were said to enjoy 'parity of esteem'. What began as an attempt to increase the power of consumers over producers — always a desirable object for those who believe in equality and freedom — ends as the concentration of power in the hands of one small powerful group. But opposition to schemes which have the appearance of extending choice whilst, in reality, only entrenching privilege should not prejudice education administrators against extensions of parents' rights and parental choice in areas where one group of parents cannot, by their superior negotiating power, prejudice the interests of another. Parents should dominate governing bodies. The representatives elected in those circumstances are more likely to be the upwardly mobile that the socially depressed. But in the management of a single school their energy and self-interest will be an indispensable engine of improvement for the whole institution. Parents, governors or not, must be given real and continuous access to teachers and the right to comment on, if not determine, the curriculum. Their close and continuous involvement may be both an inconvenience and embarrassment to the staff of the schools where the governance is changed, but extensions of democracy invariably have that effect on the centres of power which they assault.

The duty of national and local government to pass on to its voters many of the powers which once were kept within Parliament and town halls is only half of the obligation to greater freedom. The state must play a positive role in organising equality: in preventing the abrogation of rights to a single select group, in prohibiting an unreasonable distribution of resources and in encouraging the greater liberty that such a process provides. The obvious examples are the most contentious. That is why they have those characteristics. The passion aroused by discussing them is increased by the inevitable resentment generated by the intrusion of politics into such intimate family matters as health and education. It is worth repeating that it is both wrong and unattractive to moralise about the iniquity of mothers going out to work in order to pay for their sons' education or fathers who abandon smoking and drinking in order to provide their daughters with private medical care. There is no unitary morality which insists that what is right for the community as a whole must be right for every individual family within it. To excoriate the family that pays for private health or education is an error of logic comparable only with the most common justification for allowing the continued existence of the private sector. When challenged with all the sophistries about reducing pressure on public resources and setting higher standards for the state services to follow, the apologists for independent schools and pay beds always take refuge in the ultimate absurdity. Why, they ask, do we object to individuals spending their own hard-earned money on medicine and education when we take no exception to them squandering their pay on continental holidays, exotic consumer goods and flashy clothes? The answer is, of course, that such tawdry demonstrations of material success do not harm the rest of the community to any significant (or irredeemable) extent. They may proclaim a difference in wealth and remuneration; but they do not entrench and accentuate by dividing education and medicine between the private haves and the public have-nots. Nor do the fripperies of conspicuous consumption produce the damaging result which is undoubtedly the consequence of the existence of private education and private medicine. The socialist complaint about their existence does not concern personal morality of those who take advantage of them. It concerns the effect on the public at large.

The existence of private sectors in both health and education has four indisputable effects.

1. Private sectors are in themselves a declaration of the divisions in society and a manifestation of the social acceptability of those decisions. They are an endorsement of the idea that even in the provision of life's basic services, a superior level of provision is available for those who can afford its expense. The demonstration that society allows such discrepancies between the quality of help which it makes available to different classes of citizens encourages the belief that differences between the classes are natural and different levels of life chances are inevitable and right.

2. They provide a conduit through which the favoured minority can keep in constant touch with opportunities to increase their good fortune. Private medical schemes, having treated a specific condition, offer a general level of health assessment and concern which is not possible on the public service. The private sector of education offers opportunities for employment which are only obliquely related to merit and which are not available on similar terms to products of the state system. It is the antithesis of the double detriment which operates against the poor by preventing them from buying cheaply in bulk or obtaining cheap credit. It is a double privilege which perpetuates itself and grows upon itself.

3. They absorb a disproportionate share of scarce resources which, if they were spread more evenly, could distribute health care and education according to need and merit rather than against the criteria of the greatest ability to pay.

4. They isolate the influential from the failings and inadequacies of the public system and therefore deny that system the benefits which it would enjoy were its interests to be espoused by those who control public spending and investment. The public health and education services would undoubtedly improve if children of senior civil servants attended state schools and the wives of stockbrokers and newspaper editors were forced to wait for medical care in overcrowded and dilapidated outpatients' departments.

By any reasonable analysis, the existence of a private system in both education and medicine does more than offer the recipients of private provision a superior service. It depresses the service provided in the public sector. The generality of men and women are not simply relatively disadvantaged. There is an absolute reduction in the standard of provision which they would receive from a unified system. There is no echelon or trickle-down effect. The level of provision generally available (and the chance, in reality, to choose better education and health care) would, for a majority of men and women, be improved. The abolition of private medicine and private education would, by any sensible analysis, increase the *sum of liberties*. It would reduce the freedom of prospective Old Etonians; but for those children who, in truth, have not even a distant prospect of Eton College, new horizons would be created as their educational opportunities improved. To shrink from the assault on private medicine and private education is either to lack courage or to neglect a real chance to extend the totality of freedom.

To neglect that chance is to debilitate society as well as to penalise a majority of men and women within it. For the alienation that comes from class differences has done chronic damage to the material as well as the moral prospects of Great Britain. In Britain, wrote Matthew Arnold, 'inequality is a religion'. It is a religion which must bear much of the responsibility for a century of decline. 'On one side', Arnold explained, 'inequality harms by pampering; on the other by vulgarising and depression. A system founded on it is against nature, and, in the long run, breaks down'. It was for that reason that he urged the readers of *Culture and Anarchy* to 'choose equality and flee greed'. We should do the same. For to choose equality is to choose freedom as well.

Giles Radice — Labour's Path to Power (1989)

Without the 'new' revisionists of Giles Radice's generation, 'New' Labour would not exist today. By articulating the argument that democratic socialists should accept the competitive market economy on the grounds of principle, not pragmatism, Radice helped to prepare the ground for Labour's ideological transformation in the 1990s. His was a passionate call for 'second-stage' revisionism.

This amounted, in effect, to the completion of the original revisionist project instigated by Hugh Dal-

ton and Evan Durbin in the 1930s, though it is important to be clear about how far this re-thinking both upheld and diverged from central tenets of that original analysis. This shift also accompanied the policy and organisational changes that Neil Kinnock instituted during his leadership, especially from 1987 to 1992.

Radice was born in London in October 1936. He was educated at Winchester, and Magdalen College, Oxford, and began his career as Head of Research at the General and Municipal Workers Union (GMWU). He successively fought the Chester-le-Street by-election in 1973.

In 1978, Radice was appointed as Parliamentary Private Secretary to Shirley Williams at the Department for Education. However, Labour's defeat at the 1979 General Election, and the rapid swing to the left, brought an abrupt end to his ministerial ambitions. In 1981, many of Radice's natural allies including Shirley Williams and Roy Jenkins split to form the Social Democratic Party (SDP). Yet he chose to stay and fight, resolving to build up the Solidarity Group of MPs, and determined to halt the Party's drift to the left.

In 1981, Radice was appointed opposition spokesman for Foreign Affairs, for Employment (1982–3), and as chief spokesman on Education in the Shadow Cabinet (1983–7). In fact, he was one of the most influential post-war Labour politicians never to hold office, as much of his career coincided with the party's self-imposed exile in the 1980s and early 1990s.

Radice's published works include What Needs to Change *(1996), and many books and articles on the case for British integration into the European Union. His Fabian pamphlet* Southern Discomfort *was a landmark in the rise of 'New' Labour. He argued: 'the language we use as politicians is totally alien to most of the voters, particularly those we want to attract in the South. If you talk about opportunity for all, that is the language people can understand. If you talk about equality, they think it is about levelling down and taking from them and it becomes a negative idea.'[4] Tony Blair once described him as 'a Blairite before Blair'.*

In Labour's Path to Power, *Radice provided essential theoretical justification for Labour's eventual acknowledgement of the merits of a market economy – unprecedented in the historical development of Labour policy. Labour had to, 'demonstrate its credentials as a fully fledged revisionist party, capable of learning from the past, analysing the changing trends'. It ought, 'to have the honesty to come to terms with the market and admit that in many areas the competitive model, providing it is adequately regulated, works well in the allocation of goods and services'.*

---

[4]   Radice & Pollard (1993).

Radice was convinced that Labour's reticence on this central issue helped to instil a widespread fear among the public that its goal was the construction of a sclerotic command economy founded on state ownership and control. The historic re-drafting of Clause IV of the Party constitution in 1995 removed this ambiguity once and for all, and in an important sense, did complete the work of revisionist social democracy.

However, by apparently abandoning its traditional egalitarian aspirations founded on redistributive taxation and high levels of public expenditure, critics have argued that Labour was rejecting this tradition altogether. The lively debate continues as to whether 'New' Labour is actually 'neo', or alternatively 'post' revisionist — though the view that the party has betrayed its heritage by discarding any commitment to greater equality would be forcefully refuted by many social democrats, including Radice.[5]

Selected Text[6]

The Case for Revisionism

After three successive defeats, the Labour party needs a change. The main argument of this book is that, if Labour is to have a chance of mounting a serious challenge to Conservative political supremacy, it will have to become a fully fledged revisionist party, not so much in the classic sense of breaking with a Marxist past, but in the wider sense of being prepared to reassess its values, strategies and policies in the light of rapid economic and social change. The Labour party has always been a variegated, ideologically confused party. Though in the past it has been able to get away without defining its position, the party is now paying a heavy price for its pragmatism. Unless it is prepared, like its sister Continental parties, to adapt in a principled way to changing circumstances, it is in danger of becoming a permanent minority party. If Labour is to gain power over the next decade, it has to set out an alternative political agenda which will be relevant to the needs of the 1990s and around which a new progressive majority can rally.

---

[5]   This debate is explored extensively in my introduction to this volume.

[6]   Radice, G., *Labour's Path to Power: The New Revisionism*, London: Macmillan, 1989. [Footnotes in this section are editorial.]

The Revisionist Heritage

Revisionism has a rich intellectual heritage within the European Socialist movement. The earliest revisionist was Eduard Bernstein, the German Social Democrat. In March 1899, he wrote his major book *Evolutionary Socialism*, which set out for the first time a powerful revisionist critique of Marxism. In this work, which had a profound impact not only on the German Social Democrats, but on other European Socialist parties, Bernstein decisively refuted the Marxist theory that capitalism was about to collapse.

He pointed out that, contrary to Marx's predictions, the working class were becoming better off, the numbers of capitalists were growing and there was no evidence of any general economic breakdown. Bernstein's explanation for the failure of Marxist predictions to materialize was that Marx had underestimated the economic and social consequences of a free political system upon its mode of production: 'In all advanced countries we see the privileges of the capitalist bourgeoisie yielding step by step to democratic organisations ... Factory legislation, the democratisation of local government ... the free trade unions and systems of cooperative trading from legal restrictions, the consideration of standard conditions or labour in the work undertaken by public authorities — all these characterise this phase of evolution'.

Bernstein also firmly rejected the Marxist concepts of revolution and 'the dictatorship of the proletariat'. 'Is there any sense', Bernstein asked, 'in holding to the phrase "dictatorship of the proletariat" at a time in which Social Democracy has in practice put itself on the basis of parliamentarianism, equitable popular representation and popular legislation, all of which contradict dictatorship?' He showed that increasingly Socialist and working class parties were winning votes at national elections and seats in national parliaments, that at local government level they were beginning to run things and that trade unions were making significant industrial gains. Democracy, he concluded, was both essential to the development of Socialism and a key Socialist objective.

Finally, Bernstein criticized the unscientific nature of Marxism. He accused Marx of ignoring economic and social improvements because they refuted his theories. The problem with *Das Kapital*, argued Bernstein, was that it aimed at being a scientific inquiry and also at proving a theory laid down before its drafting: 'It thus appears that this great scientific spirit was, in the end, a slave to a doctrine'. It was also unscientific to believe that Socialism could have a 'final goal'. To Bernstein, Socialism was rather an ethical framework and a way of changing things: 'To me that which is generally called the ultimate aim of Socialism is nothing; but the movement is everything'. The priority for Socialists in the here and now was to extend political and social rights by democratic means.

Anthony Crosland saw himself as Bernstein's successor. He wrote: 'I am revising Marxism and will emerge as the modern Bernstein'.[7] His most important book, *The Future of Socialism*, published in 1956, certainly shaped the thinking of a whole generation of British Socialists. It was ambitious in conception, wide-ranging in scope, and written with wit, lucidity and authority. Even today the brilliance and sharpness of Crosland's mind stand out clearly from its pages.

Crosland's message was that the harsh world of the 1930s had been transformed by the war and the post-war Labour government. The Marxist theory of capitalist collapse, so firmly believed by Socialist intellectuals in the 1930s, had clearly been disproved. On the contrary, output and living standards were rising steadily. At the same time, the commanding position of the business class had been reduced by the increased powers of government and improved bargaining strength of labour. Managers, not owners, now ran industry. The combination of rising living standards, redistributive taxation and welfare benefits and services had substantially reduced primary poverty. Crosland argued that, in the new situation, ownership of the means of production was largely irrelevant: 'I conclude', he wrote, 'that the definition of capitalism in terms of ownership . . . has wholly lost its significance and interest now that ownership is no longer the clue to the total picture of social relationships: and that it would be more significant to define societies in terms of equality, or class relationships, or their political systems'.

One of the key points about *The Future of Socialism* was the clear distinction it drew between ends and means. 'Ends' were defined as the basic values or aspirations and 'means' as describing the institutional or policy changes required to promote these values in practice. It was incorrect to try and define Socialism in terms of a policy like nationalization which, as Crosland pointed out, had been applied for very different purposes in Nazi Germany and the Soviet Union. The revisionist task was to subject means to searching scrutiny in the

---

[7]   Crosland wrote to his friend Philip Williams, at the age of twenty-five.

light of changing conditions. As he pointed out, 'the means most suitable in one generation may be wholly irrelevant in the next'.

Modern socialism, Crosland concluded, was about improving welfare and promoting social equality: 'The Socialist seeks a distribution of rewards, status, and privileges egalitarian enough to minimise social resentment, to secure justice between individuals and to equalise opportunities; and he seeks to weaken the existing deep-seated class stratification with its concomitant feelings of envy and inferiority, and its barriers to uninhibited mingling between the classes'. Significantly Crosland gave first priority to educational reform, including introducing comprehensive secondary education reform and opening up entry to private schools: 'If Socialism is taken to mean a "classless society", this is the front on which the main attack should now be mounted'.[8]

Nearly twenty years after the publication of *The Future of Socialism* and two years before his death, Crosland restated the revisionist position: 'Socialism, in our view, was basically about equality. By equality, we meant more than a meritocratic society of equal opportunities ... we adopted the "strong" definition of equality ... We also meant more than a simple ... redistribution of income. We wanted a wider social equality embracing also the distribution of property, the educational system, social class relationships, power and privilege in industry — indeed all that was enshrined in the age-old Socialist dream of a more "classless society"'.

It is relatively easy to criticize these two great revisionist thinkers. Both Bernstein and Crosland were over-optimistic about economic improvements. In one celebrated passage, Crosland proclaimed, 'I no longer regard questions of growth and efficiency as being, on a long view, of primary importance to socialism'. Both were inclined to be over-complacent about Conservative opposition to Socialist ideas and policies. Bernstein's 'capitalist bourgeoisie yielding step by step' was matched by Crosland ruling out 'a wholesale counter-revolution' by the Conservatives. Neither had much to say about international context in which Democratic Socialists had to work. Though Bernstein eventually broke with the SPD over their support for the German war effort, he had not foreseen the coming of the 1914–18 war and on 4 August 1914 voted for war credits. Crosland became Foreign Secretary but he used frequently to say that he was not interested in foreign affairs and he certainly did not write any-

[8]   See Crosland (1956 and 1974).

thing of note about them. Specific policies or methods with which Bernstein and Crosland were associated or admired have either failed to live up to their hopes or have come under attack. Thus Bernstein passionately believed in cooperatives and Crosland was a somewhat uncritical advocate of public expenditure (though he latterly added qualifications).

But the shortcomings and inadequacies of the Bernstein and Crosland models do not undermine the revisionist case. Far from it. Both actively encouraged new thinking, new strategies and new policies. Indeed, the whole point of revisionism is that it cannot be a final position. By definition, it is provisional, always open to reappraisal.

The revisionist approach is made up of a number of crucial processes. First, analysing what is actually happening as opposed to what a particular dogma says ought to happen or what one would like to happen; secondly, distinguishing clearly between values and methods; thirdly, subjecting values and methods to scrutiny — and, if necessary, being prepared to modify these in the light of changing conditions; fourthly, supporting open and pluralistic procedures, by which ideas and policies are not only tested against criticism but changed in the light of that criticism. In short, revisionism is a radical cast of mind, a critical way of evaluating human affairs and politics, in order to develop strategies and policies which take account of change.

Continental Revisionism

All the most successful Continental Socialist and Social Democrat parties are revisionist — both in the narrower technical sense of having broken with Marxism and in the broader sense of the being prepared to rethink, re-examine and reassess their direction and policies.

The classical revisionist statement is the 1959 Bad Godesberg programme of the German Social Democratic Party (SPD). In this programme, the SPD not only sent a signal to the West German electorate that it had broken with its Marxist past but also created a modern Socialist identity which was in tune with the post-war world.

The SPD, which had expected to dominate the politics of post-war Western Germany, had been beaten by the Christian Democrats (CDU) in three successive federal elections — in 1949, 1953 and 1957. It was against the background of electoral defeat that the SPD's leading politicians and thinkers worked out a new political programme which was adopted by an overwhelming majority at a special party conference at Bad Godesberg.

A key feature of the socialism of Bad Godesberg was its commitment to values: 'Freedom, justice and solidarity which are everyone's obligations towards his neighbour and spring from our common humanity are the fundamental values of Socialism'. The programme also underlined support for democracy and opposition to dictatorship, whether of right or left: 'Socialism can be realized only through democracy and democracy can only be fulfilled through Socialism'. Willi Eichler, the main author of the programme, called it, 'an ethical revolution'.[9]

Echoing Crosland in *The Future of Socialism*, Bad Godesberg gave a high priority to social welfare and stressed the responsibility of the state in social affairs: 'Established fundamental rights do not only protect the freedom of the individual in relation to the state; they should also be regarded as social rights which constitute the basis of the state. The social function of the state is to provide social security for its citizens to enable everyone to be responsible for shaping his own life freely'. It outlined an ambitious plan of social reforms, including extensions of social security and health protection, expansion of the housing programmes, reduction in working hours, more codetermination, and opening up education to provide better life chances and greater redistribution of income and wealth.

But the crucial difference between the Bad Godesberg programme and previous party programmes was the abandonment of comprehensive public ownership as an objective and the acceptance of private ownership and the market over large parts of the economy. 'Free choice of consumer goods and services, free choice of working place, freedom for employers to exercise their initiative as well as free competition are essential conditions of a Social Democratic economic policy . . . Private ownership of the means of production can claim protection by society as long as it does not hinder the establishment of social justice'. But the acceptance of the market was not unconditional. There was a key role for Keynesian policies: 'The state cannot shirk its responsibility for the course the economy takes. It is responsible for securing a forward-looking policy with regard to business cycles and should restrict itself to influencing the economy

---

[9]   See Sassoon (1996) for an excellent account of revisionist social democracy in Germany.

mainly by indirect means'. And the state had to intervene to prevent abuse of economic power: 'The most important means to this end are investment control and control over the forces dominating the market'. It added that where, 'sound economic power relations cannot be guaranteed by other means, public ownership is appropriate and necessary'. The formula which best sums up the Bad Godesberg approach is, 'as much competition as possible — as much planning as necessary'.

In a discussion of the significance of Bad Godesberg, a leading British journalist has acutely observed:

> If socialism is prominently about the socialisation of production, the Bad Godesberg Programme kills it off. If socialism, on the other hand, is concerned with something different — the emancipation of men and women so that all have an equal right to shape their society and to control their own lives — then Bad Godesberg can be presented as a fresh vision of socialism.

For the SPD, Bad Godesberg did not lead immediately to electoral success. It was not until 1966 that it joined the 'Grand Coalition' with the CDU and not until 1969 that it was able to form an SPD-led coalition, with Willy Brandt as Federal Chancellor. But the impetus to new thinking and new policies by Bad Godesberg enabled the SPD to win four successive elections and to dominate West German politics in the 1970s.

In the 1980s, after two successive election defeats, the SPD is once again taking stock. A draft party programme (the Ilsee draft) was drawn up in 1986 and a definitive programme will be discussed and adopted in Lübeck in 1989.[10] As a revisionist party, the SPD is very much aware that it needs to come to terms with recent changes in West German society and to adapt its direction and policies, especially on the environment and the economy, to the new world of the 1990s.

Almost all the major European Socialist parties have brought out a new statement of aims within the last fifteen years. After their 1979 election setback the Spanish Socialists (PSOE) had an intense debate about the future direction of the party. At an extraordinary party congress in September, Felipe Gonzalez, who had resigned as leader following the defeat of his amendment at the May party congress, persuaded his party to drop Marxism from its statement of aims. The way was thus open for Spanish socialists to present themselves as a

---

[10]   In fact, the programme was not formally adopted by the SPD in 1989.

democratic reformist party and to build up an electoral majority by attracting new support beyond PSOE's traditional base. PSOE won both the 1982 and 1986 elections with large majorities, and is now the predominant party in Spain.

In 1980, the French Socialists (PS) brought out the Projet Socialiste on which Francois Mitterrand based his presidential manifesto, the 110 propositions, in his successful bid for the Presidency in 1981. The Mitterrand approach was a blend of Keynesian expansion, French-style public ownership and industrial intervention, and policies of redistributive social spending characteristic of Scandinavian Social democracy but less well known in France.[11]

A critic could argue, with some justice, that the 1981 Mitterrand programme, with its emphasis on 'Keynesianism in one country' and its extensive social programmes, was inappropriate to the recessionary world of the early 1980s. But what has been remarkable is the extent to which the French Socialists have learnt from their mistakes. The *Propositions pour la France*, put forward by the Socialists at the 1988 Presidential election (won once again by Francois Mitterrand), was a realistic document which gave priority to selective industrial intervention to boost research and training, without committing the party to further nationalisation or even renationalising industries privatised by the Chirac government. However, the Socialist minority government, under Michel Rocard, underlined the party's continuing commitment to social justice and solidarity by introducing an increased social minimum benefit and wealth tax and by its emphasis on democratising and expanding education.

Both the Austrian Socialists and the Swedish Social Democrats produced new statements in the 1970s. In 1978, the Austrian Socialist party (SPOE) firmly set out its commitment to Socialist values and to Keynesian policies to combat recession; its resolve was justified by the triumphant election victory of 1979 and its continuing strong position in Austrian politics during the 1980s. Even so, the Austrian Socialists, as the 1978 Party Congress showed, are once again reconsidering their direction in the fiercely competitive world of the late 1980s. The Swedish Social Democrat party document, which confirmed the party's support for full employment and the welfare state, was followed by the election defeat of 1976. But defeat led to fresh thinking and in 1982 Olof Palme, the Social Democrat leader, put forward the so-called 'third-way', a new economic strategy,

---

[11] See Sassoon (1996).

designed to stimulate production, investment and employment, which not only assisted the party to win the 1982 election but also restored economic growth. In the late 1980s, after two further election victories, the party is once again reassessing its policies, particularly on taxation.

The circumstances in which these revisionist statements were made were often different. Some were responses to electoral defeat; others were put forward on the threshold of power; yet others were produced by parties in power to reassert the relevance of their policies. But, whatever the circumstance in which they were conceived, all have certain features in common. Each analyses current economic and social trends and provides a coherent intellectual and ideological framework. Within that framework, each describes the most important means and methods and outlines a few key policy areas. Above all, each statement seeks to establish for its party a clear political identity in the light of changing conditions.

The Price of Pragmatism

Unlike most of our European sister parties, the British Labour party has never officially been a 'revisionist' party. This is partly because, in contrast to these other parties, Labour's origins owed little to Marx. Clause IV (iv) of the party's constitution and the first statement of aims *Labour and the New Social Order*, both drafted by Sidney Webb in 1918, ingeniously combined Fabian collectivism, Guild Socialist cooperation, trade union 'labourism' and progressive 'Social' liberalism into an attractive new synthesis which sustained the party for the next forty years. These key declarations committed Labour not only to 'common ownership', the establishment of a welfare state, and a fairer distribution of income and wealth, but also to parliamentary democracy. From the first, the British Labour party firmly rejected the revolutionary Marxism which was so attractive to other Socialist parties, particularly the German Social Democrats and the Austrian Socialists.

It is this difference which, to a considerable extent, explains why Labour did not follow the 'Bad Godesberg' route. When after the 1959 defeat, the then leader, Hugh Gaitskell, tried to persuade the Labour party to amend Clause IV in favour of a more selective approach to public ownership, he was defeated, though an anodyne declaration of principles was adopted at the 1960 conference. He was defeated partly because of faulty tactics and partly because he had underestimated the sentimental attachment of his trade union allies to the clause. But perhaps the most important reason for his defeat was that, despite its ambiguous and incomplete nature, Clause IV (iv) was not a revolutionary Marxist statement which simply had to be changed if Labour was to have any chance of victory in the future.

Labour's electoral successes in the 1960s seemed to justify the more pragmatic tactics of his successor, Harold Wilson, who preferred to change the Labour party by stealth. But Labour has paid a heavy price for the victory of pragmatism.

First, in contrast to most other European Socialist parties, it has never officially come to terms with private ownership, the mixed economy and the role of the market, though in practice, of course, it has for many years accepted their existence. The consequence of this confusion is that it has failed to develop a credible model of state intervention and has not benefited as much as it should have done from the overwhelming popular support for the welfare state. It has also been vulnerable to the attacks from the Conservatives and the claims of the fundamentalists that Socialism stands for state ownership.

Secondly, again in contrast to most of the continental Socialist parties, Labour has failed to reassess its direction in the light of changing conditions. After the Wilson attempt to make Labour the natural party of power in the 1960s came unstuck, Labour went through the 1970s on the defensive, even though it was in government for much of the time. The civil war of the early 1980s and the Social Democrat (SDP) breakaway led not to a far-reaching reappraisal but to an uneasy equilibrium which did not convince the electors.

As the 1980s draw to a close, it is more essential than ever that Labour becomes a fully fledged revisionist party, capable of learning from the past, analysing the changing trends, and carving out for itself a new political identity, which will help create a new majority.

The unpleasant facts have to be faced. The party has suffered three successive defeats: at both the 1983 and 1987 elections it finished far behind the Tories. What is more, the party's declining class base and its disturbing political weakness in the South leaves it in serious danger of becoming a permanent minority party, incapable of mounting a challenge to Conservative supremacy in the 1990s.

Fundamental long-term economic and social shifts are changing British society. The old world of heavy industry and mass production is shrinking rapidly and is being replaced by a far more varied pattern, based on distribution, financial services and computer and information technology industries. Manufacturing today accounts for less than a quarter of the labour force, compared with a third in 1971. In the same period, the proportion in the service sector has risen from a half to over two-thirds.

There have been corresponding shifts in occupation. Significantly, the majority of the employed are now in white-collar jobs. Prosperity, home and share ownership have all risen substantially. Britain in the 1990s will be a 'two thirds, one third' society, in which the vast majority of the population will have a stake in the land, while not only the poor but the manual working class will be in a minority.

Profound changes which also affect Britain are taking place in the world outside. The two superpowers are being driven by necessity towards mutual accommodation, with all that could mean for Europe. The balance of economic power is beginning to shift away from the Atlantic towards the Pacific basin. Within Europe, the drive towards a single European market and closer economic and monetary integration has major implications for national decision- making.

Labour has to come to terms with this rapidly changing world. The truth is that Labour's pragmatism, which is at one and the same time complacent, defensive and confused, is no longer enough. The party can no longer hope to muddle through. It has to have the intellectual honesty and courage to face up to change, to be clear about its objectives and to explain how it intends to achieve those objectives. Labour has to become a *revisionist* party, prepared to rethink, reassess and revise. Only a clear, unequivocal and up-to-date statement of what the party stands for will provide the intellectual basis for victory in the 1990s.

A Revisionist Party?

At the 1987 Brighton conference following its election defeat, the Labour party, for the first time since the early 1960s, began to look as though it might become a revisionist party. It committed itself in principle to a rigorous review of its main policies. If there were those who argued that more would be required than a policy review, it was good news that Labour was to re-examine its policies in order to make them relevant to the world of the 1990s.[12]

---

[12] Radice was writing prior to the publication of the Labour Party statement *Meet the Challenge, Make the Change* in 1989, and the completion of the policy review process instigated by Neil Kinnock.

In the period since the Brighton conference significant progress has certainly been made. For the first time since the adoption by the party of Clause IV (iv) in 1918, Labour has published a statement of 'Democratic Socialist Aims and Values'. Reports were produced by the seven review groups under the title 'Social Justice and Economic Efficiency'. Leading figures in the party have given their commitment to the process of review and reassessment. Neil Kinnock himself called on the party to shape and develop policies 'to match new times, new needs, new opportunities, new challenges' and, in a major speech at the 1988 Blackpool conference, courageously argued that Labour had to come to terms with the market economy.

But, as after the 1959 election, the process of revision has aroused some hostility in the party, a hostility expressed most vocally by the far left but not confined to it. The unsuccessful campaign for the leadership by Tony Benn and Eric Heffer in 1988 was specifically designed to exploit this hostility.

In part the discontent comes from the old confusion to which Crosland referred in *The Future of Socialism* between ends and means. To many Labour party activists, the review process amounted to a frontal attack on what they believed to be the central tenet of Socialism — the commitment to public ownership. Yet privately the same activists would freely admit that public ownership, at least in the old Morrisonian style, had not been uniformly successful. Long ago, Bernstein warned the SPD against the danger of 'cant' — using words as a substitute for thought . . .

. . . Despite the hesitation, hostility and conservatism of some sections of the party, it is essential that the leadership does not allow itself to be deflected from a fundamental reappraisal of Labour's direction and policies. For there is some way to go before the party can be satisfied that it is in a position to put forward a credible alternative agenda which will set the stage for the 1990s.

The overall message from the statement 'Democratic Socialist Aims and Values' and the policy review is still confused. The statement of aims' principled commitment to the importance of freedom as a value as well as the more grudging acceptance of the mixed economy is certainly a step forward. From the policy reviews, there is the recognition that market processes 'spur competition, stimulate innovation and widen consumer choice', that straightforward renationalisation of privatised companies will be inappropriate, and that Labour will have to adopt a more realistic policy towards

Europe. But there is as yet no decisive answer to the question 'What does Labour stand for?'

Over the next two or three years, the Labour party must decide on its overall direction if it is to mount a serious challenge for power in the 1990s. it will have to begin by recognizing that economic and social change has significant implications for the way in which Labour interprets its values, draws up its strategies and revises its policies.

The growing disparity between individual, groups and regions in Mrs Thatcher's Britain makes Labour's traditional commitment to social justice and fairness more than ever relevant. But the fact that, in contrast to the 1930s and 1940s, the disadvantaged groups are in a clear minority means that an appeal based on social justice alone is unlikely to be successful. Hence the need to emphasize Labour's commitment to the greater freedom and opportunity which prosperity undoubtedly brings, while stressing that there will be no lasting security for the majority unless they recognize their common obligation to the depressed minority. A balance of values will be required.

Drawing on an idea which, since R.H. Tawney, has always had an important role in socialist thought, Labour should champion the concept of citizen rights — in politics, in welfare, at work and in the market. Rights challenge the inequalities, disparities and division of a 'two thirds, one third' society. They help to humanize the process of change and civilize the workings of the market. At the same time, because they give all citizens (including those who may be more prosperous but cannot be certain of high quality education or good health provision or basic rights at work or in the market) an instrument of empowerment, they provide the basis for a programme which is likely to appeal not only to the impoverished minority but also to the aspiring majority.

Labour must also have the honesty to come to terms with the market and admit that, in many areas, the competitive model, provided it is adequately regulated, works well in the allocation of goods and services. Once the party has demonstrated clearly and unequivocally that it supports a properly regulated and effectively functioning market in large parts of the economy, it is in a far stronger intellectual and political position to point to those areas in which the market system performs so imperfectly that, in the interests of the community, there has to be selective collective intervention. The case for a basic 'floor' of rights will also become more powerful.

It will also be important for the Labour party to reassert its commitment to and support for democratic institutions. Even John Nott, a former Conservative Cabinet Minister, has warned that the Conservatives, under Mrs Thatcher, are revealing an increasingly authoritarian streak. So Labour must champion the cause of democratic reform — strengthening individual rights, providing new checks on the executive and reinvigorating parliamentary and local democracy.

There are two other issues, which, like those already outlined above, must also be tackled by the Labour party. The first is to ensure that the welfare state is efficiently managed and that services are run in the interests of consumers. The second is to develop an external policy which is based on a realistic assessment of British power and interest and which takes seriously our obligations as neighbour and partner.

If Labour is to get the full political benefit from its review of policy, it has to be certain its reappraisal has been rigorous and honest. The party cannot afford any 'no go' areas. That is why later sections of this book consider the merits and shortcomings of Keynesianism, the case for incomes policy and the strengths and weaknesses of the welfare state. There must be no 'sacred cows'. That is why I examine defence policy, trade union legislation and the relationship between the unions and the party itself. Policy options should not be ruled out because they are supported by people outside the Labour party or even by other political parties. It is for this reason that there is a discussion in this book of the case for a Bill of Rights, a written constitution, proportional representation and the integration of tax and benefits. The only valid test is whether or not policies are in line with basic values and will, at the same time, be relevant to the Britain of the 1990s.

For if Labour is to become electable in the 1990s it must be a revisionist party, capable of producing new ideas and strategies — and, above all, of setting a fresh political agenda which will help to create a progressive majority over the next decade.

Revisionism Ascendant? New Labour's Old Roots

Gordon Brown — Equality: Then and Now (1997)

Gordon Brown is among the most prominent 'New' Labour modernisers, vigorously supporting Neil Kinnock's policy changes and organisational reforms, and John Smith's stand on 'One Member, One Vote' in 1993. In a succession of speeches and articles written during the last twenty years, Brown has explored the main areas of ideological revision for the Party, and emerged as its leading contemporary revisionist thinker.

In contrast to previous generations, he was not constrained by political debts to different sections of the party, nor did he see his role as primarily one of compromise or unity. Instead, alongside Tony Blair, he believed that Labour needed further radical reform if it was to be elected, and felt it was the responsibility of the leadership to drive that process. The Party must exist not only to defend the gains of the past: it must forge a new future for itself and the country.

Gordon Brown was born in February 1951 in Kirkcaldy, Scotland. At the age of 16, he was admitted to Edinburgh University where he became rector (1972–5), and later completed his doctorate (1982).

A part-time lectureship and work as a television producer followed. But he was consumed by politics, securing election to the National Executive of the Scottish Labour Party in 1977, and contesting Edinburgh South in the 1979 General Election. In 1983, he was elected to represent Dunfermline East at the age of 32.

His rise through the ranks of the PLP in opposition was rapid. In 1985 he was appointed as an opposition Trade and Industry Spokesman, then Shadow Chief Secretary to the Treasury (1987–9), Shadow Trade and Industry Secretary (1989–92), and Shadow Chancellor (1992–7). He made his name in opposition by lacerating Nigel Lawson during a parliamentary debate in 1988. But his outstanding achievement was to redefine Labour's 'tax and spend' commitments prior to the 1997 election.

Brown has easily matched the post-war Labour Chancellors including Stafford Cripps and Roy Jenkins. His policies combine a traditional focus on social democratic redistribution, higher public expenditure and full employment, with encouragement for enterprise, and a role for the private sector in the provision of public services where it can do so more effectively than the state. Financial stability, and a growing economy could, through budget surpluses, meet redistributive objectives. Economic competence and social justice go hand in hand.

His publications include The Red Paper on Scotland *(ed. 1975 with Dr Henry Drucker),* The Politics of Nationalism and Devolution *(1980),* Scotland: The Real Divide *(ed. 1983),* Maxton *(1986), and* Where There Is Greed *(1989).*

In the essay, 'Equality: Then and now', Brown sets out the case for a modern socialist egalitarian commitment.

In place of the inadequacies of state socialism, Brown wishes to embrace the fundamental ideas of early ethical socialism — including its emphasis on the need for society to act together on behalf of the individual, and to apply such ideas to the conditions of modern British society. Far from abandoning its past, Labour has returned to its traditional values, territory that it should never have abandoned.

This recapturing of Labour's ethical socialism draws upon values derived from that heritage such as community and mutual responsibility, as well as more familiar social democratic ideals of social justice and equality of opportunity. It draws a connection too with post-war social democracy, arguing that the publication of The Future of Socialism, *'marked a decisive moment in the post-war Labour history'.*

It was right to define equality as the fundamental value that divides Labour from the Conservatives. But the key question was how to apply these egalitarian values to the world of the 1990s. Brown advocated the further extension of educational and employment opportunities necessary to vigorously promote equality of life chances. This renewal of the party was to transform the landscape of British politics, and offered hope to social democratic parties around the world.

Selected Text[1]

When I was asked to make this contribution on the legacy of Anthony Crosland, I felt both challenged and daunted. Daunted because no one could ever encapsulate his life, his thinking and his achievements — and his sheer humanity — better than Susan Crosland has herself in her remarkable biography. And challenged because Crosland's vision of equality cries out to be restored to its proper place alongside freedom and solidarity in the trinity of socialist values.

When *The Future of Socialism* was published in 1956, it marked a decisive moment in post-war Labour history. No other post-war contribution to Labour thinking has had such an impact and no one who has read it — and his later works — can fail to be impressed by Crosland's intellectual vigour and his clarity of thought or moved by his deep political commitment.

I want to argue that there are three essential elements to Crosland's rich and lasting legacy to Labour: First, he defined equality as the fundamental value that divides the Labour Party from the Conservative Party. You can agree or disagree with Tony Crosland on equality. You may take the view he goes too far or not far enough. You may think he gave too little emphasis to equality for women and that he over-emphasised social and economic equality at the expense of equality in political power. But since 1956, any serious discussion of the politics of equality must take as its starting point and have as its compass *The Future of Socialism*, his greatest work.

At root, Crosland believed — as I will suggest — in a society in which nobody is deprived of the chance of realising their potential. For him, it was the duty of government not just to attack entrenched privileges that held people back but to vigorously promote equality in life chances and his objective, a classless society, and to do so across the economy, politics and our culture. What he said is — I believe — more relevant than ever today and it is how we apply egalitarian values to the world of the late 1990s that I want to address my thoughts.

---

[1]   Brown, G. , 'Equality: Then and now', in D. Leonard, *Crosland and New Labour*, London: Macmillan, 1999. Revised and expanded version of platform speech, Memorial meeting (13 February 1997).

Crosland's second legacy is to make a socialist's central focus his or her essential values, not any particular method of achieving those values. Means may change from time to time, but essential objectives endure. Nationalisation — as he showed in 1956 — was, at best, a means. Equality was his principled objective.

Thirdly, and this is his inspiration for today, he set out to establish a socialist position that was both intellectually rigorous and practically credible for the world as it actually exists. The key to understanding Crosland's legacy for us today is that he was a political thinker who was prepared to grapple with all the day-to-day challenges of practical politics. And in more than 30 years of active politics he never ceased to argue his case or defend his decisions — even as a Cabinet minister — from socialist principle.

There have been left-of-centre politicians who have espoused socialism but fail to meet the test of credibility. There have been those who have presented themselves as credible by abandoning socialism. The real challenge of left-of-centre politics is to be socialist and at the same time credible, a challenge which Crosland met triumphantly, rejecting all sorts of gesture politics along the way. It is the challenge which we in the Labour Party, inspired by Anthony Crosland, fully understand and fully intend to meet.

I want to look at the way the world has changed since Crosland wrote and I want to suggest that far from marginalizing the issue of equality, these changes mean that the case for equality is even stronger. I will argue that what happened in Britain over the two decades of Conservative rule — the Tory exaltation of inequality — has made it all the more necessary to make the philosophical case for equality.

I want to translate, into the context of the 1990s, Crosland's idea of democratic equality — a concept that offers more than equality of opportunity, but something other than equality of outcome. And finally, I want to identify the policies that flow from this insight and in particular I will suggest that the only possible starting point today for those who are serious about equality — indeed the pre-condition for tackling inequality — is tackling unemployment.

The Changing Context for Equality

Today's world is, of course, quite different from the world of 1956 in which Crosland first formulated his policies for equality and therefore a new approach will be required, applying our socialist ethics to addressing its inequalities. In 1956 the UK economy was largely a closed economy subject to national controls — import controls, credit controls, demand management by the Treasury — effective within national boundaries. In 1956, under a Conservative government, exchange controls meant that an individual could take just £30 out of the country.

Now we operate in an open, global market in capital and credit where billions of pounds flow in and out of Britain each day. Against this, the old national levers of power which Crosland thought important have less and less influence. And the effect of global competition in good markets mean that, inevitably, national economic policy must focus less on managing demand and more on supply-side measures necessary for competitiveness — such as promoting long-term investment and education.

When Crosland wrote, physical capital was more important to a firm than its employees, human capital. In 1956 there were less than 50 computers, most of them in Oxford and Cambridge, and now there are over 10 million computers in Britain. So today we live in an information economy where knowledge is the real source of value and it is skills and ideas that are the assets that matter. The truly indispensable form of capital is intellectual and human capital — not just at the top of a business but throughout the firm.

In 1956 there was one dominant model of employment in the labour market — men working for 40 hours a week for 40 years of their lives in the same job. Today we have a labour market in which almost half the workforce are women, people are working part-time as well as full-time and there are no jobs for life but, at best, a working life of many jobs.

Finally, the most important change of all is that the assumption of full employment, which Crosland could make even in his later works for the 1970s, has gone. In 1956, just 1 per cent of people were unemployed and even in the early 1970s when Crosland wrote his later works, the figure averaged just 3 per cent. Today, nearly one in five working age families have nobody in employment.

If Anthony Crosland had been writing today , I believe it is to the issue of workplace generated poverty and inequality that he would have turned his thoughts. I believe that Crosland with his luminous realism would have recognised the need to change in the context of a changing economic world.

In the same way that in 1956 he argued persuasively that socialism did not require a command economy but that, in a national economy, markets could be made to work in the public interest, today in an international economy, he would argue that cooperation in economic policy is essential. Just as Crosland defended the mixed economy in the 1950s, making the case for a mix of public and private ownership, so today public and private sectors need to work together in partnership for shared objectives.

In the same way that Crosland argued in 1956 that increased public ownership was not synonymous with the public interest, so today a rise in public spending does not necessarily equate with meeting the public interest. Indeed in 1975, he himself questioned who benefited from spending and expressed concern that 'we have made the painful discovery that a shift from private spending to public spending does not necessarily increase equality.'

In particular, I think he would have recognised that the record since 1979 shows that increased spending does not necessarily increase social justice: that you can tax, spend, borrow ... and fail. Indeed, I believe he would have seen that today a new welfare state is needed to bring employment and educational opportunities to those denied it.

So what makes for inequality — and the weapons that we must fashion to achieve greater equality — have changed. But the cause of equality endures. So before I turn in more detail to the question of how we achieve greater equality in the changed world of the 1990s, let us address the fundamental questions central to all that Crosland wrote: What form of equality should we aim for and why?

The Case for Equality

The Future of Socialism was written at a time when equality was not under attack. Tony Crosland did not therefore feel the need to make the philosophical case for equality. Raymond Plant has suggested that, by failing to build an intellectual and a popular consensus for Croslandite social democracy, we allowed its collapse in the 1970s. And after 20 years in which New Right ideology which has worshipped inequality has dominated the political landscape, it is now more important than ever that we argue the case for equality from first principles.

Today, we argue for equality not just because of our belief in social justice but also because of our view of what is required for economic success. The starting point is a fundamental belief in the equal worth of every human being. We all have an equal claim to social consideration by virtue of being human. And if every person is to be regarded as of equal worth, all deserve to be given an equal chance in life to fulfil the potential with which they are born.

Crosland wrote of the importance of potential in *Socialism Now*. And in doing so he took issue with the old view — used to justify inequality in educational opportunity — that intelligence was a fixed quantity, something given in limited measure in the genetic make-up of the new-born child. Crosland was right. Intelligence cannot be reduced to a single number in an IQ test taken at the age of 11. People cannot be ranked in a single hierarchy and talent cannot be regarded as fixed. So people should not be written off at 7, 11 or 14 or indeed at any time in their life. It is simply a denial of any belief in equality of opportunity if we assume that there is one type of intelligence, one means of assessing it, only one time when it should be assessed and only one chance of succeeding.

But we have still to act on the consequence of recognising these facts: that people have a richness of potential to be tapped, that their talents take many forms — skills in communication, language, and working with other people as well as analytical intelligence — that these talents can develop over a lifetime, and that to get the best economy we need to get the best out of people's potential. And if we are to allow each person to develop that potential which exists within them, it is clear that we need to develop a more demanding view of equality of opportunity than a one-off equality of opportunity up till age 16.

I believe that everyone should have the chance to bridge the gap between what they are and what they have it in themselves to become. But what is right on ethical grounds is, in the 1990s, good for the economy too. In our information-age economy, the most important resource of a firm or a country is not its raw materials, or a favourable geographical location, but the skills of the whole workforce. And so prosperity for a company or country can be delivered only if we get the best out of all people, and that cannot happen without continuous and accessible equality of opportunity.

Indeed, I would suggest that Britain's economic weakness is not attributable to neglect at the top of the educational pyramid, but has arisen because we have given insufficient attention in education and employment policies to the latent and diverse potential of the population as a whole. In the industrial age, the denial of opportunity offended many people but was not necessarily a barrier to the success of the economy. Today, in an economy where skills are the essential means of production, the denial of opportunity has become an unacceptable inefficiency, a barrier to prosperity.

And once we take this view that what matters on ethical and economic grounds is the equal right to realise potential, we reject — as Anthony Crosland did — both an unrealisable equality of outcome and a narrow view of equality of opportunity. Indeed, we reject equality of outcome not because it is too radical but because it is neither desirable nor feasible.

Crosland himself wrote of 'the rent of ability', recognising that incentives for effort are essential in any economic system: greater incomes for some justified by the contribution they make to the society as a whole. Indeed I would go further: pre-determined results imposed, as they would have to be, by a central authority and decided irrespective of work, effort or contribution to the community, is not a socialist dream but other people's nightmare of socialism.

It denies humanity, rather than liberates it. It is to make people something they are not, rather than helping them to make the most of what they can be. What people resent about Britain is not that some people who have worked hard have done well. What angers people is that millions have been denied the opportunity to realise their potential. It is this inequality that must be addressed. Just as we join Crosland in rejecting an unattainable equality of outcome, so we refuse to narrow our horizons to a limited view of equality of opportunity.

There was an old idea of equality of opportunity in which it meant a single chance to get your foot on a narrow ladder, one opportunity at school till 16 followed by an opportunity for 20 per cent to go into higher education. And for millions of people in Britain it has meant that if you missed that chance it was gone forever. It is the equal opportunity only to become unequal: as Crosland wrote 'only a few exceptional individuals hauled out of their class by society's talent scouts, can ever climb'. It is, in the words of Tawney, the invitation for all to come to dinner in the sure knowledge that circumstances would prevent most people from attending.

Whether done on the basis of birth or academic qualifications, the potential of all is clearly denied when we entrench the privilege of a few. So Crosland correctly concluded that a narrow equality of opportunity was not enough if we were to prevent the entrenchment of unjustifiable privilege, and sought a broader view of equality that complemented rather than conflicted with the importance he attached to personal liberty. He proposed what he called a democratic view of equality — one that sought to prevent the permanent entrenchment of privilege from whatever source it came. This more demanding view of equality of opportunity — democratic equality — had, as he said in *The Conservative Enemy*, 'revolutionary connotations'.

So what, in the 1990s, does this concept of democratic equality mean for me?

First, it demands employment opportunity for all because work is central not just to economic prosperity for Britain but to individual fulfilment. And there must be a permanent duty on government to relentlessly pursue this objective.

Secondly, we must as a society ensure not just a one-off educational opportunity in childhood, but continuing and lifelong educational opportunity for all — second, third and even fourth chances so that people are not written off if they fail at school and are not left behind by the pace of technological change.

Thirdly, life-long opportunity must be comprehensive, extending beyond education and employment, involving genuine access to culture — and, most importantly, a redistribution of power that offers people real control over the decisions that affect their lives.

While Crosland did write about industrial democracy, he said less about the state or about an equal right to participate in the decisions that affect our lives. In the 1940s people accepted services handed down from the state — for example, housing. They now want to make their own choices over their own lives and rightly see themselves as decision-makers in their own right and they want a government that will enable them to make decisions for themselves and give them power over their lives. So the issue for socialists is not so much about what the state can do for you but about what the state can enable you to do for yourself.

Political reform is central to this; it must enable people to have the chance to participate in decisions that affect them. This is about more than the concept of a classless society, it is about power and therefore about a truly democratic society. Proponents of democratic equality must also — even in a global marketplace — address wealth and income inequalities. I believe that these inequalities can be justified only if they are in the interests of the least fortunate.

Crosland took his stand against inequalities of social status and wealth. He viewed the question of income inequalities as of lesser importance, but he thought that great inequalities of wealth, and particularly inherited wealth, could not be justified as a source of enormous social and economic advantage. But Crosland also saw the distinction between the private ownership of property that simply furthered privilege and the private ownership of property that allowed people control over their lives. So he was ahead of his time on the Left in wanting a more general diffusion of property among the entire population. Indeed, he was right to say in *The Conservative Enemy* that 'If the property is well-distributed, a property-owning democracy is a socialist rather than a conservative ideal.'

Democratic equality means we tackle unjustifiable inequalities, but it also, of course, pre-supposes a guaranteed minimum below which no one should fall. Our minimum standards must include a minimum wage, a tax and benefit system that helps people into work, the best possible level of health and social services for all and the assurance of dignity and security for those who are retired or unable to work through infirmity.

Putting Equality into Practice

When it came to power, this government was clear that those who support democratic equality must begin by tackling the biggest source of poverty and inequality — unemployment. Employment opportunity for all is hollow when one working age family in five has no one earning a wage. This contrasts with 11.5 per cent in the USA, 15 per cent in Germany and 16 per cent in France. In some inner cities — such as inner-city London or Glasgow for example — there are constituencies where 30 per cent and up to 35 per cent of working-age families have nobody in work.

A far-reaching modernisation of the welfare state was essential, starting with an assault on youth unemployment and long-term unemployment among men and women. So within two months of taking office, the government put in place a massive programme of employment opportunity — a new deal for those excluded from the chance to work. The programme covers the young unemployed and long-term unemployed as well as other groups who have faced permanent exclusion from the labour market — such as single parents and the long-term sick and disabled who want to work.

The new deal for the unemployed is the first building block of the new welfare state of the 1990s. The second element of our modernisation is to re-establish the work ethic at the centre of our welfare system. This involves a reform of the tax and benefit system to make work pay. So in the 1998 budget, the government announced whole-sale reform of the tax and benefits system to tackle the unemployment and poverty traps facing low-paid families. This includes a reform of National Insurance and a new Working Families' Tax Credit which will guarantee a minimum income for working families with children. These reforms will be underpinned by the National Minimum Wage.

The third element is to give priority to education. As well as creating work, a modern employment policy must also be improving people's skills and helping them into new jobs. In the new economy, that will require not just the one-off acquisition of a skill but the continuous acquisition of new skills. So hand in hand with increased employment opportunity goes life-long educational opportunity. Greater educational opportunity will come through an expansion of the numbers going into further and higher education and lifelong learning opportunities will come through our University for Industry, and the creation of Individual Learning Accounts.

So real equality in life chances is what the government seeks. And let me conclude by saying how we are tackling inequalities in opportunities and potential facing women. The days of men-only economic policies — full employment for men, educational equality only for men and a welfare state for men — are over. An economy in which women cannot fulfil themselves in work will be an inefficient economy.

But still nowhere is the gap between the rhetoric of equality of opportunity and the real world of inequality greater than in achieving political, economic and social opportunities for women. Prevented from securing the jobs they want, too often denied childcare which would enable them to gain financial independence, and often debarred even from enjoying a second chance in education, our modernisation of the welfare state will ensure that it becomes far more responsive to the needs of women — allowing them to combine family responsibilities with employment and gain new skills.

Since coming to office, the government has not only established the first national programme of opportunities for work for lone parents, it has for the first time said that employment opportunities will be available not just to the registered unemployed, but also to the partners of the unemployed — mainly women. The government has also invested substantial extra resources in after-school childcare and with new childcare tax credit in the Working Families' Tax Credit, we are tackling the problem of the affordability of childcare.

And with extra resources provided for child benefit, the government is supporting all families with children. Taken together, these measures are the first steps to providing a genuine chance for women to balance work and family responsibilities.

So the government is putting forward a radical agenda for equal opportunity. It is a far-reaching conception of equal opportunity in which we believe, a modern conception for the modern world. And it tackles the causes of inequality at the root — dealing not simply with the consequences of poverty but addressing the causes — unemployment and low skills.

Conclusion

I would argue that our commitment to equality is as strong as ever. We are applying it, however, in the new circumstances we face. That means never being diverted from egalitarian ends, but being aware that policies may change to take account of changed times. So our policies are credible because we build from a platform of stability of tax, spending and borrowing.

There is no alternative to this iron commitment. But it is socialist because we are talking about toughness for a purpose — an egalitarian purpose:

- Giving unemployed people opportunities currently denied to them.
- Making work pay for all families.
- Lifelong educational opportunities for everyone to acquire new skills.

I have outlined what I see as some of the egalitarian policies of the 1990s. This is the agenda we are pursuing in government. And I hope and believe it is an agenda which does justice to Tony Crosland's intellectual and political memory.

Postscript

Social Democrats Fighting Back

What does revisionism have to say to us about the future of the Labour Party, and Britain?

In the last century Labour underperformed, despite high hopes that it could quickly become the dominant political party given its demographic advantages in British society. Even in 1950, 70% of the electorate were still officially classified as working-class.[1] There were no significant religious or ideological divides within the British labour movement leading to the divisions common elsewhere in Europe. Yet for much of the twentieth century, the party remained hopelessly confused about British capitalism, and was unable to clarify its aims and purposes in power.

The identification of Labour with nationalisation and public ownership, the defining feature of the post-war Labour Government, had become destructive by the early 1950s. It instilled a widespread fear among the public that Labour's goal was the construction of a sclerotic command economy founded on state ownership and control.

The electoral victories of 1945 and 1964–6 broke the historical sequence of defeats. The Attlee Government helped to produce a reformed and humanised capitalism that appeared successful for fifteen years. However, the economic deterioration of the sixties and seventies caused numerous problems for the party. The reversion to Labour's ideological past born of the 1970 General Election defeat

---

[1]   See Gamble (2003).

only worsened its doctrinal sterility.[2] The 'glad, confident morning' of 1945 lay far behind it.

The impact of these disputes, which fundamentally concerned the very nature and identity of the historical Labour Party and its ability to become an instrument of radical change, damaged Labour more profoundly than the simple fact of its unpopular and outdated policies.

Labour could not emerge as the natural governing party within the British state because these internal divisions and ideological ambiguities prevented it from undertaking the drastic re-orientation of policy required to modernise Britain's post-war economy and society. Ramsay Macdonald personified the myth of treachery, given substance in 1931. It was reinforced after 1945 since it was believed Labour had failed to use its parliamentary majority to implement radical socialist measures. Disillusion and cynicism were never far away, as successive Labour Governments failed to satisfy their supporters, or meet their expectations. The party was unable to escape the ethos of perpetual opposition.

Labour constantly struggled to develop a reputation for economic competence, and was instantly blamed whenever the pound was devalued (1931, 1949, 1967,1976). This perceived inability to manage the economy weakened Labour's electoral appeal, and was ruthlessly exploited by its political opponents.

The incorporation of the working-class into the existing state by 1939 preserved property rights, but put major obstacles in the path of a successful capitalism. No consensus emerged on how to revive Britain as a leading capitalist economy, as British politics was dominated by continuing disputes over the rival merits of private and public enterprise, the size of the state, and the limits of taxation.

When it was founded in 1906, Labour had no incentive to make a national appeal. It aspired to be a party that secured the right of the working-class to organise, to develop its own institutions and its own unions, and for the right to parliamentary representation. Its purpose was not to secure power replacing either the Conservative or Liberal parties within the state, but to defend trade union free-

---

[2]   Between 1971 and 1973, the Labour Party Conference supported public ownership of banking, insurance, building societies, the building industry, finance houses, road haulage, shipbuilding, and ship repairing. At the 1973 Conference, it was proposed to create a National Enterprise Board to purchase controlling interests in profitable firms.

doms.[3] As Henry Pelling has described, 'The early components of the Labour Party formed a curious mixture of political idealists and hard-headed trade unionists'.[4]

As Labour evolved in the twentieth century, it was racked by dissension about what type of party it was and aspired to be, arousing passionate and intense internal dispute. Was Labour a party of class struggle seeking to re-cast property relations, or a party of responsible moderation seeking to create a universal and redistributive welfare state?

Serious conflicts emerged when Labour did achieve power, as key elements within the labour movement adopted a strategy of permanent opposition to established capital. The trade unions' power was largely defensive. Like the party itself, they could not resolve the internal conflict of whether to support a socialist programme replacing capitalism; or negotiate an effective system of corporate representation, securing the permanent influence of the labour interest within the institutions of the state.

The left appeared to believe that Britain's problems could be ascribed to the structural contradictions of weaknesses in capitalism, not to the adjustment deficiencies of the British state and British culture.

This was an entirely inadequate basis on which to construct a dynamic, competitive industrial economy. Labour lost power in 1951 just as the long boom in the British economy was taking effect, enabling the Conservatives to remain in office for thirteen years. A long spell of post-war Labour Government would have had a profound effect on the structure of power within the Labour Party, as well as the British state.

Instead, under the Conservatives Britain was fundamentally weakened from the early 1950s. It failed to revitalise its education system, or to invest sufficiently in public infrastructure. The new Conservative Government cut projected capital investment in education between 1952–8 from £468 million to £378 million. The result — average class sizes in secondary schools were over 50:1 in the 1950s. By 1955, over half the 15–18 age group were not in any form of education or training; of those entering employment, 71% did so to

---

[3]   Pelling (1965).
[4]   Pelling (1965).

jobs offering no craft or career training whatsoever.[5] The fruits of growth as the global economy recovered in the mid–1950s were therefore squandered. The Conservatives were able to resume their role within the British state with only a brief interruption, while Labour was consigned to opposition — the familiar routine of moral certainty, but political sterility.[6]

Labour's ultimate aim should have been to emerge as the vehicle to revolutionise British society as a party of reform, re-casting the dominant terrain of British politics and British society.

Until 1970, both parties sustained a large public sector in Britain reflecting the 'Butskellite consensus'.[7] But the state did not fulfil the developmental role that characterised other economies in Western European. It was an Anglo-American state that removed the barriers to free market exchange, and sustained the institutions that define and defend individual property rights, while fulfilling extensive international commitments.

It did not revitalise infrastructure, ensure closer ties between finance and industry, nor did it harmonise the interests of capital and labour driving a more dynamic private sector, restoring competitiveness and improving the rate of growth.[8] If it had, a reforming Labour Party may have more convincingly averted Britain's decline than the firestorm of Thatcherism that transformed British capitalism in the 1980s.

In those circumstances, Labour could have matched the ambitions envisaged for it by its founders, emerging as a mass party within the British state leading Britain on the road to social democracy. It could have refashioned, and indeed uprooted, many long established features of the British political landscape, exploiting the internal inconsistencies of British Conservatism.

Embracing 'modernisation' implies rejecting traditional attitudes and established institutions, deeply alien to Conservatives. Economic restructuring requires a cross-class coalition, ensuring an equitable distribution of the costs and benefits imposed by industrial change. Fundamentally, Conservatism serves to suppress ingenious British characteristics such as innovation, creativity, and even entrepreneurial vigour.

---

[5]   See Barnett (2001).

[6]   See Gamble (2003).

[7]   See Dutton (1991).

[8]   See Marquand (1988).

For much of the twentieth century, revisionists were urging Labour to alleviate the precarious foundations of British prosperity. Revisionist ideas demanded the full-scale modernisation of Britain's institutions, of which the Conservatives proved themselves incapable.

In the 1930s, Tawney, Dalton and Durbin confronted a stagnant and inefficient British economy of mass unemployment. What Labour needed to provide, as they saw it, was a strategy for industrial modernisation built on collectivism and indicative planning that could put Britain back to work, ending decades of protracted economic instability heightened by structural weaknesses in the world economy.

The generation of New Fabian economists in the 1940s set out to dismantle the Treasury orthodoxy that post-war Britain could succeed only by implementing severe cuts in its welfare state and public services — rebuilding its economic backbone through cheaper exports. They argued, in contrast, that only by fulfilling pent-up demands for more ambitious public provision could the British state undertake the modernisation of the economy and society that were required by 1945.

As Labour attempted to break out of its vacillation and evident ambiguity of purpose in the 1950s, Gaitskell, Crosland and Jay sought to end, decisively, the damaging distraction of Labour's unattainable aspiration to nationalise the capitalist system and create a new, though hitherto unspecified economy founded on the socialisation of production.

The battle to revise Clause IV was lost in 1959–60. But Crosland set out in *The Future of Socialism* a decisive contribution to debates about equipping post-war Britain for success as a modern industrial economy. Critically, this accommodated social and cultural themes, seeking to modernise civil society as much as the formal economic and political structures of the state, and promoting in Labour's politics, 'a trace of the anarchist and the libertarian'.[9]

Generations of revisionists sought to counter the immobilism of left and right, taking great leaps forward in socialist thinking. But the bursts of intellectual energy and fresh thinking depicted in these essays proved to be exceptions to the rule. It is a familiar, though over-stated criticism, that leading revisionists remained wedded to the established structures of the British state. Both David Marquand

[9]   Crosland (1956).

and J.P. Mackintosh sought to revive revisionist social democracy by formulating a strategy for the modernisation of the British state, embracing devolution, decentralisation and a break up of the old party system.

Social democracy, and the modernisation of Britain's economy and society are inextricably linked. There are strong grounds for believing that Labour's social democratic strategy for national renewal could have triumphed in the twentieth century over conservative forces.

First, it would have strengthened Labour in winning the battle for hegemony within the British state. This is the fundamental strategic aim of politics — a fact seldom understood in the twentieth-century Labour Party. As R.W. Johnson suggests, British national culture was a conservative culture by 1939.[10] The superiority of the British, deference, and status hierarchy defined its character. The identity of the Conservative Party is inseparable from the history of Britain's *ancien regime*.[11] It was the traditional establishment of the crown, aristocracy, high church, the law and the military. Conservatism viewed the British state as its state, and only fleetingly did Labour seem prepared to challenge this ethos.

It is a battle to re-cast institutions and to re-define prevailing ideas, destroying the old consensus, while forging a new settlement to which others must then adapt and respond. In 1945–50, Labour began to succeed in these terms as the Second World War discredited the British ruling-class, and Britain's national consciousness briefly embraced collectivism. But the opportunity was lost.

The centre-ground is not a given — it is contested, and constructed, by politics itself. Hegemony is a strategy to define the political centre in progressive terms, shifting the gravity of British politics permanently to the left, reshaping the British national culture, instead of being content to administer within parameters established by Labour's opponents.

Second, the electorate would have regarded Labour, in its identity and interests, as the party that could best avert Britain's post-war decline. Wilson's 'New Britain' of 1964–6 evoked this theme. But regrettably the alliance of the scientific revolution and the British socialist tradition did not amount to a plausible strategy for modernising the British economy and state. In the face of repeated pressure

---

[10]   Johnson (1985).

[11]   Nairn (1981).

on sterling, it was forced to abandon its expansionist ambitions in 1967.[12] Had it succeeded, Labour might have owned the future as an effective and competent governing force in twentieth-century Britain. But these historical ambitions were thwarted.

So what does all this mean for our contemporary understanding of 'New' Labour?

'New' Labour is clearly the embodiment of historic revisionist ambitions, rather than a suspect deviation from recognisably Labour or social democratic traditions.[13] It is the culmination of a long-standing battle instigated by leading social democratic intellectuals and politicians to re-make the historical Labour Party, in which conscience rather than class is the key to radical politics.

'New' Labour is an unfinished revolution. For Labour, dominance rests on ensuring the narratives that define its politics become the narratives of British politics itself. In abandoning the Utopian expectation that capitalism will one day be transcended, Labour must affirm its status as an agent of radical transformation pursuing specific and feasible reforms.

The party has instigated a period of constitutional innovation and experimentation since 1997 with potentially far-reaching implications for how Britain's nations govern themselves, augmenting the economic reforms of the 1980s. When the Conservatives left office in 1997, great questions about Britain's future relationship with Europe and the world, the future relationship between nations of the United Kingdom, the future of Britain's constitution, and indeed questions about the very cohesion of British society, were all unresolved.

British society and its institutions have been transformed by successive shocks since 1979. As Andrew Gamble suggests, 'The post-war compromise between capital and labour has been reshaped, and successive constitutional reforms have profoundly altered the essential character of the British state.'[14] Talk of 'decline' among the political class is now seen as irrelevant, and rather parochial.

Yet, many critics argue that Britain has not averted the structural causes driving the contraction in its post-war economy and world

---

[12] See Gamble (1981).

[13] See Fielding (2003).

[14] Gamble (2003)

role, and threatening the continuation of British prosperity.[15] Unreformed institutions based on an antiquated, and indeed deferential view of British society are said to no longer meet the challenges and pressures of the age.

It is a stark fact, according to the literature exemplified by Anthony Sampson's *Anatomy of Britain*, that Britain remains a profoundly unequal society, where opportunities are too often determined by socially inherited privilege.[16] This has prevented Britain from moving decisively beyond economic decline and structural crisis in the post-war period, as John Kay has testified.[17]

Britain has inevitably grown materially wealthier since the 1950s. This is reflected in its improved social capital as a nation, its better-equipped schools, new recreation facilities, and local authority housing built to higher standards than ever before.

There has been progress on libertarian reform, and the evolution of popular culture has transformed the traditional class structure.[18] By the late 1970s, participation in university education had increased five-fold since Crosland's time at the Department for Education and Science (DES), with twice as many part-time students and greater numbers of women and students from ethnic backgrounds.[19] As John Vaizey noted at the time of Crosland's death, the average standard of living was 'emphatically higher' than anybody could have anticipated, 'when the guns stopped firing in 1945'.[20]

But there was no immutable law that dictated Britain's uninterrupted progress towards greater equality. The Institute for Fiscal Studies reported that Britain had become far more unequal in the 1980s and 1990s: a 'parade of dwarfs and a few giants'.[21] Poverty still casts a long shadow in contemporary Britain, as social divisions stretch back through successive generations. The UK's productivity and growth performance is constrained by inefficiencies that arise from such inequities. The paralysis of Britain's post-war political economy originates in these entrenched social divisions.

---

[15] See, for example, Hutton (1996).

[16] Sampson (2004).

[17] Kay (2003).

[18] See McKibbin (1990).

[19] Pratt (1997) .

[20] Vaizey (1983).

[21] *Guardian* 28 July 1997.

The widening of wage inequality and income distribution since the 1970s is simply extraordinary. Between 1979 and 2001, salaries for the top ten per cent of earners increased three times more than for those on the lowest incomes. 3.8 million children in Britain live in poverty. A child in Britain is five times more likely to be poor than a child in Denmark. The percentage of households with children in relative poverty has increased from 14% to 32% since 1979, among the highest in the OECD. Britain has the highest proportion of children living in poverty in the European Union, despite the enormous progress made by the Labour Government since 1997.[22]

This has forced many commentators to ask is Britain a country where too many elites are simply closed to outsiders, bedevilled by endemic poverty of aspiration among the least affluent?

The pluralist social democratic ideal of a middle-class society has not been achieved. Since the late 1960s, the education system has entrenched the advantages of the privileged despite some narrowing of the attainment gap since 1996–7.[23] The lion's share of intergenerational upward mobility has resulted from changes in occupational structure and more white-collar jobs, rather than greater openness.[24]

This presents a decisive opportunity for 'New' Labour to become the vehicle for radical social reform — no longer reticent about its aims and purposes in power — fulfilling Britain's potential as a successful European society. The enabling and developmental state that Labour seeks to construct is inclusive of all its citizens, maximises participation in economic activity, and secures comparative advantage in the world economy through equality of opportunity and the fundamental redistribution of life-chances. It rests on the belief that redistribution requires moral foundations, a 'fairness code',[25] affirming that opportunities are matched by obligations.

This enabling state is conscious of the damage done to social cohesion when collectively financed services are available to those who are not entitled to them. It insists, for example, that absentee fathers have a responsibility to pay for their children; it demands regular school attendance; it recognises that devices such as league tables and parental preference encourage families to become actively

---

[22] See Esping-Andersen (1999a).

[23] See Esping-Andersen (1999a).

[24] See Esping-Andersen (1999a).

[25] Denham (2004).

involved in their children's education, rather than sinking into powerless passivity. It affirms that the welfare state should be there for those who need it, who are entitled to it, and who use it responsibly.

The social contract enables the state to remain in touch with people's lives. It connects effort with reward, encourages virtuous behaviour, sanctions infringements of the fairness code, and it views the enlargement of opportunity in the lives of the majority, not just the poor, as central to its purpose. It shares the conviction of earlier idealists like Durbin and Tawney, 'that man is by nature a gregarious social animal and not simply a selfish lone hunter'.[26]

A moral system arises neither from the market, which is amoral, nihilistic, subversive of all values except the values of free exchange; or from collective provision that suspends moral judgement as a matter for private individuals.[27] The social contract embraces the *quid pro quo* of mutuality as Tony Blair has stated it:

> The left have undervalued the notion of responsibility and duty, and it is time we understood how central it is to ourselves... It is rooted in the understanding that the individual does best in a strong and decent community of people with principles and standards and common aims and values. We are the party of the individual because we are the party of community.[28]

This reflects what the philosopher Adrian Oldfield describes as,

> The sense of belonging and commitment. The commitment is to others who share interests, or positions, or purposes, and it is also to those who, for whatever reason, are unable to look after their own interests or pursue their own purposes. It is to seek the good of others at the same time as, and sometimes in neglect of, one's own good. It is to approach relationships in the Aristotelian sense of 'concord'. It is this that creates the sense of community; and it this that creates citizens.[29]

The argument of this book is that the under-performance of the post-war Labour Party and the under-performance of the British state have coincided. 'New' Labour can complete the revisionist project instigated by Gaitskell, Crosland, and Jay in the 1950s. This establishes a successful social democracy, and the modernisation of the British economy and state, as coterminous.

---

[26]   Reisman (1997).

[27]   Marquand (1996).

[28]   Blair (1994a).

[29]   Oldfield (1990).

If Britain since 1979 has experienced several structural convulsions to its economy and constitution, it needs a third revolution: a social revolution capable of ending the stubborn persistence of social inequalities in Britain. Only then, it is argued, will Britain at last overcome its underperforming capitalism, its anachronistic *ancien regime*, and its failing public services.

Most commentators agree that 'New' Labour has yet to match the successive structural transformations instigated by the Thatcher administrations of the 1980s. Yet governments are defined by their institutional legacies. 'New' Labour needs to invent new social and economic institutions, and reallocate resources and assets, on a scale that matches the privatised industries, the National Lottery, council house ownership, and the saving schemes introduced under the Conservatives.

It is sometimes said that the English do not have revolutions, only evolutions.[30] But revolutions come in various forms, and 'New' Labour — and whatever follows it — has an unparalleled opportunity to establish a new political, ideological, economic and cultural order in Britain.

Lasting institutional reform is the key, building on the transformation of Britain's public services. Britain has not witnessed the relentless intrusion of markets, as seemed inevitable in the 1980s. New forms of collectivism and state intervention have steadily been embraced, that make explicit the two-way relationship between individual entitlement, and civic responsibility.

In these circumstances, not only can the British state secure itself from the relative decline that has cast a shadow over Britain's national life since the nineteenth century. Labour is most likely to fulfil its destiny as the pre-eminent progressive party in British politics.

---

[30] Taylor (1965).

Appendix

*'A Manifesto' Published by the
Campaign for Democratic
Socialism (1962)*

1. We are long-standing members of the Labour Party who are convinced that our Movement cannot afford another Scarborough. Rank-and-file opinion must now assert itself in support of Hugh Gaitskell and of those Labour MPs — the great majority — who are determined to resist and then reverse the present disastrous trend towards unilateralism and neutralism.

2. This is the culmination of a long period in which the voice of moderate opinion in the Labour Party has been drowned by the clamour of an active and articulate minority. As Socialists who are loyal to its central tradition yet aware of the changed conditions of the nineteen-sixties, we seek to reassert the views of the great mass of Labour supporters against those of doctrinaire pressure groups.

3. By the central tradition of the Party we mean a non-doctrinal, practical, humanitarian socialism — a creed of conscience and reform rather than of class hatred. The British Labour Movement owes its inspiration to British radicals, trade unionists, co-operators, nonconformists and Christian socialists, not to Marx or Lenin. We oppose the narrow definition of socialism which is being insinuated as orthodox party doctrine, not only because it repels a growing number of Labour sympathizers but, above all, because it betrays the Party's ethical, reformist heritage.

4.   We believe that the Labour Party should be a broadly-based national party of all the people, as the early pioneers saw it. To their vision we wish to return. A democratic socialist party must be based predominantly on working people. But a purely sectional, one-class party would face electoral suicide; more important, it would be a betrayal of the ideal of a classless society.

5.   The historic partnership between the Party and the trade unions is as basic and natural as that between Conservatives and big business. But, in the interests of both partners, responsibility for policy-making should be simplified and clarified; the Party must be seen to represent all sections of society, and it must be made absolutely clear that no one has the power to instruct, control or dictate to the Parliamentary Labour Party.

6.   The object of political activity is to achieve political power. We are not utopians, prepared to wait indefinitely for the socialist millennium; nor are we a sectarian faction, contemptuous of the ordinary voter. We want an effective Labour Party, capable of winning elections and implementing its policies. But the Party will have no opportunity of putting its principles into practice unless it adapts itself to the realities of social change, so that it represents the new, emerging society and not the society of thirty years ago.

7.   We are glad to see people better-off, and have no patience with those who are comfortably-off themselves yet seem to resent the prosperity of others. Though profoundly critical of many defects in our affluent society, we much prefer it to the poverty-ridden society of the past; we want to reform it, not repudiate it.

8.   We insist particularly on more concern for the less fortunate, greater equality of personal wealth, and more stress on public as against private interests. Growing prosperity will be self-frustrating unless increasing private incomes are matched by greater collective provision for roads, schools and hospitals, by constructive planning for the renewal and growth of our towns and the preservation of our countryside, and by a long-overdue effort to conserve and develop our cultural resources. In reasserting a sense of community amid the excesses of individualism, Labour would mobilize the latent idealism and moral sense of the British people.

9.	We believe passionately that socialists should always strive to enlarge the area of human freedom. We are on the side of the individual citizen in conflict with arbitrary authority, of the consumer against monopoly and vested interests, and of the minority group seeking to live its own life in its own way. We urge the need for more reason and less prejudice in our approach to current social evils.

10.	We do not believe our mixed economy to be in serious danger of sudden collapse or massive unemployment. But we resent its lack of enterprise and technical innovation; it is a disgrace that the rate of economic growth in Britain is now the slowest of any advanced industrial country. The fault lies partly with Conservative policies, but also with our hierarchical, old-fashioned social structure with its built-in conservatism and unevenness of educational opportunity. We seek a more fluid and open social system, which would give us both a more dynamic economy and a less class-ridden society.

11.	We maintain that Labour's social and economic objectives can be attained by purposive government planning, a bolder use of tax policy, and educational reform. Recognizing that public, co-operative and private enterprise all have a part to play in the economy, we regard the public ownership of particular industries or services as a useful technique to be justified on its merits.

12.	We believe in the ultimate necessity of world government. While the world remains divided into two blocs, we adhere to Labour's traditional policy of seeking peace through collective security, and fully accept our obligations under NATO (though not additional self-imposed obligations such as a national independent deterrent). We have great respect for the conscientious pacifist who faces the consequences of his policy, but very little for the wishful-thinking ostrich who expects justice, freedom or equality to survive under a Communist monopoly of nuclear weapons. We therefore recognize that the West must retain the nuclear deterrent until all governments — not merely our own — can be brought to face the desperate need for collective disarmament.

13.	We favour two radical changes in Britain's relations with the outside world. First, as a matter of conscience as well as of policy, we urge a great new effort to share our prosperity with the under-developed countries of Asia and Africa. Secondly, we are convinced Europeans, certain that Britain's destinies are inextricably bound up with those of a resurgent and united Europe.

14. We do not expect all who associate with us to accept every word of this manifesto: we hope they will share the spirit in which we face the future. We are radicals and progressives. Our enemies are conservatism — everywhere, prejudice — everywhere, and tyranny — everywhere. We interpret socialism not as an arid economic dogma, but in terms of freedom, equality, social justice and world co-operation. We believe that the British people, who rightly mistrust doctrinaire utopianism, will always respond to an idealistic appeal to remedy real evils by practical and radical reform.

Bibliography

The edited extracts featured in this collection are as follows:

Brown, G. , 'Equality: Then and now', in D. Leonard, *Crosland and New Labour*, London: Macmillan, 1999. Revised and expanded version of platform speech, Memorial meeting (13 February 1997).

Crick, B., *Socialist Values and Time*, London: Fabian Society, 1984.

Crosland, C.A.R., 'The meaning of socialism', in *The Future of Socialism*, London: Cape, 1956; rev. edn 1964.

Dalton, H., *Practical Socialism for Britain*, London: Routledge, 1935.

Durbin, Evan, *The Politics of Democratic Socialism*, London: Routledge, 1940.

Gaitskell, H., *Socialism and Nationalisation*, London: Fabian Society, 1956.

Hattersley, R., 'Choose equality', in *Choose Freedom: The Future for Democratic Socialism*, London: Penguin, 1987.

Healey, D., 'Power Politics and the Labour Party', in R.H.S. Crossman (ed.), *New Fabian Essays*, London: Turnstile Press, 1952.

Jay, D., 'Social justice and social purpose', in *Socialism in the New Society*, London: Longman, 1962.

Jenkins, R., *The Labour Case*, London: Penguin, 1959.

Luard, E., 'Socialism at the grassroots: Community socialism', in *Socialism Without the State*, London: Macmillan, 1979.

Mackintosh. J.P. 'Has Social Democracy failed in Britain?' *Political Quarterly*, July 1978.

Marquand, D., *The Unprincipled Society*, London: Heinemann, 1988.

Radice, G., *Labour's Path to Power: The New Revisionism*, London: Macmillan, 1989.

Tawney, R.H., *Equality*, London: Bell & Sons, 1930.

Secondary Sources

Arblaster, A., 'Anthony Crosland: Labour's Last Revisionist?', *Political Quarterly*, vol. 48, no.4, October-December 1977

Barnett, C., *The Verdict of the Peace*, Oxford: OUP, 2001.

Beckerman, W., *The Labour Government's Economic Record 1964–70*, London: Duckworth, 1972.

Bevan, A., *In Place of Fear*, London: MacGibbon & Kee, 1951.

Blair, A., 'Forging a New Agenda', *Marxism Today*, October 1991.

Blair, A., *Socialism*, London: Fabian Society, 1994.

Blair, A., Speech to the Labour Party Conference, Blackpool, 4 Oct. 1994a.

Bernstein, E., *Evolutionary Socialism*, London: 1899.

Bernstein, G.L., *The Myth of Decline: The Rise of Britain Since 1945*, London: Pimlico, 2004.

Brivati, B., *Hugh Gaitskell*, London: Richard Cohen, 1996.

Brivati, B. and Heffernan, R., *The Labour Party: A Centenary History*, London: Macmillan, 2000.

Callaghan, J., *The Retreat of Social Democracy*, Manchester: MUP, 2000.

Clarke, P., *Liberals and Social Democrats*, Cambridge: CUP, 1978.

Clarke, P., *A Question of Leadership: From Gladstone to Thatcher*, London: Penguin, 1991.

Coates, D., *Labour in Power*, London: Longman, 1980.

Cole, G.D.H., *A History of the British Labour Party from 1918*, London: Routledge, 1948.

Crick, B., 'Socialist Literature in the 1950s', *Political Quarterly*, 31 (1960), pp. 362–8.

Crosland, C.A.R. 'The Arrogance of Austerity', *The Listener*, Vol. 54, 8 December 1955, p. 975.

Crosland, C.A.R. *The Future of Socialism*, London: Jonathan Cape, 1956.

Crosland, C.A.R, *The Conservative Enemy*, London: Cape, 1962.

Crosland, C.A.R, *Socialism Now and Other Essays*, London: Cape, 1974a.

Crosland, C.A.R., 'A Social Democratic Britain', in Leonard (1974).

Crosland, S., *Tony Crosland*, London: Cape, 1982.

Crossman, R.H.S, *Planning for Freedom,* London: Hamilton, 1965.

Dell, E., *A Strange Eventful History: Democratic Socialism in Britain* London: Harper Collins, 2002.

Denham, J., 'The Fairness Code', *Prospect*, June 2004.

Drucker, H.M., *Doctrine and Ethos in the Labour Party*, London: Allen & Unwin, 1979.

Durbin, E., *The Politics of Democratic Socialism*, 2nd ed., 1954.

Dutton, D., *British Politics Since 1945: The Rise and Fall of Consensus*, Oxford: Blackwell, 1991.

Esping-Andersen, G., *Social Foundations of Post Industrial Economies*, Oxford: OUP, 1999.

Esping-Andersen, G., *Three Worlds of Welfare Capitalism*, Oxford: OUP, 1999a.

Fielding, S., *The Labour Party: Continuity and Change in the Making of 'New' Labour*, London: Palgrave, 2003.

Foot, M., *Aneurin Bevan*, London: Davis-Poynter, 1973.

Freeden, M., *The New Liberalism: An Ideology of Social Reform*, Oxford: Clarendon Press, 1978.

Gaitskell, H.,' Introduction' to Durbin (1954).

Gamble, A., *Britain in Decline*, Basingstoke: Macmillan, 1981.

Gamble, A., *Between Europe and America: The Future of British Politics*, London: Macmillan Palgrave, 2003.

Gould, P., *The Unfinished Revolution*, London: Little Brown, 1998.

Gray, J., *After Social Democracy*, London: 2000.

Haseler, S., *The Gaitskellites: Revisionism in the Labour Party 1951–64*, London: Macmillan, 1969.

Heffernan, R., *New Labour and Thatcherism*, London: Macmillan, 2000a.

Heffernan, R., 'The Politics of the Parliamentary Labour Party' in Brivati and Heffernan (2000).

Hinden, R., 'The New Socialism', *Socialist Commentary*, November 1956.

Hobhouse, L.T., 'The Contending Forces', *English Review*, vol. 4, 1909–10.

Howell, D., *British Social Democracy*, London: Croom Helm, 2ed. 1980.

Hutton, W., *The State We're In*, London: Random House, 1996.

Jay, D., *The Socialist Case*, London: Faber & Faber, 1937.

Jeffreys, K., *Anthony Crosland: A New Biography*, London: Richard Cohen, 1999).

Jenkins, R., *What Matters Now*, London: Fontana, 1972.

Jenkins, R., *A Life at the Centre*, London: Macmillan, 1991.

Johnson, R.W., *The Politics of Recession*, London: Macmillan, 1985.

Jones, T., *Remaking the Labour Party: From Gaitskell to Blair*, London: Routledge, 1996.

Kay, J., *The Truth About Markets: Their Genius, Their Limits and Their Follies*, London: Allen Lane, 2003.

Keynes, J.M., *The General Theory of Demand*, London: 1936.

Leonard, D. (ed.), *Socialism Now*, London: Jonathan Cape, 1974.

Labour Party, The, *Meet the Challenge, Make the Change*, London, 1989.

Lipsey, D. & Leonard, D., *The Socialist Agenda*, London: 1981.

Mackintosh, J.P., 'Socialism or Social Democracy', in Marquand (1982).

McKibbin, R., *The Evolution of the Labour Party, 1910-24*, Oxford: OUP, 1974.

McKibbin, R., *Classes and Cultures: England 1918–51*, Oxford: OUP, 1990.

Mandelson, P. & Liddle, R., *The Blair Revolution*, London: Faber, 1996.

Marquand, D., 'Inquest on a movement: Labour's defeat and its consequences', *Encounter*, July, 1979.

Marquand, D. (ed.), *J.P. Mackintosh on Parliament and Social Democracy*, London: Longmans, 1982.

Marquand, D., *The Unprincipled Society*, London: Fontana, 1988.

Marquand, D., *The Progressive Dilemma: From Lloyd George to Kinnock*, London: Heinemann, 1991.

Marquand, D., 'Moralists and Hedonists', in *The Ideas That Shaped Post-War Britain*, ed. D. Marquand & A. Seldon, London: Fontana, 1996.

Marquand, D., *Decline of the Public*, Cambridge: Polity, 2004.

Middlemass, K., *The Politics of Industrial Society*, London: Deutsch, 1979.

Morgan, K.O., *Labour People: Leaders and Lieutenants: Hardie to Kinnock*, Oxford: OUP, 1987.

Nairn, T., 'The Twilight of the British State', in *The Break-up of Britain*, London: Verso, 1981.

Nettleship, R.L., *Works of T.H. Green, three volumes*, London: Longmans Green, 1885–8.

Nield, R., 'Prosperity and Reform', in *Where? Five Views on Labour's Future*, London: Fabian Society, 1959.

Oldfield, A., *Citizenship and Community: Civic Republicanism and the Modern World*, London: Routledge, 1990.

Pelling, H., *Origins of The Labour Party*, Oxford: OUP, 1965.

Perkin, H., *The Rise of Professional Society: England since 1880*, London: Routledge, 1989.

Pimlott, B., *Harold Wilson*, London: Harper Collins, 1992.

Plant, R., 'Democratic Socialism and Equality' in Lipsey and Leonard (1981).

Pratt, J., *The Polytechnic Experiment*, Oxford: OUP, 1997.

Radice, G., *Southern Discomfort*, London: Fabian Society, 1993.

Radice, G., *Friends and Rivals: Crosland, Jenkins and Healey*, London: Little Brown, 2002.

Rawls, J., *A Theory of Justice*, US: Belknap Pr, rev. edn., 1999.

Reisman, D., *The Mixed Economy*, London: Macmillan, 1997a.

Reisman, D., *Crosland's Future: Opportunity and Outcome*, London: Macmillan, 1997.

Rodgers, W.T. (ed.), *Hugh Gaitskell, 1906–63*, London: Thames & Hudson, 1964.

Sampson, A., *Who Runs this Place? The Anatomy of Britain in the 21st Century*, London: John Murray, 2004

Sassoon, D., *One Hundred Years of Socialism*, London: The New Press, 1996.

Shaw, E., *The Labour Party Since 1979: Crisis and Transformation*, London, Routledge, 1994.

Stedman-Jones, G., 'Why is the Labour Party in such a mess?' in *Languages of Class: Studies in English Working-class History1832–1982*, Cambridge: CUP, 1983.

Tawney, R.H., *The Acquisitive Society*, 1921.

Tawney, R.H., *The Attack and Other Papers*, Nottingham: Spokesman Books, 1981.

Taylor, A.J.P., *Essays in English History*, Oxford: Clarendon, 1965.

Townsend, P., *Poverty in the United Kingdom*, London: Penguin, 1975.

Vaizey, J., *In Breach of Promise: Five Men who Shaped a Generation*, 1983.

Williams, P., *Hugh Gaitskell: A Political Biography*, London: Cape, 1979.

Williams, P. (ed.), *The Diary of Hugh Gaitskell, 1945–56*, London: Jonathan Cape, 1983.

Wilson, H., *The New Britain*, London: Penguin, 1964.

Wright, A., *British Socialism*, London: Longman, 1983.

Wright, A. and Gamble, A. (eds), *The New Social Democracy*, Oxford: Blackwells, 1999.

Index